Engl... ...ology
Book

Roger of Hereford's *Judicial Astrology*

Translated and edited by

Chris Mitchell, PhD

Almuten Figuris Publications
Leicester, UK
2021

Almuten Figuris Publications is a trading name of Chris Mitchell Astrology Services

First published in 2021 by Almuten Figuris Publications, Leicester.

www.almuten.co.uk

A catalogue record for this book is available from the British Library.

ISBN 978-1-7398093-0-0

ACKNOWLEDGEMENTS

I would like to thank João Coelho and Levente László for their help in deciphering some of the more obscure parts of Roger's text, to Cat Keane for the cover design, to Dr Bernadette Brady for setting me on the Roger of Hereford path in the first place, to Nicholas Whyte for kick-starting awareness of Roger with his excellent MPhil dissertation, to Dr Richard Jones for being a fantastic PhD supervisor, to Dr Nick Campion for his support, and – as always – to my partner Phil Shine for his love and forbearance as I spent long hours at the keyboard hammering away!

Images: Front cover image includes a folio of Roger's *Judicial Astrology* showing a horoscope, from Oxford, Bodleian Library Selden Supra 76, f.17v. Images illustrating the astrolabe are with the permission of the Master and Fellows of St John's College, Cambridge, and are copyright Dominic Ford and Katie Birkwood.

ABOUT THE AUTHOR

Chris Mitchell has been a practising astrologer since the late 1990s, and has a PhD from the University of Leicester. He is a tutor on the MA Cultural Astronomy and Astrology course at the University of Wales Trinity Saint David, and holds a diploma in Medieval Astrology from Astrologos. He has been actively involved in promoting and teaching astrology since 2000, is on the boards of both the Astrological Association and the Association of Professional Astrologers International, and has given talks to groups and conferences in Europe and the US.

The topic of Chris's PhD was examining the twelfth-century manuscript that is the topic of this book, identified as the first astrology textbook in England. This involved transcribing and translating it, an undertaking that had never been done before. Although Chris's thesis analysed the manuscript in some detail, it did not provide a full translation. The aim of this book is to offer that complete translation, as well as a description of the techniques; this book is aimed at astrologers rather than academics.

CONTENTS

PRELUDE

Two thirteen-year-old boys were having a fistfight in the classroom, surrounded by a gaggle of cheering classmates. A smaller boy at the back of the room, acting as lookout, sounded the warning as the teacher approached and the children quickly ran to their seats with an innocent look on their faces. The teacher, known only as "Master Roger", rolled his eyes as he walked into the class – he'd heard the commotion, of course, and shrugged it off. They were bright kids, and he wasn't going to discipline them for letting off steam. After all, they were sitting down now, quiet as mice, and it was time for the class to begin.

"Why is astrology the finest of all the arts?" asked Roger. A couple of hands shot up. "Is it because the whole of nature can be represented by just seven planets and twelve signs, instead of having to test everything individually?" asked one boy, the class swot. "Yes, very good, William, but what else?" Another boy, who'd been looking out of the window and apparently not paying attention – the one who'd started the fight, in fact – smirked and butted in. "It's because you can tell the future and that gives you power over other people!" The teacher nodded benignly. "Very good, Robert, I'm glad that somebody has been listening to my lessons."

This depiction of children being taught astrology is not a scene from Harry Potter, but a reconstruction of a real class in a real school in twelfth-century England. The school in question was the Cathedral School at Hereford; it is still an active school, and is one of the oldest schools in the country. The teacher was known simply as "Master Roger", and to later historians as "Roger of Hereford". The subject being taught – horoscopic astrology – was new, too, at least to scholars in Christian Europe. Roger was teaching cutting-edge stuff – he'd read the latest texts from the Islamic world that had recently been translated into Latin, and had compiled these exciting new techniques into a textbook for his students – the first such textbook in England.

Figure 1.1: Hereford Cathedral.

I can sense eyebrows being raised reading this. One might expect a school attached to a cathedral to be focusing on religion, or teaching children to sing hymns. Why would a schoolteacher in the twelfth century have been teaching children astrology?

Surely the Catholic Church – and England was entirely Catholic, as it would be for another four centuries – has always been thoroughly opposed to astrology, as it is today? On top of that, why would Islamic texts be taught in a Christian school, at a time when Christians and Muslims were fighting over Jerusalem in the Crusades?

However, as astrologers, we may have more practical questions than that. Never mind WHY Roger was teaching astrology – we want to know WHAT he was teaching. Are there any exciting new techniques in Roger's textbook? Can we use these techniques today and incorporate them into our own astrology practice? The answer to both of these questions is "yes". Roger didn't directly innovate – all his techniques came from somewhere, but several have been lost and are unfamiliar to most astrologers today. Many seem quite strange techniques, but do they work? The only way to answer that question is to try them yourselves, and see!

Figure 1.2: Hereford Cathedral School.

I'm fairly confident that you won't have seen Roger's textbook before. This is because it has never been published, and has never been translated into English, or any other language. Roger was teaching in an English school but, like all English scholars of the time, he wrote in Latin. He was writing in the 1170s, long before the printing press, so his textbook exists only in a small number of manuscripts spread across Europe – all handwritten, which is what "manuscript" literally means. Producing the book that you are reading now wasn't a simple case of looking at an earlier translation and commenting on it. It meant hunting down the existing 22 manuscripts, comparing them, working out the scrawling Latin handwriting with its many abbreviations and then translating that Latin into English. In common with most twelfth-century texts, the wording is confusing to a modern ear, even when translated into English, and the techniques are sometimes obscure so the book needs to be analysed to make sense of it.

The lengthy business of hunting down Roger's manuscripts and making sense of them occupied me for the best part of a decade, and was the topic of my PhD, which you can freely download.[1] However, the thesis goes into a lot of academic detail about the format of the manuscripts, an analysis of the Latin, and an examination of Roger's sources and techniques – but it doesn't give a complete translation of what Roger wrote. I started off doing my PhD with the aim of hearing what Roger had to say and making this information available to astrologers today, so after completing my thesis I was very keen to produce a book aimed at astrologers, not academics – which I hope is what I've done with this book.

What I've aimed to do in this book is to give Roger a voice – a modern voice, where instead of talking to you in Latin or archaic English, he can go through his techniques and explain them to you in modern English. Roger's original text doesn't have many worked examples, although as a teacher Roger probably would have done worked examples in the class in front of the students, so I've included numerous examples in this book. I want to recreate for you the experience of learning astrology in Roger's classroom, but from the comfort of your own twenty-first-century home rather than a hard classroom bench.

So – sit in your favourite chair, grab a cup of tea, and let Roger teach you his version of astrology starting off with simple techniques and building on them, and look at the examples I've provided to illustrate them. Then try them out for yourself. Roger was a brilliant teacher, but he's been silent for over eight hundred years. Now, at last, we can let him speak again!

---

[1] Chris Mitchell, 'Roger of Hereford's *Judicial Astrology*: England's First Astrology Book?', PhD thesis (2019), https://doi.org/10.25392/leicester.data.11793636.

CHAPTER ONE: ENGLISH ASTROLOGY

The title of this book is *England's First Astrology Book*, and the prelude claims this was written by a teacher called Roger of Hereford in the twelfth century. I think it's only fair to qualify the title a little here. After all, Saint Bede "The Venerable", writing in the year 725 in north-east England, described the zodiac[2] while Figure 1.3 shows an eleventh-century calendar produced in Canterbury depicting zodiac symbols on each page and gives the date when the Sun moves into a new sign.[3] They predate Roger, and are surely astrological? This is true to an extent; medieval English monks needed to be able to calculate the date of Easter, and that involved understanding the cycles of the Sun and Moon and how they interact. This complicated subject was called **computus**, from the Latin word for calculation, and its practitioners in monasteries could tell you what sign the Sun and Moon was in on any given date. However, as astrologers we tell our clients that there's more to an astrological chart than one's Sun sign and Moon sign, and this is where astrology fell short in England, and Western Europe in general, prior to the twelfth century. Computists could calculate the position of the Sun and Moon, but no other planets. A limited astrology existed, but not horoscopic astrology as we know it – it was impossible to draw up a full astrological chart for a particular date and time and interpret it.

That all changed in the twelfth century, and the fascinating story of how we in the West rediscovered the art of drawing up astrology charts is the topic of Chapter Two. In this chapter, though, we'll have a look at a potted history of schooling in medieval England, some Christian attitudes towards astrology then, and how a teacher in Hereford was allowed to teach a subject as controversial as astrology in a school attached to a cathedral.

---

[2] Bede, *Bede: The Reckoning of Time*, Faith Wallis (trans.) (Liverpool: Liverpool University Press, 1999), pp.56-58.

[3] London, British Library, Cotton Tiberius B V/1, f8.v.

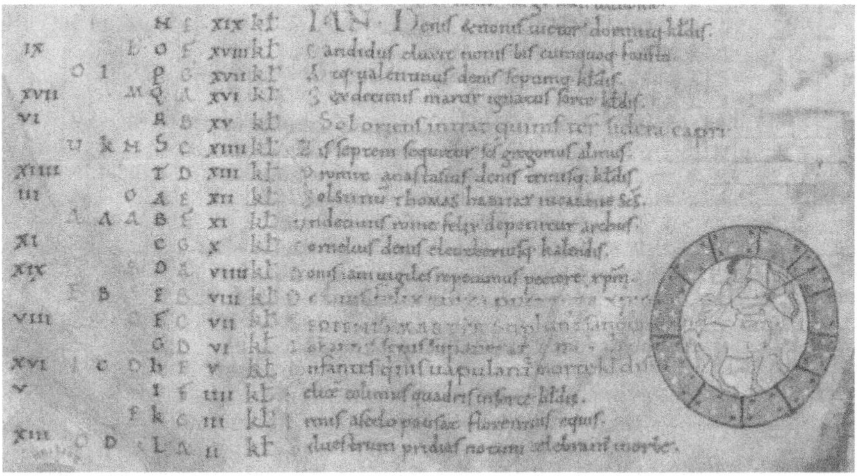

Figure 1.3: Eleventh-century calendar for December showing Sagittarius, and the date of the Sun's ingress into Capricorn. British Library Cotton Tiberius B/V1 f.8v.

The birth, death, and rebirth of horoscopic astrology

Human beings have been watching the sky for thousands of years. Cave paintings appear to depict stars, and numerous books have been written demonstrating how ancient monuments such as Stonehenge align to the solstices. When we talk about astrology as modern astrologers, however, we usually refer to drawing up charts that show the positions of planets at the time of a particular event. That event may be a person's birth, or a particular occasion such as the crowning of a monarch or the inauguration of a president. Such a chart is often known colloquially as a horoscope, and the term **horoscopic astrology** simply means the practice of drawing up an astrological chart, regardless of its purpose. Creating a chart involves calculating the position of planets at a given date and time along an arc in the sky called the **ecliptic**, which is simply the path along which the Sun appears to move from Earth's perspective. Because of the way the solar system formed billions of years ago, planets tend to stick more or less to this same path – they may deviate by a few degrees above or below it, but in general an astrological chart will simply show the position of a planet along the ecliptic. Since the ecliptic is a circle, there is no obvious starting point, and so one has to be defined. In modern Western astrology, that starting point is usually the position of the Sun at the spring equinox. In Vedic astrology, used in India, that starting point is based on the position of certain stars. Whichever system is used, that 360-degree circle is divided into twelve equal segments called **zodiac signs**, and are called, in this order, Aries, Taurus, Gemini, Cancer, Leo, Virgo, Libra, Scorpio, Sagittarius, Capricorn, Aquarius, and Pisces. The system of starting the zodiac at the spring equinox is called the **tropical zodiac**, and the system based on stars used in Vedic astrology, and by some Western astrologers too, is called the **sidereal zodiac**. These two zodiacs differ by about 24 degrees in the early twenty-first century, and continue to drift by about a degree every 72 years, but the notation used is similar. For example, the opening ceremony for the London Olympics took place at 21:00 British Summer Time on 27 July 2012. At that time, the Sun was at 5°10′ Leo, and Mars was at 13°33′ Libra using the tropical zodiac. In the sidereal zodiac, there are various systems that differ from each other slightly, but the one favoured by the Indian government, called the Lahiri zodiac, put the Sun at 11°08′ Cancer, and Mars at 19°31′ Virgo at the moment of the opening of the London Olympics.

The definition of zodiacs was not always so neat, however. The names of the signs used today in astrology mostly derive from the astrology practised in Babylon in Mesopotamia about 3,000 years ago, where constellations of stars were identified and given names such as "The Great Bull of Heaven" and "The Scorpion", today called Taurus and Scorpio. Constellations do not fit neatly into precise thirty-degree boxes, and Babylonian astrology would identify a planet by describing it as being, for example, "in the horns of the Great Bull of Heaven". Babylon changed hands in the intervening years – first being conquered by the Persian ruler Cyrus the Great in the sixth century BCE, and the Persian Empire then being defeated by Alexander the Great in the fourth century BCE, seeing Babylon end up under Greek rule. Many of the astrological concepts of Babylon found their way into the Greek astrology of that period, now known as **Hellenistic astrology**, which took the rather loose signs of Babylonian astrology, codified them into precisely defined thirty-degree segments of the tropical zodiac, and retained the names of the constellations that approximately corresponded to them. This innovation made horoscopic astrology possible; rather than Jupiter appearing in "the horns of the bull", Hellenistic astrology made it possible to give a precise location for Jupiter within a tropical sign. Figure 1.4 shows the night sky on

1 November 207 BCE at 21:00 in Alexandria, Egypt; Jupiter is in the horns of the Great Bull of Heaven (Taurus), while Figure 1.5 shows this same event on an astrological chart set to the tropical zodiac, with Jupiter at 17°01′ Taurus.

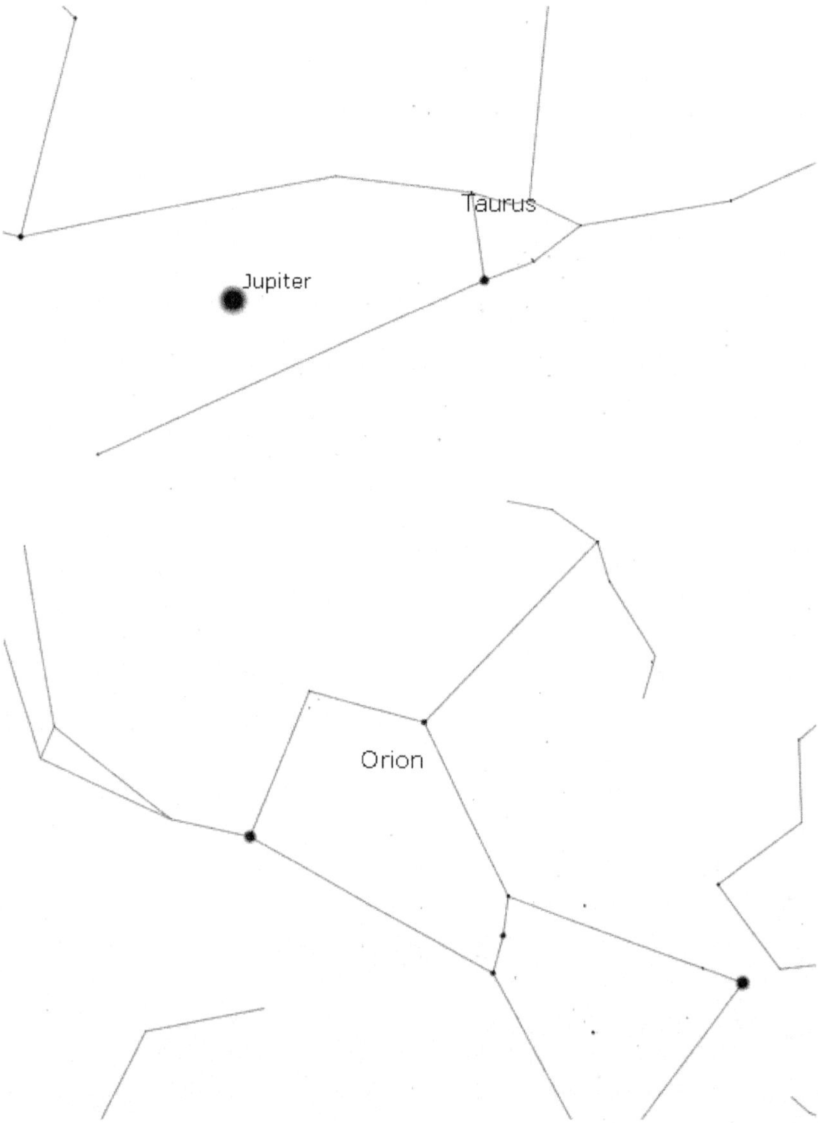

Figure 1.4: Jupiter in the night sky at 21:00 on 1 November 207 BCE in Alexandria, Egypt, showing Jupiter in the horns of Taurus.

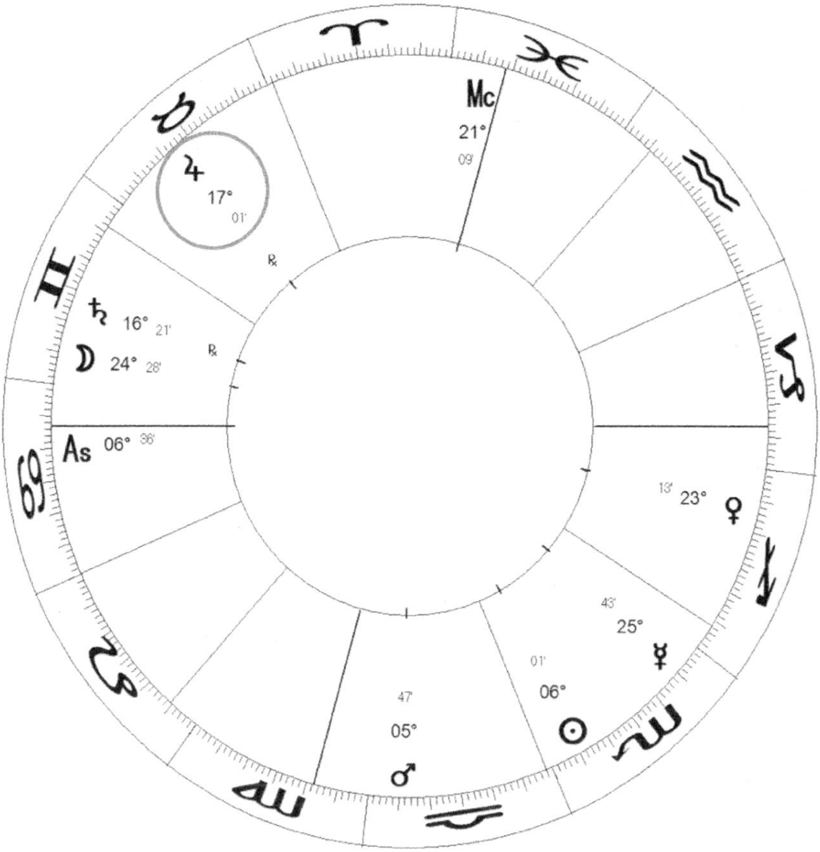

Figure 1.5: The same event represented on an astrological chart using the tropical zodiac, showing Jupiter at a precise position in the zodiac: 17°01′ Taurus.

Hellenistic astrology became widely used and after the Roman Empire conquered Greece it was adopted in the Roman Empire, so when historians talk of Hellenistic astrology, Latin texts are included alongside Greek texts. One Hellenistic author who was to have a major influence on later astrology was Claudius Ptolemy. Ptolemy lived in Alexandria, in Egypt, which was part of the Roman Empire at the time, and he wrote in Greek. He wrote on many topics, but two are relevant to our story. His *Almagest* was a book on astronomy in which he described all the known constellations in such incredible detail that his definitions were adopted in the twentieth century by the International Astronomical Union when they formalised the boundaries of constellations. He also described the model of the heavens used by the Greeks, which was a geocentric system of perfect circles in which all planets, and the Sun and Moon, orbited the Earth. In fact, a simplistic model of planets orbiting the Earth in perfect circles was not sufficient to describe the actual movement of planets, and Ptolemy was well aware of this, so his model was more complex than that and involved circles within circles called **epicycles** to explain why planets sometimes went retrograde. Although this geocentric system is not factually correct, the model works in terms of providing accurate positions of planets, and *Almagest* described the method of working these positions out. His *Tetrabiblos* was a book on astrology, describing many techniques that would be familiar to modern astrologers: the signs of the zodiac, descriptions of the planets, aspects between planets, and rulerships. Modern astrologers would immediately recognise his examples that trines are easier than squares, that Saturn is harder work than Jupiter, and that Venus rules Libra. There were numerous other Hellenistic authors, but I mention the existence of these two books because, armed with these, an astrologer could calculate the positions of planets for any given date and time, draw up an astrological chart, and interpret it. Hellenistic astrologers were able to do practical horoscopic astrology, and it was an established and perfectly acceptable practice in the Roman Empire.

If it was used in the Roman Empire, was astrology practised in Roman Britain? Almost certainly. The *Historia Augusta* is a set of works describing the lives of Roman emperors, and was probably written in the late Roman period. Its reliability is, admittedly, a little suspect, but it is still considered a useful source of information. Volume one is about the life of the emperor Hadrian, who ruled Britain in the year 122 and initiated the building of a wall near the current border between England and Scotland named after him, describing him as a proficient astrologer who wrote his own horoscopes every year.[4] With astrology such a part of day-to-day life in the Roman Empire, it is very likely that officials in Roman Britain would have had astrologers among their retinue.

---

[4] Aelius Apartianus, *Historia Augusta, Volume I: Hadrian,* David Magie (trans.), Loeb Classical Library 139 (Cambridge, MA: Harvard University Press, 1921), pp.50-51.

There's a popular image that the Roman Empire subsequently collapsed, as though this were a single dramatic event. The reality is a lot more complex. The Roman Empire was a victim of its own success, and by the third century had become too large to be ruled by a single emperor, and the emperor Diocletian appointed a co-emperor in 286, splitting the Empire into a Western half and an Eastern half. The Western empire struggled to control its provinces, and declined over the fourth and fifth centuries, and in 476 the last Western emperor was deposed, marking the final end of the Western Roman Empire. The Eastern part of the empire, however, survived for another thousand years.

Both parts of the Roman Empire had adopted Christianity in the period between Diocletian and the final collapse, as had many of the tribes that subsequently took over the territories in the West formerly under Roman rule. Despite the collapse of Roman rule in the West, the Pope, based in Rome, was the spiritual head of all Christians in the region, and Latin – the language of the Western Roman Empire – remained the language used for religious services, writing, and as a common language when different tribes needed to communicate with each other. Although many of the Germanic tribes that had taken control in former Roman provinces had adopted Christianity, this wasn't the case in Britain. Britain had split into a number of kingdoms, and much of the country had been taken over by a number of Germanic tribes, collectively known as Anglo-Saxons, and who eventually created the English nation. England as such didn't really exist in the sixth century, but there were a number of Anglo-Saxon kingdoms. Although the kingdoms had pagan rulers, Christianity was tolerated and was a minority religion; indeed, King Æthelberht of Kent had married the Christian daughter of the king of the Franks. The Pope considered that Æthelberht was ripe for conversion as a result of this, and in 597 he sent a monk called Augustine (not to be confused with Saint Augustine, who was an earlier theologian and bishop) to Britain to convert Æthelberht to Christianity. This was successful, and Augustine founded churches, establishing Canterbury Cathedral, and becoming the first Archbishop of Canterbury.

The establishment of Christianity in England had a profound effect on education. Since the local population hadn't been Christian up to this point, they spoke no Latin. As missionaries successfully converted many of the population to Christianity, it was necessary to teach these new converts the skills needed to be good Christians – they needed to be able to sing in choirs, and those among them destined for the priesthood needed to learn Latin, the language of the Roman Catholic church. In order to do this, schools were set up and in time most cities had song schools, designed to teach choirboys Gregorian chant, and grammar schools to teach boys Latin grammar so that they could become monks and priests. It seems that teaching Latin was considered more important, or perhaps simply more difficult, than teaching chanting, and so song schools were considered the poor cousins of grammar schools.[5] Being a priest required more skills than simply knowing Latin, and grammar schools thus provided teaching in a broad range of subjects. This led to a split where in many cases, song schools were run by monks, but grammar schools were run by ordinary clergy and would allow the general public access. The school at Canterbury was one such example. The school that arose in Hereford much later was another.

The decline of the Roman Empire and the subsequent Christianisation of England also had an impact on astrology. While the idea of predicting the future from the position of planets was perfectly acceptable in pagan Rome, the early Church was opposed to it on two grounds. Firstly, astrology clearly had pagan origins – the planets themselves had the names of Roman gods, which made the Church wary. Secondly, Christianity required its practitioners to believe in free will – if God will judge us all eventually and God is fair and just, then humans have to be given the ability to choose good or evil. If everyone's actions were predetermined by the predictable motions of planets, there was no room for free will, and hence no room for salvation. The focus on Christianity had another side-effect – the Roman Empire in its heyday had been bilingual, with Roman scholars well-versed in Greek as well as Latin. Most of the texts on astrology came from Greek sources, and were written in Greek. Roman scholars had no problem reading and understanding these, but after the decline of the Roman Empire in the West, knowledge of Greek was gradually lost. Some classical non-religious texts on natural science were copied, but these were texts written in Latin by classical authors such as Pliny. Hence by the time schools were being developed in

---

[5] Arthur Leach, *The Schools of Medieval England* (London: Methuen, 1915), p.7.

England, the texts available were restricted to writings by the Church fathers, and a handful of texts on science and philosophy from classical Latin authors; as most of the astrological texts were written in Greek, these fell by the wayside. Some texts dealing with astronomical and astrological concepts were written in Latin and so survived – Pliny's *Natural History*, for example, describes the zodiac and a number of astronomical concepts, including an accurate measurement of the distance between the Earth and Moon.[6] However, Pliny's book does not give details on how to calculate planetary positions, and so not only was astrology met with disapproval by the Church, but without the necessary mathematics, the art of chart calculation was lost.

Despite the disapproval of the Church towards astrology, the Christian Church couldn't simply outlaw any form of sky-watching, because there was one thing that Christians had to do that seemed very astrological: the observance of the most sacred Christian festival of Easter. Since the Gospels recount that Christ was crucified on the eve of Passover, which is a Jewish festival that always falls on the day of a Full Moon, early Christians agreed that Easter should fall on the first Sunday after the Full Moon after the spring equinox. This needed to be calculated in advance, since Christians were obliged to observe a period of frugal living, Lent, for forty days prior to Easter. Working out New Moons and Full Moons involved being able to calculate cycles of the Sun and Moon to see when they coincided – the computus referred to at the beginning of this chapter – which is far from simple, and which exercised the minds of Christians from the earliest days. By the eighth century, schools had sprung up all over England, often attached to monasteries and cathedrals, and one such was at Jarrow in north-east England. One boy who attended Jarrow from the age of seven was Saint Bede. Bede had a particularly sharp mind, and wrote widely on natural science and computus, including providing methods of calculating the position of the Sun and Moon in the zodiac. Despite this, he had the traditional Christian

---

[6] Pliny, *Natural History, Volume I: Books 1-2*, H. Rackham (trans.), Loeb Classical Library 330 (Cambridge, MA: Harvard University Press, 1938), II.85, p.228, gives the distance as 2 million stades, equivalent to 370,000 km. The average modern value is 384,400 km.

suspicion of astrology, warning his readers to avoid using astrology for divination as it was "alien to our faith".[7]

The need to look at planetary cycles to be able to calculate Easter meant that there were cracks in the edifice of Christian objections to astrology. As well as calculating Easter, using celestial events for weather forecasting, navigation, and farming were also permissible – it was using astrology for divination that was considered taboo. Isidore of Seville, a bishop writing in the seventh century, said that astrology was "partly natural, and partly superstitious", and it was only the superstitious element that was condemned.[8] However, the distinction was somewhat irrelevant – since the art of chart calculation had been lost, would-be astrologers couldn't do predictions anyway, if all they could do was calculate the position of the Sun and the Moon. There was no need for the Church to come down hard on astrologers, because nobody could do horoscopic astrology anyway, and when it came to suspect pagan practices, there were bigger heretical fish to fry.

By the time of Bede, England was no longer a backwater at the edge of an empire and it had developed links with other scholars in mainland Europe. Education was quite sophisticated for its time, and by the early ninth century the standard of scholarship was sufficiently high that Alcuin, a scholar at York, was invited by Charlemagne to his court at Aachen, where he allegedly taught Charlemagne to read and write, and sent word back to York for more books, as they weren't available in Aachen. Charlemagne, as Holy Roman Emperor, had contacts all over Europe and even had contacts with the Islamic caliph in Baghdad, who presented him with a water clock.[9]

English education appears to have taken another leap forward after the Norman Conquest of 1066, although schools had been growing anyway in Anglo-Saxon England. In particular, "secular" cathedral schools run by lay clergy rather than monks became more prominent after the Conquest, and as

---

[7] Bede, *The Reckoning of Time*, pp.15-16.

[8] Isidore of Seville, *Etymologies*, S. Barney, W.J. Lewis, J.A. Beach, O. Berghof (eds) (Cambridge: Cambridge University Press, 2006), 3.xxvii, p.99.

[9] Kocku von Stuckrad, 'Interreligious Transfers in the Middle Ages: The Case of Astrology', *Journal of Religion in Europe*, 1, no.1 (2008), pp.49-50.

secular schools had a more flexible curriculum, individual schools had their own specialties. Hereford in particular built up a reputation for teaching astronomy and astrology, and the difference in attitudes among different schools and their clergy is shown up wonderfully in the story of Gerard, Bishop of Hereford from 1096 to 1100. Gerard studied astrology, and when he was promoted to Archbishop of York in 1100, he continued his habit of reading part of his astrology book (it was *Mathesis*, by the Hellenistic astrologer Firmicus Maternus, which had recently become available in Latin), which caused the cathedral at York to accuse him of being a necromancer. One day he sat in the cathedral garden, where he died peacefully in his sleep, and his servants found him dead with *Mathesis* under his pillow. They were so outraged at this that they refused to bury him in York Minster and buried him outside the gates. The scandalous behaviour of studying astrology in York was seen as perfectly normal in Hereford![10]

England, then, had moved from being a provincial backwater after the end of the Western Roman Empire to a country with a strong education system, and, following the Norman Conquest, cathedral schools rose to greater prominence, and had more links with mainland Europe. By the end of the eleventh century, knowledge of the sciences in Western Europe had increased a little, with more texts available including a handful of astrological texts – but the holy grail of being able to do real astrology, to cast charts, was still out of reach.

All this was to change in the twelfth century in what is sometimes dubbed "the twelfth-century renaissance". The Islamic world had had access to the lost classical texts of the Roman Empire for several centuries – the story of how this happened is the topic of the next chapter – and a huge translation movement saw these texts translated into Latin, making them available to scholars in Christian Western Europe for the first time. These texts included astrological texts from the Hellenistic period, and also Arabic texts with techniques that had originated in Greece, Persia, and India, and which had been adapted by Arabic scholars, giving rise to a unique astrology, which we now call **medieval astrology**. The texts also, vitally, included those

---

[10] Chris Pullin, 'Cathedrals as Centres of Learning' in A. Johnson and R. Shoesmith (eds), *The Story of Hereford* (Woonton, Herefordshire: Logaston Press, 2016), p.82.

mathematical texts that gave details of how to calculate planetary positions, now vastly improved by Arabic techniques to provide better accuracy. At last, the secret of casting astrological charts had been rediscovered.

The role of the Church

Earlier, we saw that the Church had condemned astrology, but its condemnation was rather half-hearted. Astrology was confusingly divided into "natural" and "superstitious", and it was only its use for divination that was really condemned. In many ways, the Church only paid lip service to the condemnation because nobody could actually do real astrology – the knowledge of casting a chart wasn't available, so there was no point in wasting energy attacking a practice that couldn't be performed, when there were far more worrying instances of folk magic to be dealt with. In taking its eye off the ball, the Church let astrology in. The need to look at cycles of the Sun and Moon meant that observing planetary cycles was acceptable, and led to monks studying scientific issues that must surely have made them wonder about cycles of other planets too. Tentative contacts between Christians and Muslims in Islamic Spain meant that the Christian West became aware of some Arabic science, and in particular an instrument called an astrolabe, which could be used for navigation, telling the time, and astronomy. The astrolabe was enthusiastically embraced in the West, and one person instrumental in its introduction was Gerbert d'Aurillac, a French scholar with a keen interest in all matters scientific, who went on to become Pope Sylvester II in 999. Once the door had been opened to Arabic astronomy, other related texts became of interest, which is how genuinely astrological texts like Firmicus Maternus' *Mathesis* found their way into the Christian West in the eleventh century – this is the book that the scandalous Archbishop of York was reading when he died. *Mathesis* is a genuine astrology textbook, with useful tips such as "Mercury in the third house will make priests, magicians, healers, and astrologers".[11] Useful, but incredibly frustrating for the budding astrologer, since without the ability to calculate the position of Mercury, you can't tell whether you have it in the third house or not.

The Church, then, underwent a curious shift. It moved from condemning astrology to allowing limited study of it for calculating Easter, and then it supported schools that taught wider scientific topics related to it. Then a Pope introduced an Arabic astronomical instrument to Christian scholars, and a

---

[11] Firmicus Maternus, *Ancient Astrology Theory and Practice: Matheseos Libri VIII*, J.R. Bram (trans.) (Park Ridge, NJ: Noyes Press, 1975), III.VII.6, p.100.

Hereford bishop started reading astrology books. By the early twelfth century, the study of astrology became even more open. A Spanish Jewish convert to Christianity called Petrus Alfonsi moved to England, became King Henry I's physician, and collaborated with the prior of Malvern, a man called Walcher, on translating some astronomical tables written by a ninth-century Persian scholar called al-Khwarizmi. This Persian scholar was a formidable intellect – his book on mathematics, called *Kitāb al-ğabr* or *The Compendious Book on Calculations*, which solved complex issues like quadratic equations, is where we get the word "algebra" from. His very name – al-Khwarizmi – was transcribed into Latin as "Algorismus", and is where we get the word "algorithm" from. The planetary tables that he drew up three hundred years before Walcher and Alfonsi translated them were the missing link that Western scholars needed to draw up astrology charts. Ironically, this was the key that made horoscopic astrology possible – the very aspect of astrology that the Church was scared of – all made possible by a prior of that same Church!

The twelfth-century translation movement then took off, with large numbers of Arabic texts being translated into Latin. This movement was a Europe-wide one, but it's fair to say that English scholars punched above their weight. Adelard of Bath translated more tables, learned Arabic himself so he could translate an astrological text, and taught astrology to King Henry I's grandson, the future King Henry II. Henry I himself promoted astrology and astronomy both in his own court and at the cathedral school at Hereford.[12] Robert of Ketton, from Rutland, collaborated with a Croatian scholar, Hermann of Carinthia, and was probably also his lover.[13] It is likely that they met Abraham ibn Ezra when they were both in Spain and then southern France; ibn Ezra was a Jewish rabbi and scholar and practising astrologer, who later on ended up in London.[14]

The once-sceptical Church, then, unwittingly opened the floodgates of a huge astrological translation movement, which meant that the horoscopic

---

[12] John Tolan, *Petrus Alfonsi and his Medieval Readers* (Gainesville: University Press of Florida, 1993), p.42.

[13] Ben Dykes, *Hermann of Carinthia: The Search of the Heart* (Minneapolis: Cazimi Press, 2011), p.30.

[14] Charles Burnett, *The Introduction of Arabic Learning into England* (London: British Library, 1997), pp.57-58.

astrology once practised in the Roman Empire had come home to Europe, and could be practised once again.

Teaching astrology

In order to practise astrology, it needs to be taught. By the latter half of the twelfth century, scholars had access to a wide range of astrological texts, and the ability to calculate charts. How was this information disseminated? In England, the answer was through the cathedral schools that already existed, and in particular the cathedral school at Hereford, which already had a reputation for astronomy. This is where the hero of our story, Roger of Hereford, comes in. By 1176, Roger had been teaching computus at the cathedral school in Hereford for many years, and already had a reputation as an innovator. He'd realised that standard computus didn't always give the right answer for determining a New Moon and developed a "natural computus" to take this into account. Messing around with computus was a controversial thing to do, and he tells us his students were "locked in battle" discussing it.[15] He now also had access to brand new astrological texts recently translated from the Arabic – and then taught these to the kids at the cathedral school. How do we know they were kids, and not adults? We don't know for sure. However, this was only a couple of decades before Oxford University became fully established in England, and there were already universities elsewhere in Europe at this time, and at Oxford many undergraduates started their studies at 14 years of age, not 18 as it generally is today; in Paris, students could start at 13. As cathedral schools were the forerunners of these universities, it is likely that their students would have been a similar age.

The astrological texts in Roger's possession came from a number of different Arabic sources, and many of these texts were reference works rather than a textbook designed to teach astrology in a structured manner. Roger realised that this was confusing, and so he compiled the information he had into a single textbook, with a logical structure. He tells us, in his prologue, that he has done this and that it's the first time anyone has put all this information together into a single volume – in other words, he has just produced the first astrology textbook in England.

[15] Jennifer Moreton, 'Before Grosseteste: Roger of Hereford and Calendar Reform in Eleventh and Twelfth-Century England', *Isis,* 86.4 (1995), p.572.

This textbook doesn't cover everything; in particular, it doesn't tell you how to calculate the position of planets, but he assumed you knew how to do that because he had produced such tables himself. He didn't cover natal astrology. This textbook was on horary astrology, and in Chapters Five and Six we'll look at what this textbook said, how he taught it, and look at each technique in detail – and then you can put these techniques to use in your own practice.

CHAPTER TWO: ARABIC ASTROLOGY

The decline of the Western Roman Empire meant that practical astrology – the ability to draw up a chart – was lost for centuries in Christian Western Europe until the twelfth century, when a host of texts suddenly became available, translated from Arabic into Latin. Many of these texts had originated in the Roman Empire in the first place, so how did scholars in the West rediscover them via the medium of Arabic? The answer lies in what was happening in the other part of the Roman Empire – the Eastern Roman Empire. The capital of the Eastern Roman Empire was Constantinople (modern-day Istanbul), and after the decline of the Western Empire, the Eastern Empire became known as "Byzantium" in the West, although its own citizens continued to simply call it the Roman Empire. It continued for nearly a thousand years after the fall of the Western Empire, until Byzantium itself fell to the Ottoman Empire in 1453.

In the West, astrological texts fell into obscurity because they were mainly written in Greek, and knowledge of Greek became lost. However, this was not the case in Byzantium, where Greek remained the day-to-day language. This meant that Greek texts from the classical world continued to be studied and understood there. Like the West, Byzantium was Christian, and shared the same mistrust of astrology that the Church authorities in the West demonstrated. However, while the Church in the West didn't need to expend much time in tackling the potential heresy of studying astrology because the texts weren't available in the first place, in Byzantium it was a far hotter topic. The ideas of Plato, a Greek philosopher from the fifth century BCE, were broadly accepted by the Christian church despite being a pre-Christian philosophy, because his notion of the soul fitted in with Christian belief. However, later followers of Plato, called Neoplatonists, broadened these ideas, some of which were treated with suspicion by the Church. According to popular legend, the Byzantine emperor Justinian banished pagans from the Empire in 529, including astrologers, who fled to the court of King Chosrau in Gundeshapur in Persia. This dramatic legend is a lot more nuanced than that, however. Justinian did indeed close the Academy in Athens, run by Neoplatonists, and some of its pagan scholars did move to Persia, taking their classical Hellenistic ideas with them. However, some returned, and other schools of philosophy continued in Byzantium.[16] There were, nevertheless, regular migrations of scholars from Byzantium to the Persian Empire, and Hellenistic astrology texts were translated into Persian. The Persian Empire also had links with India, and so Indian astrological techniques were also known in Persia.

A century later, a new religion arose in the deserts of Arabia – Islam. The prophet Muhammed reported receiving a revelation from God in 609 or 610, and in 622 he and his followers migrated from Mecca to Medina; this migration is known as the Hijra, and this date is the one on which the Islamic calendar is based. Islam grew very rapidly, and in 633 Muslim armies launched an attack on the Persian Empire, and by 654 Persia was under Muslim control. This gave the new Muslim rulers access to those astrological texts from Byzantium, Persia, and India, and in the eighth century a translation movement was in full flow, translating numerous scientific, medical, and astrological texts into Arabic. One might wonder why Islam did not have the same mistrust of astrology, with its pagan roots, as the early Christian church. In fact, it may have done; little is known of the status of astronomy in very early Islam, and many of the translators were Persian and Jewish, initially working in the court of the caliph al-Mansur in Baghdad, and appear to have been an elite who were mistrusted by some religious clerics. However, the obvious usefulness of many of the texts to the expansion of the Islamic empire, especially in science and medicine, overrode the qualms that clerics may have had. Indeed, al-Mansur employed a team of astrologers to elect the most auspicious date to lay the foundation stone for his new capital city of Baghdad itself. This team, which included the Persian Jewish astrologer Māshā'Allāh, elected 30 July 762 as the best date.

Further evidence that astrology was not entirely uncontroversial can be seen by later translations. The ninth-century Arabic scholar Abū Maʿšar devoted two chapters of his *Great Introduction to Astrology* to justifying astrology. He did this by recourse to Aristotle, a Greek philosopher from the fourth century BCE, whose concept of a "Prime Mover" sounds remarkably like a monotheistic God. Aristotle accepted the influence of planets, and since

---

[16] Alan Cameron, 'The last days of the Academy at Athens', *Proceedings of the Cambridge Philological Society* 195 (1969), pp. 7-29.

Aristotle was to a certain extent accepted within Islam, then astrology was considered acceptable too. However, the fact that Abū Maʿšar needed to write a justification suggests that astrology was not automatically considered acceptable.[17]

Whatever the reason for the initial enthusiasm for these foreign astrological texts in early Islam, translation of philosophical, mathematical, astronomical, and astrological texts into Arabic continued for several centuries. Māshā'Allāh was a prolific author of the late eighth and early ninth centuries, writing at least 26 works incorporating Indian and Persian astrological practices together with Hellenistic techniques. His contemporary Sahl bin Bishr, another Persian Jewish astrologer, produced a number of works that were, to use Ben Dykes' term, "reader-friendly" and were influential for many centuries.[18] Abū Maʿšar's *Great Introduction*, mentioned above, and his condensed *Abbreviation to the Introduction*, were written in the ninth century and were extremely influential later on in the Latin West. Al-Qabisi's *Introduction to Astrology* was written in the tenth century, and in the eleventh century, despite attacks on astrology by philosophers such as ibn Sina (known as Avicenna in the West), ibn Sina's contemporary, al-Biruni, compiled an astrological encyclopedia in 1029.

There was, then, a long tradition of translating astrological texts. Since these texts included Hellenistic, Persian, and Indian concepts, Arabic astrology became a genre in its own right. It wasn't simply Hellenistic astrology that had been blindly copied by uncomprehending scholars, it was a living art used on a daily basis. It incorporated Hellenistic concepts such as "lots", which it developed and expanded into what later became known as "Arabic Parts". It took the "nakshatras" of Indian astrology and adapted these into Arabic "lunar mansions". It adopted the Persian concept of Jupiter/Saturn conjunctions and their shift into different elements as markers for long-term world events in mundane astrology. It took the idea of dividing a horoscope

---

[17] Keiji Yamamoto and Charles Burnett (eds), *The Great Introduction to Astrology by Abū Maʿšar* (Leiden: Brill, 2019), Chapter 2, 'The second chapter: on the existence of the science of astrology', pp.53-79, and Chapter 5, 'The fifth chapter: on giving arguments concerning the confirmation of astrology and the refutation of everyone who claims that the planets' movement has no power and no indication for the things coming to be in this world', pp.107-149.

[18] Ben Dykes, *Works of Sahl and Māshā'Allāh* (Minneapolis: Cazimi Press, 2008), p.viii.

into quadrants based on the Ascendant and Midheaven espoused by the Hellenistic author Vettius Valens and popularised by the later Hellenistic astrologer Porphyry, and developed new house systems. While horoscopic astrology had been lost in the Latin West, it was alive and vibrant in the Islamic world.

The Islamic world bordered the Christian world in both the east and west, and this provided an interface between the Islamic world and Christian Europe for astrological ideas to cross. Despite mistrust and conflict between the two religions, there were links between Constantinople and Baghdad. In the eighth century, Theophilus of Edessa, a student of the caliph's astrologer, moved from Baghdad to Constantinople in 775.[19] In the other direction, Leo the Mathematician ended up at the court of the caliph in 830, who was sponsoring translations of Hellenistic astrology texts.[20] In the West, the border was in Spain, the southern part of which had been under Muslim control since the early eighth century. The new Muslim rulers permitted Christians and Jews to remain, and so Muslim cities in Spain had Christian bishops. Some of the interactions between Christians and Muslims were, of course, hostile – Muslim armies attacked France at the Battle of Tours in 732, laying waste to the area before being driven back. Some interactions were friendly, however. The bishop of Córdoba in Islamic Spain in the ninth century lamented the fact that young Christians in the city couldn't write a letter in Latin, but could write excellent poetry in Arabic![21]

These borderlands provided a fertile environment for the transmission of ideas. In Chapter One, we met the French scholar Gerbert d'Aurillac, who went on to become Pope Sylvester II in 999, and who introduced the Arabic astrolabe into the Christian West. It was rumoured that he studied in Córdoba – almost certainly untrue, but he did have links with Muslim Spain via a Jewish intermediary, which enabled further transmission of some astrological texts. Jewish scholars were a major source of transmission of

---

[19] Nicholas Campion, A History of Western Astrology Volume II - The Medieval and Modern Worlds (London: Continuum, 2009), p.20.

[20] John Freely, *Aladdin's Lamp: How Greek Science Came to Europe Through the Islamic World* (New York: Alfred A. Knopf, 2009), p.71.

[21] Dorothee Metlitzki, *The Matter of Araby in Medieval England* (New Haven: Yale University Press, 1977), p.5.

ideas, too, since Jews lived in Muslim countries, and many Christian countries also had Jewish communities. The Jewish rabbi and scholar Abraham ibn Ezra was born in Muslim Spain and would have been fluent in Arabic, but travelled throughout Europe, including England. We saw in Chapter One how a Jewish convert to Christianity, Petrus Alfonsi, who was born in Muslim Spain, moved to England to help the prior of Malvern translate an Arabic astronomical table. One particularly relevant event for the transmission of Arabic astrology into the Christian West came in 1085 when Toledo, near modern-day Madrid and a great centre of Islamic learning, fell to the Christians. The Spanish king who took over Toledo, Alfonso VI of Castile, encouraged its Arabic and Jewish scholars to stay, and Christian scholars flocked to Toledo to learn Arabic and translate Arabic texts on medicine, science, and astrology into Latin. This was a turning-point for astrology in the West. As we saw in Chapter One, the twelfth century saw a flood of astrological texts translated from Arabic into Latin, and this chapter has given an insight into why these texts were in Arabic in the first place, and how they found their way into the Latin West. Astrology had come full circle. The Hellenistic astrology used in the Roman Empire centuries earlier had moved east in the face of Christian antipathy, been adopted and modified by the new Islamic empire, and this revamped Arabic version of Hellenistic astrology was translated into Latin and became the medieval astrology taught in the Latin West in cathedral schools and universities. Astrology flourished in Christian Europe once again.

CHAPTER THREE: STRUCTURE OF ROGER'S BOOK

Getting hold of a book to read is easy in the twenty-first century. If I hear that Liz Greene's book on Saturn is well worth reading, it's easy enough for me to get hold of a copy. The author has a clearly defined name that she uses: Liz Greene. I don't need to know that she was born Elizabeth Leigh in New Jersey, USA and that she got her PhD from the University of Bristol, because she is always known as "Liz Greene", and not "Elizabeth the American", or "Leigh of Bristol" so I don't need to agonise over whether I've got the right author. The book has a clearly defined title: *Saturn: A New Look at an Old Devil*. I don't need to worry about trying to find the opening words "In the tale of Beauty and the Beast..." of the introduction to her book, or "A traditional reading of Saturn in the signs and houses may be found in a number of textbooks", which are the opening words of Chapter One of the book, because no catalogue will use that system for identifying a book. I can even discuss the issues the book raises with a friend who lives in another country by referencing the chapter or page number, provided we both have the same edition.

Medieval manuscripts didn't have those luxuries. They didn't have titles. The authors often didn't sign their names. If the same author wrote more than one manuscript and they happened to be bound together in the same volume, later librarians couldn't always tell where one manuscript ended and the other began. Roger's textbook is no exception. There was no clear definition of a "book", either. Manuscripts were all copied by hand, and scribes would sometimes copy lots of manuscripts from different authors. They may have been bound together into a single **codex**, which is just a volume of manuscripts, often organised by theme, and placed in a cathedral or monastic library. Then, centuries later, they may have been rebound in a completely different order, with other manuscripts added to a codex and others removed. These later codices are the ones that are sitting in university libraries today, and most of the catalogues describing these codices were compiled in Victorian times, and aren't always correct. Trickier still, although there are some helpful websites, there's no such thing as a "universal catalogue" with all manuscripts in. Roger's manuscript was copied a lot, and there are 22 existing copies (unfortunately, nobody has located his original twelfth-century version – the oldest existing copy is from between 1240 and 1250, a few decades after Roger wrote the original). To find the manuscript, you need to know which library it's in – and then get hold of that library's catalogue and hunt through it to find the possible text you want. As they didn't generally have actual titles, cataloguers simply made one up, or used the first line of the text as a title. For example, Cambridge University Library has two copies of Roger's textbook. One is in the catalogue as "GG vi.3, Liber Mgri Rogeri de Hereford de Judiciis siderum et Astrologie", the other is exactly the same text but the cataloguer assumed it was two different texts, so appears as "II i.1, Liber Magistri Rogeri de Herfordia de judiciis Astronomie" and "Liber de Tribus generalibus Judiciis Astronomie ex quibus cetera omnia defluunt editus a Magistro Rogero de Herfordia". The library at Dijon has a copy of the same text too, which is listed in their catalogue as "Quoniam circa tria fit omnis astronomica consideratio".

Confusing? It gets worse!

To add to the confusion, Roger's text is laid out in a way that is confusing to our modern mindset. He starts his textbook with a prologue, which states why he's written the book and how it's laid out. He's written the book, he tells us, because the techniques he describes come from lots of different sources (although he doesn't tell us which ones), so he's putting them together into a single volume to satisfy the needs of his students. In terms of layout, he says that his book is in four parts, and he lists them: simple judgements, intentions, elections, and the method of judgement. This sounds simple enough, but the text isn't quite as clear-cut, because immediately after the prologue, Roger's book has a very lengthy reference section describing planets, signs, and various techniques. We'd be forgiven for thinking that is the first part – but it isn't. It was quite usual in medieval texts to include reference material as a sort of primer, but it's considered a separate item to the main text; indeed, several of the manuscripts leave it out altogether. After the reference material, Roger launches into what some catalogues assume is an entirely different manuscript – but in fact, the next section is the first part that Roger promised, on simple judgements. Parts two and three – the section on intentions, and the following one on elections – are also highlighted quite clearly in most of the manuscripts. However, the fourth part, which Roger promised would be on the "method of judging", is so short that it's hard to tell whether it's a separate part or not. I did eventually find evidence that it was, but it really does give the sense of Roger running out of steam for his last two pages, and simply jotting down a few observations, in stark contrast to the earlier sections, which go into a lot of detail. Maybe the new term was starting, and Roger was keen to get his book out there!

These discrepancies have caused all sorts of problems. Roger also wrote another work on astrology describing its "four parts", which is an astrological miscellany and entirely different to the textbook. However, as described above, the textbook was also, according to Roger, "in four parts", leading many librarians and scholars to confuse the two works. Some of Roger's other works are attributed to "Rogerus Infans" and "Roger Yonge", again highlighting the problem of authors being known under different pseudonyms – surnames were something of a novelty in medieval times.

To avoid all this confusion, therefore, I've taken all 22 existing manuscripts, resolved the discrepancies in the text (thankfully, most of them were very similar to each other) and laid it out in a clearer order. I'm ignoring any of Roger's other nicknames, and calling him "Roger of Hereford". The textbook doesn't have a formal title, so I've given it one: *Judicial Astrology*. It's clear from the sections in it that Roger is focusing on horary astrology, which is where a chart is cast for the moment that a question is asked, and then used to answer the question. Horary was very popular in medieval times, because there were no clocks, and it was often hard to establish an accurate natal chart.

In this book, I've followed Roger's stated layout, and relegated the lengthy (but, frankly, not very exciting) reference section to Appendix One. I've also written a primer (not related to Roger's work at all) giving the basics of medieval astrology in Appendix Two, so if you're not familiar with the principles of medieval astrology, I'd recommend reading this before tackling Roger's material in the following chapters.

The layout in this book looks like this:

Ch 4	Prologue	Roger's introduction, telling us why he's written this book and why astrology is the finest of all the arts
Ch 5	Simple judgements	Some basic principles of horary astrology
Ch 6	Intentions	How to find out why your client is really visiting you
Ch 7	Elections	How to elect the best time to do something
Ch 8	Method of judging	A few closing comments and miscellaneous techniques
App 1	Reference	Reference material from Roger
App 2	Medieval astrology primer	My primer on medieval astrology if you're not familiar with the general principles

In each chapter, I've let Roger speak to us first, and then I've commented on what he's said. He spoke to his students in Latin, and wrote in Latin, so I'm paraphrasing Roger's Latin text so he can speak to us in modern English. Roger's words are in a box, to make them stand out.

CHAPTER FOUR: PROLOGUE

The rules of judicial astrology are described in a number of sources, but to make it easier to explain I've collated them all into a single book – the textbook you're reading now. It was a difficult task, but astrology is such an important subject I was compelled by the superior merits of this art to undertake it.

Astrology underpins everything else – without it, all the other arts and sciences would be like the dead branch of a tree that doesn't bear fruit. The heavenly bodies provide little nuggets when you dig into them. Numbers, measurements, proportions – investigating these gives you insight into everything (except for the mysterious ways of God, of course).

Why would you want to study astrology? It's obvious! It rewards you by showing you future events, and things that are hidden from most people – and that gives you power over other people! So, apart from the Mind of God Himself, who brought astrology itself into existence, astrology is the most defined, certain, and excellent of all the arts.

Roger's opening statement tells us that he's written this book to gather together a lot of material on judicial astrology – the astrology of making judgements, which in the case of his book means horary astrology – that he's found in other sources. As we saw in the first two chapters, there was always the danger that the pagan origins of astrology presented a potential threat of heresy to monotheistic religions like Islam and Christianity, and many authors of astrological works felt the need to justify their study. Roger starts his prologue by explaining that he was "compelled by the superior merits of this art" to compile his book, and goes on to justify why he considered astrology to be the greatest of the arts, but – like the Arabic authors – throws in statements to ensure he exempts the actions of God from the laws of astrology.

However, that's as far as he goes. Abū Maʿšar devoted two fairly large chapters to defending astrology against accusations of blasphemy. Roger gives us a couple of throwaway lines before bluntly extolling the virtues of astrology, and pointing out that its usefulness is obvious – knowing the future and knowing about hidden things gives you power over other people. That doesn't sound very pious, but it sounds like an excellent technique for piquing the interest of schoolkids in a classroom!

Roger now expands on his reasons for calling astrology the "most defined, certain and excellent art":

> **Defined:** there are boundless things in art and science, some relating to individuals, some relating to groups, but these can all be narrowed down by means of seven planets and twelve signs.
>
> **Certain:** in all other sciences we deal with variable matter subject to the material world and the laws of physics. Let's say you carry out an experiment on something from nature, like a rose – we can learn from that, but a rose changes according to time and place, and a rose is just one thing we could investigate, out of countless numbers of possibilities. Now consider the heavenly bodies – finite, incorruptible, and unalterable. If we can learn about a rose by some small experiment, something changeable, think how much more certain we can be when dealing with the experience of the whole of invariable matter – the heavenly bodies. We can use reason and study the principles of number, measurements, movements, and seasons, and understand the mathematics of proportion to do this. The other sciences, however, investigate individual effects looking at each case separately. Just as we can use our senses to detect the whiteness of snow, the sweetness of honey, and the warmth of wine, the other sciences can investigate individual things – but this does not prove that these scientific conclusions are universal, applying everywhere. For instance, consider the qualities of something – beautiful, sweet-sounding, fragrant, or gentle. The Sun, Moon, or another planet represents these qualities too, qualities that increase when the planet is rising, and weaken when setting. This applies when the planet is rising literally, or when it is doing so in a chart. Calculations, investigations, measurements, and proportions add refinements, and then you can choose the dominant themes.

> The other arts have their fruit, but the fruit of astrology is universal judgement (except for the miracles of God, which can never be subject to the laws of nature).

Astrology is "defined" as it is able to narrow everything down to seven planets and twelve signs, and "certain" since while experiments in the natural world can give limited information about physical things, astrology gives knowledge of the whole universe. Thus, Roger explains that astrology uses universal rules, while other sciences look at individual effects, which may explain specific cases but cannot be universally applied. Astrology, on the other hand, provides a universal understanding of everything. Again, Roger needs to add the caveat that the Will of God Himself is the exception, as this always stands outside nature.

Medieval philosophy, based on Plato and Aristotle, saw the Earth surrounded by planetary spheres, and that the heavenly bodies beyond the Moon were pure and incorruptible. The Moon could be seen to be visibly pockmarked, of course, so the Moon was the dividing line between a pure heaven and a corrupt Earth. This is why Roger was so passionate about astrology – looking at pure heavenly bodies had to be better than trying to work out nature by looking at corrupt things on Earth. It's a very Platonic worldview.

> Up until now, nobody had collected these universal rules of the astrologers together, so that's what I'm doing now. With this in mind I have produced tables of hours, natures of the signs, times of the planets and houses, debilities of the planets, planetary conditions, reception in the chart, strength of planets in signs and the amount of strength they have. Then I have divided this work into four parts: the first part concerns simple judgements, the second part intentions, the third part elections and the fourth part the method of judging.

Roger therefore ends his prologue by reasserting his claim that he is the first person to combine the rules of astrology into a single volume, containing initially reference material and then a book in four clear parts – thereby creating the first horary astrology textbook in England. Roger doesn't give his book a name, but I have – and shall refer to it as *Judicial Astrology* from now.

Roger provides only one worked example in *Judicial Astrology*, but to explain his concepts I have included many more examples that aren't in his textbook. As a teacher, he would have been likely to demonstrate examples on a wax tablet – the medieval equivalent of a whiteboard – to his students, and so they would not be included in the manuscript.

CHAPTER FIVE: SIMPLE JUDGEMENTS

Immediately following the prologue, some manuscripts have the reference material that Roger mentioned – tables of hours, planetary conditions and so on. Some manuscripts leave it out completely. It does seem that Roger considers his book to be the "four parts" that he mentions, rather than the reference material, and indeed the real meat of the book where Roger shines as a teacher does begin with the section on simple judgements. The reference material is mostly a set of facts and figures copied verbatim from Arabic sources, while the textbook material on questions has a clearer structure, starting off simply and then building up, just as modern teacher would do.

However, the reference material doesn't simply comprise lists of tables; he starts off by discussing different types of zodiac, what astrological houses mean astronomically, and how to use an astrolabe to draw up the house cusps of a chart, before launching into the natures of the signs and planets. I've put all of this material into Appendix One – although it is interesting in parts, it is very wordy and not necessary to appreciate the main part of *Judicial Astrology*.

Some manuscripts have clear headings for each section written in the margin, and some don't. In this book, I've broken each chapter up based on the structure found in the earliest existing manuscript, which is a manuscript called Selden Supra 76, dating from between 1240 and 1250, at the Bodleian Library in Oxford.

> There are three categories within judicial astrology, and everything in astrology arises from these three categories. You must select these carefully to discover what events will come about and prevail. These three categories are: bringing about a good outcome or avoiding a bad one; determining intentions and thoughts; and arranging something and electing a date. We will now examine how these things are determined.

Having told us that his book is in four parts, he rather confusingly names just three of them here, which he has already specified before: asking a question (to get a good outcome or avoid a poor one), determining intentions, and electing a date for something. Asking a question is generally referred to today as horary astrology, although the term was not in use in Roger's time; it was either referred to as "questions", or "interrogations".

Questions

First, see if there is a connection between the Lord of the Ascendant or the Moon, and the Lord of the house relating to the matter asked about. The Lord of the Ascendant or the Moon signifies the querent, and the Lord of the house relating to the matter asked about signifies the thing quesited. If the querent's significator (Lord of the Ascendant or Moon) is perfecting an aspect to the quesited's significator, the querent will strive to gain the quesited thing. Finally, if the quesited's significator is perfecting an aspect to the querent's significator, the quesited will come to the querent easily.

A key feature of horary astrology is finding certain key planets called **significators**. This is vital to any astrological judgement. For example, if someone is about to undertake a journey, they may visit an astrologer to ask about the outcome. The astrologer will cast a chart for the time the question is asked, and make a judgement according to the chart, based on the significators.

Some terminology and basic concepts are useful at this point. The person asking the question is the **querent**. The thing being asked about – it might be another person, a lost object, a journey and so on – is usually referred to as the **quesited** in most astrological texts. However, in this section, Roger refers to "the matter asked about", which he subsequently tends simply to call "res", the Latin word for the thing or matter. For this reason, I have generally used the term **matter** to refer to the matter or thing or person that the question relates to.

As a general rule in horary astrology, the querent and the matter are personified by planets in the chart. Planets are the active agents, signs determine how strong or weak they are, and houses refer to areas of life. To make a judgement about a question, it is first necessary to identify the planets that will signify the outcome. These are the significators.

Since the first house, which starts at the Ascendant, is about the person themselves, the planet ruling the sign of the Ascendant represents the querent. This planet is the **Lord of the Ascendant**. The matter being asked about is suggested by a house – if the querent is asking about a journey, that would be a ninth house matter, since the ninth house relates to long journeys. If the question was about a marriage, that would be a seventh house matter, and so on. The ruler of that house – by which is meant the planet ruling the sign that the cusp of that house is in – is the **Lord of the matter**. Finally, the **Moon**, which is fast-moving, is also used to represent the querent in addition to the Lord of the Ascendant. These three planets constitute the three main significators.

Having identified the two planets representing the querent and the matter, plus the Moon which also represents the querent, we look at aspects between these planets. The chart, however, is not a static thing. Let us assume that the querent is a man asking whether he will marry a particular woman, and the chart cast for the moment of the question is as shown in Figure 5.1. In this hypothetical example, the querent is represented by the Lord of the Ascendant and the Moon. The Ascendant is Pisces, ruled by Jupiter, so the Lord of the Ascendant is Jupiter. Thus Jupiter and the Moon represent the querent. The question is about marriage, which is a seventh house matter, and the cusp of the seventh house is Virgo, ruled by Mercury. Hence the Lord of the matter is Mercury, who represents the querent's love interest. Will the man get his woman? There is no aspect between Jupiter and Mercury – Mercury is at 1° Virgo and Jupiter at 12° Cancer, so are 49° apart – too close for a sextile aspect of 60°. However, Mercury moves faster than Jupiter. Mercury is only at 1° Virgo currently, but in a few days will have reached 12° Virgo, at which point Mercury will be exactly sextile Jupiter (who will have barely moved in that time) – there will be an aspect between them. We say that Mercury is **applying** to Jupiter. The astrologer would say that the aspect is being **perfected**, and, metaphorically, the woman of our querent's affection – the quesited – is rushing towards him, and so the matter will come to a satisfactory conclusion and the man will get what he is hoping for without striving.

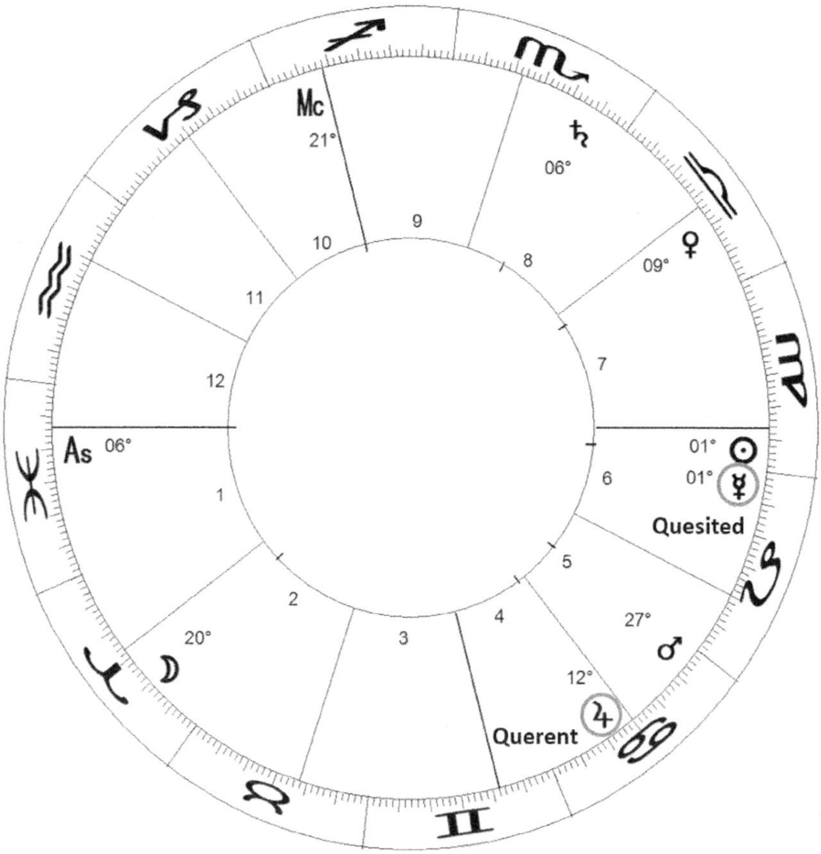

Figure 5.1: Will I marry this woman? Perfecting aspect.

On choosing a significator

> However, what happens if the Lord of the Ascendant or the Moon are impeded? In this case, if the Lord of the Ascendant aspects the Ascendant but the Moon does not, then use the Lord of the Ascendant as the significator. If the Moon aspects the Ascendant, but the Lord of the Ascendant does not, use the Moon; whichever of the two is the stronger. If neither can be used as the significator, consider if either of their rulers aspects the Ascendant. Or see if any of the other seven planets aspect the Ascendant. Whichever is strongest would be able to act as significator.
>
> If a possible connection is found, consider the degrees of the signs of the planets and how fast they are moving. Whichever planet perfects an aspect to the Ascendant first will be the planet involved in the judgement.
>
> There are two ways an aspect can happen – by house or by sign, and the aspect may be a sextile, square, trine or opposition. When aspecting by house, this will vary according to latitude, where a sign might contain two house cusps. In this case you could have a sextile aspect by house of less than 30 degrees, or from 20 degrees of Aries to 20 degrees of Taurus. For example, one house cusp could be 2 degrees of Taurus and another at 24 degrees of Taurus.

Not all examples are as clear-cut as the example about marriage above. The text had started with a simple rule to identify relevant planets, but now goes on to say that sometimes those relevant planets aren't strong enough to be candidates, for example because the planet may be in fall, or in an unfortunate house. In this case, the planet is said to be **impeded**, and Roger provides a list of impediments in the reference section, which is given in Appendix One of this book.

If the planet representing the querent, or the Moon, is impeded then the aspect cannot be perfected using that planet. A few more rules are given: to answer a question, a planet must be found that can act as significator, so if the obvious candidates for the querent – the Lord of the Ascendant and Moon – are impeded and additionally do not aspect the Ascendant and cannot be used, see if the ruler of the impeded planet or the ruler of the Moon aspects the Ascendant. If they do not, see which other planets aspect the Ascendant. There may be more than one, in which case the strongest planet is used – this is determined using a scoring system described in Appendix Two. If more than one possible planet that can be a significator is identified, the text goes on to say that one must see how fast the candidates are moving, and which planet will perfect an aspect to the Ascendant first – and that planet will be the one involved in the judgement.

Roger's comments about "house or sign" are a little confusing to our modern way of thinking, as we're used to measuring aspects along the ecliptic. If one planet is at 25 Gemini and another at 25 Aquarius, they're clearly trine, not square. However, medieval astrology paid attention not only to the ecliptic, but also to the celestial equator. This was important for a predictive technique called **primary directions**. Although Roger does not give details of primary directions, he does point out here that aspects can happen in two ways: by house or by sign. Signs are precise thirty-degree divisions of the ecliptic; houses in quadrant systems can vary in size and be more than thirty degrees or less than thirty degrees. The reason for this is that houses reflect positions in the sky on the celestial equator rather than the ecliptic. In fact, although I've translated Roger's text as saying the division is "by house" or "by sign", the Latin term that Roger uses for the former is "per celum", which literally means "by the heavens".

Illustrations demonstrating the difference between house aspects and sign aspects are given in Figures 5.2 to 5.5.

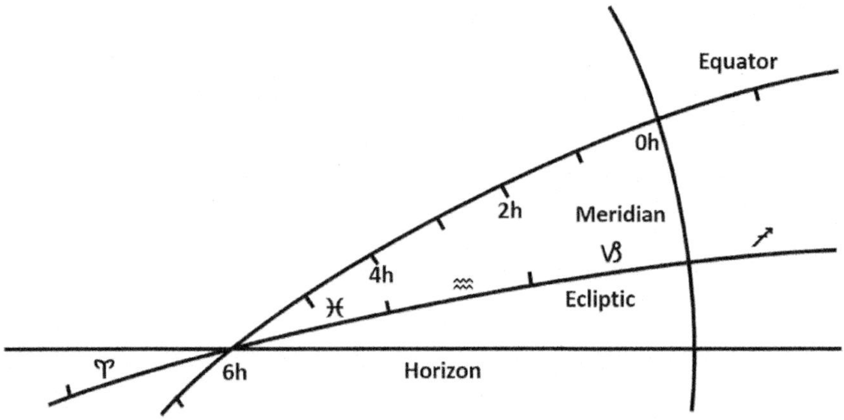

Figure 5.2: Aries rising, Capricorn culminating.

Figure 5.2 shows a diagram of the sky when 0° Aries is rising at the latitude of Hereford. 0° Aries is defined as the point where the celestial equator crosses the ecliptic. When this point rises over the eastern horizon (the Ascendant is simply the part of the ecliptic rising over the horizon), the point culminating on the ecliptic (this is the MC, which is simply the point where the southern meridian and the ecliptic cross) will always be 0° Capricorn. The distance along the ecliptic between the Ascendant and the MC in this example is exactly three signs, or 90°. The distance along the celestial equator between the point where the equator intersects the horizon and where the equator intersects the meridian is also 90°. Note that distance along the celestial equator is generally given in hours in modern astronomical texts, where one hour is equivalent to 15°.

To see what this looks like on an astrological chart, Figure 5.3 shows the chart for the spring equinox of 1176, with 0° Aries rising. The houses are of roughly equal size, and the distance between the Ascendant and the MC is exactly 90°.

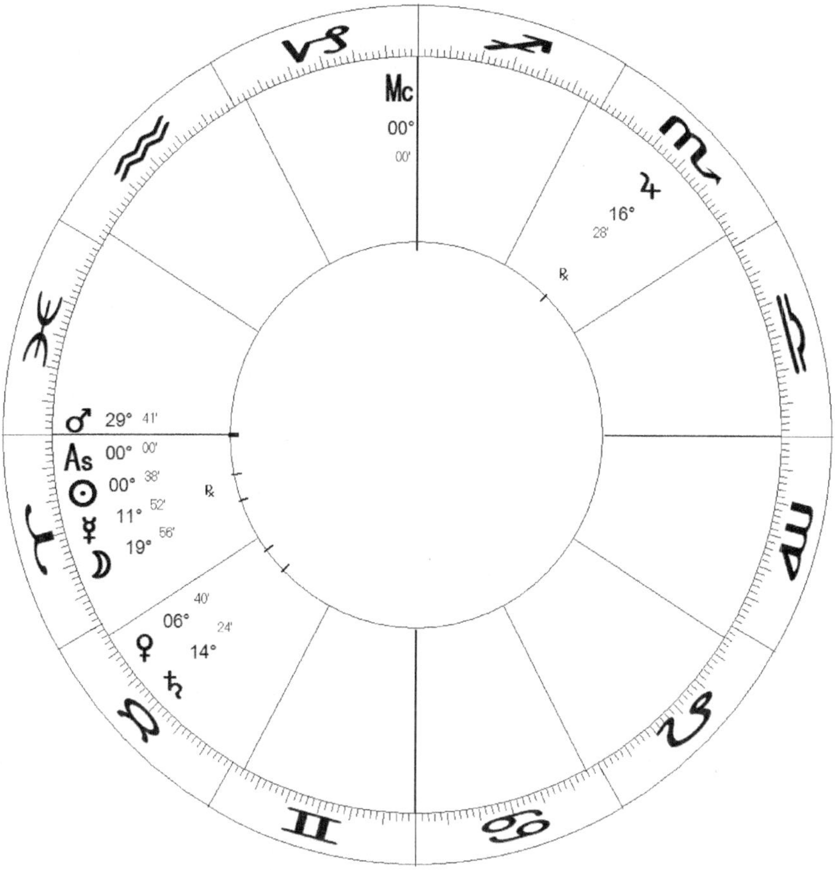

Figure 5.3: Chart for the spring equinox of 1176, with 0° Aries rising.

Figure 5.4 shows a diagram of the sky when 0° Cancer is rising at the latitude of Hereford. The distance along the ecliptic between the Ascendant and the MC in this example is just over four signs – 126°40′, in fact. However, the distance along the celestial equator between the point where the equator intersects the horizon and where the equator intersects the meridian is exactly 90°, as it was in the previous example.

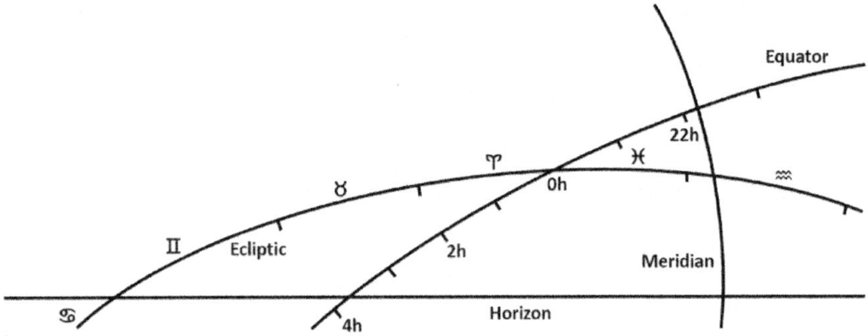

Figure 5.4: Chart for the summer solstice of 1176, with 0° Cancer rising.

Figure 5.5 shows what this example looks like on an astrological chart – this is the chart for the summer solstice of 1176. In this example, the houses between the Ascendant and MC are all more than 30° and the distance between the Ascendant and MC is 126°40′, but this still corresponds to a distance of just 90° on the celestial equator.

In this example, we can see that using positions along the ecliptic, a planet on the Ascendant and another on the MC would be making a trine, but in another sense – measuring along the celestial equator – they would be 90° apart and, in that sense, would be making a square aspect rather than a trine. In modern astrology, we generally wouldn't take that into account, but Roger makes the point that one can consider aspects along both the ecliptic and the celestial equator.

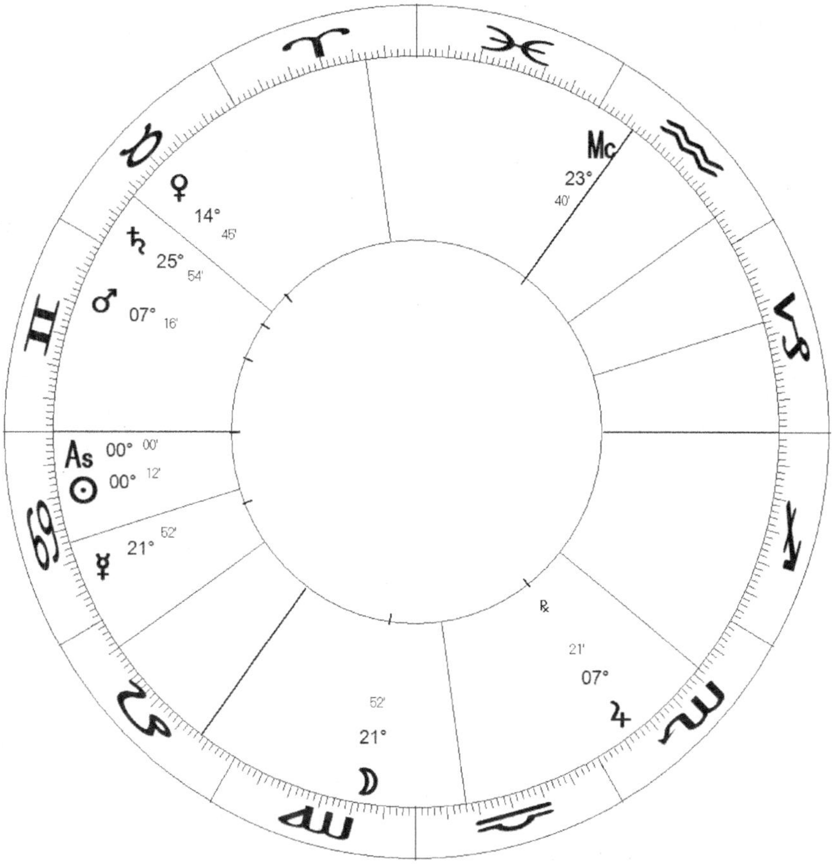

Figure 5.5: Chart for the summer solstice of 1176, with 0° Cancer rising.

Revisiting the examples given in Roger's text, two planets could be less than thirty degrees apart, but be two houses apart. An example is shown in Figure 5.6, where the cusp of the fifth house is at 2° Taurus, and the cusp of the sixth house is at 24° Taurus, as in Roger's example. The Moon is in the first degree of Taurus, and the Sun in the twenty-ninth degree; they are less than thirty degrees apart, and do not make an aspect using ecliptic degrees. However, the Moon is in the fourth house, and the Sun is in the sixth house, and so they are two houses apart. Roger's text suggests that these are "sextile" by house for this reason. In fact, this is not astronomically correct, as the distance between these two planets along the celestial equator is about 39°, not 60° since the Moon is close to the end of the fourth house, while the Sun is close to the start of the sixth. However, the idea that an aspect between two planets may be purely by the relationship of their respective houses, rather than by the number of degrees within those houses, does appear in both Hellenistic and Arabic astrology with respect to aspects by sign. It was the norm in Hellenistic astrology that aspects were by sign rather than degrees – so a planet in Sagittarius would always trine a planet in Leo, regardless of the degree position. Aspects between planets were still considered by sign in Arabic texts; Abū Maʿšar describes aspects by sign (rather than degree) in his *Great Introduction,* which states that although aspects between planets are by sign, they are stronger if the degrees of the planets within the aspecting signs are closer, and weaker if they are further apart.

Although not subsequently referred to specifically in *Judicial Astrology,* which is a book on horary astrology rather than natal, aspects between points in a chart based on the celestial equator rather than the ecliptic was an important technique in natal astrology dating back to Ptolemy. In Ptolemy's *Tetrabiblos,* the chapter on determining the length of life involves identifying a planet that acts as "prorogator", the giver of life, and to calculate how long it takes for a malefic planet to reach the degree of the prorogator. This calculation is based on the rising times of each sign, which involves converting degrees of the zodiac into degrees of right ascension measured on the celestial equator. Al-Qabisi gave a detailed description of a method that corresponds closely to Ptolemy's method, showing that the use of measurements based on the celestial equator extended into Arabic texts too for the purpose of predictive astrology.

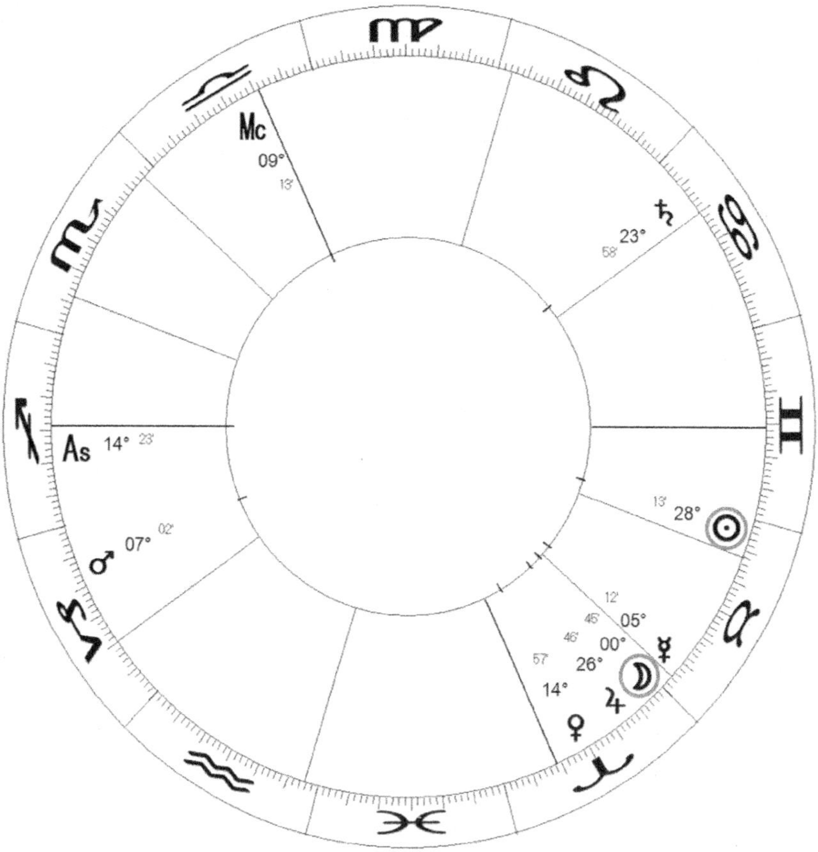

Figure 5.6: Sextile by house.

Tuning the techniques

The Moon participates with the Lord of the Ascendant in all questions except those concerning the life of the querent (in which case the Lord of the Ascendant is the stronger). If the Lord of the Ascendant is strong and not aspecting the Lord of the matter, and the Moon is weak, then the achievement will be weaker or more difficult. In a question regarding the life of the querent, if the Lord of the Ascendant were strong and not impeded by the Lord of the eighth house, then the person's life will not be impeded.

If the Lord of the Ascendant or the Moon do not aspect the Ascendant, look at all the planets that aspect the Ascendant and, see what they are applying to and what they are separating from. If there are none, then they are said to be void of course. If the Lord of the Ascendant or the Moon aspect a planet applying to the Ascendant, then whichever of these two aspects that planet and is stronger in the place of that planet is elected as the significator. Note that the strongest position is in the angles, the next strongest in succedent houses, and the weakest in cadent houses.

If there are no such connections but the Lord of the matter is in the first house and not impeded, then use the Lord of the matter to represent the querent. If in addition the Lord of the Ascendant or the Moon is in the house of the matter and not impeded, then the querent will gain the thing. If the Lord of the Ascendant or the Moon do aspect the Lord of the matter, but will perfect an aspect to another planet, the matter will come to pass but there will be a delay.

But always consider impediments, and whether the Lord of the Ascendant or the Moon, and the Lord of the matter, suggest that the querent or the matter are impeded. Friendship between the relevant planets will make the matter come more easily; enmity will signify difficulties.

> Similarly, the matter will more likely come to pass if there are stronger planets in the house of the matter. There are three ways of judging – the first, the middle and the last. The first is the Moon. The second, the faster of the Lord of the Ascendant and the Lord of the matter. The third, the slower of these two. If all are in good condition, all of the activity will be good and can be judged in the same way. If the Moon is impeded, the first part will be bad. If the second significator is impeded, then the second part will be bad. And if all are impeded then the whole of the matter will be bad.

This section of the text fine-tunes the basic technique that Roger had introduced. It starts with an example about life and death; questions about life and death were common in medieval times, and the astrology is fairly literal. The Ascendant signifies life, and the eighth house signifies death, and the first example simply says that if the planet representing the querent is strong, and the planet representing death (the ruler of the eighth house) is not doing anything unpleasant to the planet representing the querent, then the querent will not die.

For all questions, Roger has already told us that we should use the Lord of the Ascendant and the Moon to represent the querent, provided that at least one of those aspects the Ascendant. However, that ideal situation does not always apply. In that case, look for other planets aspecting the Ascendant, and see what they are applying to and separating from; if a planet doesn't apply to another, then it is **void of course**. Where there is no significator, an event does not come to pass, and the querent gets a negative answer. In determining planetary strength where a significator is found, Roger reminds us that planets in angular houses (first, fourth, seventh, and tenth) are strongest, and those in cadent houses (third, sixth, ninth, and twelfth) are weakest.

In a simple question, the ideal outcome is for the Lord of the Ascendant or the Moon (the querent) to gain what he or she is looking for, which is seen by that planet perfecting an aspect to the planet representing the matter being asked about. Sometimes that aspect will take place, but before it does the relevant planet will aspect another planet first. Again, this is fairly literal; the querent wants something, and both the querent and the thing he or she wants (the "matter") are represented by planets. If the planet of the matter is moving to the querent's planet, the querent will gain what he or she is looking for. However, if the planet of the matter meets another planet on the way, that represents a delay – in exactly the same way that someone coming to your house for dinner can be waylaid by meeting an old friend on the way.

There may be an aspect between two planets, but it is also important to bear in mind whether those two planets are friendly or hostile to each other – the concept of friendship and enmity between planets is covered in the reference material given in Appendix One. This indicates something of the nature of the matter; if the question is about whether the querent will get to speak to the king, the answer might be that she will, but that the king will not be friendly towards her.

Finally, this section of the text suggests that the matter in question and its resolution can be divided into three stages – the first part, the middle and the end. The first is signified by the Moon, the second by the faster of the Lord of the Ascendant and the Lord of the matter, and the last part the slower of those two. If all of those planets are in good condition, the entire activity will be good and can be judged in the same way; if the Moon is impeded, the first part will be bad, and so on. If all planets are in a bad condition, then the whole of the matter will be bad.

Other methods – intermediaries

We have just dealt with the first method of investigation. Now we will discuss a second method, using intermediaries. If one cannot find a connection between any of the usual three significators or their substitutes, we look for a connection between the Lord of the matter or a substitute. This is anything faster-moving, which can transfer light from one to the other. The matter will happen by this intermediary by examining it in the same way as if it were the significator. There are two ways in which light can be transferred: a body that has fewer degrees and is faster-moving than another planet can make a connection with the slower-moving planet either by conjunction or by aspect [translation], or one planet has more degrees and is faster-moving but both the slower-moving planet and it will conjunct or aspect another planet [collection].

If the Lord of the Ascendant or the Moon and the Lord of the matter are conjunct any slower planet, then the matter will be decided by a "team of judges" based on the best aspect joining them (including sextile and trine) that agrees most closely in nature (for example, by masculine or feminine) or by place in the zodiac. The above substitute will also be strong as a candidate. The closest one by degree will be favoured. Any impediment will disqualify this candidate, though, as always. Consider what is impeded – is it the thing or the querent? Above all, consider the aspects relating the two to see if the end will be achieved, or ruined.

Then remember that if there are no aspects between the Lord of the Ascendant or the Moon to the Lord of the matter but three or four planets have made a recent connection to one, judge all of them. Look at the one that most recently perfected the aspect. Any impediment will destroy the outcome, so that planet cannot be used. Look for good planets in the house of the matter or the first house. Often one can find something that bestows the matter without impediment. Look for the Part of Fortune and Part of the Future and note all the good and bad planets.

Also consider the Lord of the Part of Fortune, the ruler of the Moon, and the planet ruling the hour. In a daytime chart, consider the Sun and the ruler of the house that the Sun is in, and in a nocturnal chart the ruler of the house that the Moon is in. Then see which of all of these is the strongest in the chart. See which planet is the strongest in the degree of the Ascendant. Having discovered the significator, it will be possible to predict the outcome. Though there may be doubt about which of the planets to choose, this method will find the right candidate. Take into account, too, the New Moon or Full Moon chart prior to the spring equinox, and the next conjunction of Saturn and Jupiter to determine the outcome fully.

In summary, there are four things to enquire about: 1. The nature of the planet that is the significator and the sign it is in; 2. The sign of the Ascendant and the sign on the cusp of the house of the matter; 3. How every planet, rulers of the parts, and planetary hours participate and in what way; 4. The essential and accidental dignities of everything investigated. Careful examination of all of these will determine the outcome of the question.

Roger addresses a problem that frustrates most people when they begin to study astrology – how do you deal with all the apparently contradictory messages that a chart gives? Roger had started off with a very simple rule, then built on that by giving other techniques if the obvious candidates weren't strong enough to be used. Now he gives some other techniques, this time involving intermediaries if the usual significators can't be used. The language used in the text is quite complicated, but the principle is quite simple and best demonstrated by a non-astrological analogy. Imagine you wish to communicate with some local worthy, such as the bishop. Clearly, the easiest way of effecting this meeting is either you go to the bishop's residence, or he comes to yours. That is akin to the sort of "perfecting aspects" discussed so far. However, you are unable to travel far as your horse is lame, and the bishop is unwilling to come to you. You can still communicate with the bishop by sending a friend who will represent you – he or she can go to the bishop's residence instead, and you may still get the outcome you are looking for. The simplest way is for him or her to come to your house first, get debriefed, and then head off to the bishop's residence and pass on the message. The second method is that your friend lives halfway between you and the bishop, and so although neither you nor the bishop are willing to travel to each other's residences as that is too far, you are both willing to travel to your friend's residence and meet there. The first method is akin to the astrological technique of **translation**, and the second to the technique of **collection**.

Consider the chart shown in Figure 5.7 (this is a hypothetical example, and not an example given in *Judicial Astrology*). The querent has asked whether she will be able to get in touch with her estranged son. The querent is represented by the Lord of the Ascendant, Mars; the question is about her son, and children are the fifth house, so the son is represented by the ruler of the fifth house, the Sun. The Sun moves faster than Mars, and the Sun is at 17° Aries, and Mars is at 12° Aries. The Sun is separating from Mars, so just using the two planets as before, the querent (Mars) will not catch up with her son (Sun). However, Mercury moves faster than both of them. He is applying to Mars, and once he has overtaken Mars he will also apply to the Sun and catch up with the Sun too. This is a "translation", and is akin to the friend taking your message to the bishop. Mars (the querent) will never catch the Sun, but Mercury can pick up the message from Mars and pass it on to the Sun.

Note that although in this example Mercury makes a physical conjunction to both planets, the same principle would apply by aspect, too. If Mars were at 12° Aries as it is in this diagram, the Sun were at 17° Gemini and Mercury were at 10° Gemini, exactly the same rule would apply. The Sun would still be separating from Mars, but Mercury would perfect a sextile aspect first to Mars, and then perfect a conjunction to the Sun. It would still translate, and the outcome will be successful.

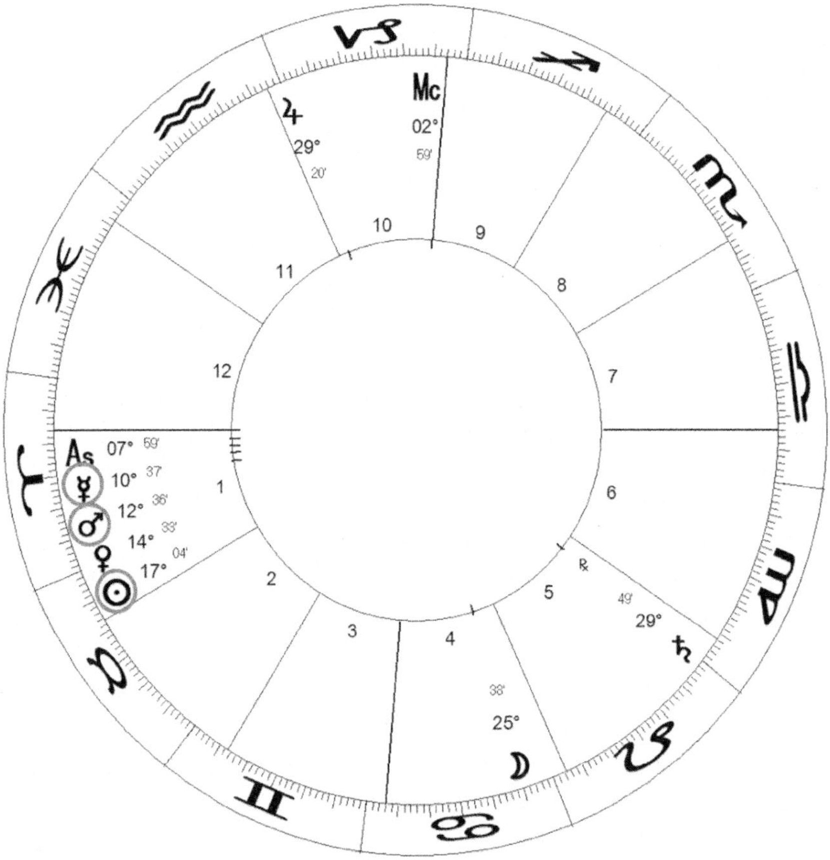

Figure 5.7: Will I see my son? Mercury translating from Mars to the Sun.

To illustrate the concept of "collection", consider the chart in Figure 5.8 in a hypothetical question about marriage. The querent has asked if she will marry a particular man. The querent is represented by the Lord of the Ascendant, Mars. The quesited is represented by Venus, ruler of the seventh house. There is no aspect between Mars and Venus, so with just those significators, the result she wants will not turn out. However, Venus at 13° Capricorn is applying to Jupiter at 15° Libra by square, and Mars at 10° Aquarius is also applying to Jupiter by trine aspect. Hence Jupiter will "collect" from both parties, and is akin to the example of you and the bishop meeting at a friend's house. Thus although the two main planets do not aspect, Jupiter collecting from both of them means a successful outcome.

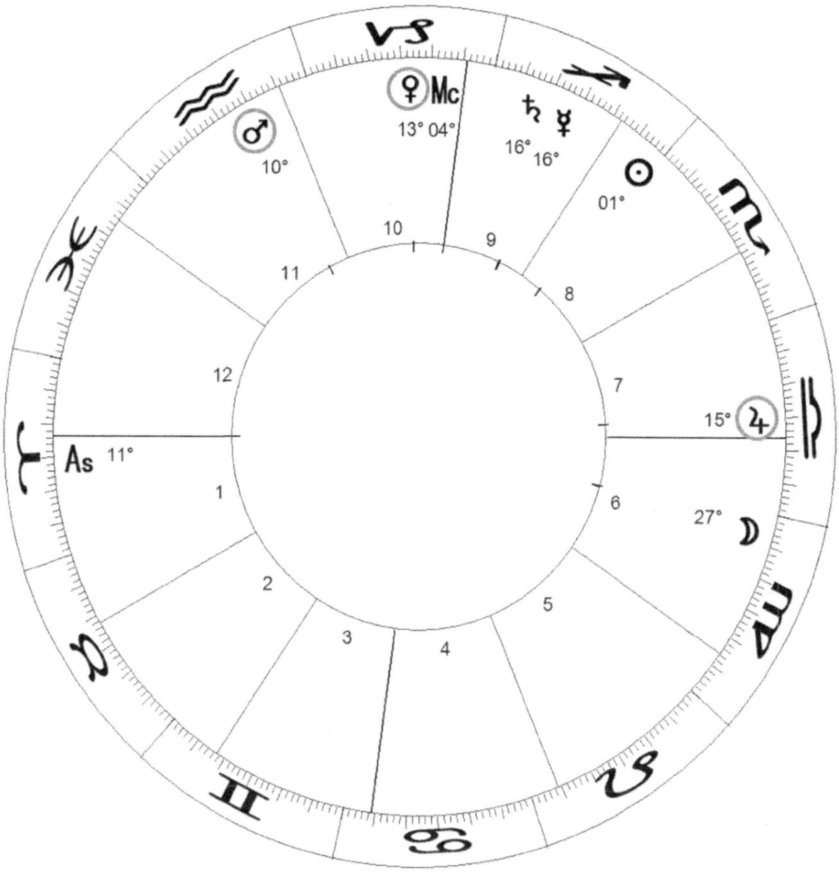

Figure 5.8: Will I marry this man? Jupiter collecting from Mars and Venus.

Intermediaries can also be used to choose the best candidate when more than one planet may be a significator. Roger uses legal terminology, likening the decision to a court case where a judge selects the best candidate.

The principle for using intermediaries is the same as for using a third planet for collection and translation – if an aspect between the querent and the matter cannot be perfected, then look for other planets that will be able to overcome obstacles. In some cases there will be more than one planet, and then it is necessary to choose the most powerful one. This will depend on all sorts of considerations – each planet's dignity, whether it is impeded, the nature of the aspect, whether the proposed planet is friendly to the planet it is acting for, and so on. In all cases, though, the key feature is to find a planet that will connect the querent and the quesited, and for that planet not to have any impediments.

Even if a significator is not immediately obvious, the text points out that one must also consider numerous other points and planets: the ruler of the Part of Fortune and Part of the Future (calculated points in the chart), the Sun, the Lord of the Moon, and the "Lord of the hour", which is the planet ruling the hour of the day (this is widely referred to in *Judicial Astrology* for determining intentions, and is covered in Chapter Six). One manuscript also adds the Sun and the Lord of the house he is in when a day chart, and the Moon and the Lord of the house she is in when a night chart. In addition, consider the planet that is strongest in the degree of the Ascendant – a scoring system is used to work out which planet is strongest at any given degree, described in Appendix Two.

The text summarises the techniques covered, and then adds a very brief comment that one should also consider the New Moon or Full Moon prior to the question being asked, or prior to the spring equinox, and the next conjunction of Saturn and Jupiter. Both of these techniques are widely used in Arabic and medieval astrology, but Roger doesn't mention them again in *Judicial Astrology*. This rather throwaway line in Roger's text is significant, because it clearly indicates that Roger expected his students to be familiar with these concepts, suggesting that *Judicial Astrology* was not intended as a complete textbook on astrological techniques, but was specifically a book on horary for readers already familiar with the basics.

Roger ends this section of the text with a summary, which though brief nevertheless demonstrates how detailed the analysis needs to be. Having started off with some simple rules and built on these, Roger demonstrates that simply looking at the obvious significators isn't the whole story – to get an accurate outcome, the astrologer needs to consider numerous points and charts to get the full story.

The concepts that Roger introduced here are not new, as they can all be found in various Arabic texts such as those by al-Kindi and Sahl; indeed, Roger told us in his prologue that these techniques could be found in various sources. However, the works of Sahl and al-Kindi have separate chapters for each type of question. Sahl's *On Questions*, for example, consistently presents questions house by house, so that the section on the sixth house has specific questions such as "Whether someone is infirm or not", or "On buying a slave", and al-Kindi's *Forty Chapters* has a variety of chapter headings on digging canals, building ships, and theft. As a result, these chapters are quite repetitive, with the same techniques reprised for each application. Roger, instead, synthesised the information in these books to give a general technique applicable to all questions, so that the reader could work out how to answer a question from first principles, rather than having to look up the relevant question in a book. Roger wasn't writing a reference book – he was writing a textbook of principles, and the method he uses to do this and the way he builds up levels of detail starting from a simple starting point demonstrates his skill as a teacher.

Reception

Reception in all judgements is powerful and to be noted. In this technique, a planet can "receive" another planet applying to it, if the applying planet has dignity in the receiving planet's location, or the receiving planet has dignity in the applying planet's location. The receiving planet is the slower-moving one, and the applying planet is the faster-moving one.

Reception works with five dignities. It can occur by sign rulership alone, or exaltation alone. It can also apply with triplicity, but only if this is together with either face or term; and similarly, term only with triplicity or face. These minor dignities only apply if the receiving planet or applying planet is in a strong angle. Reception is always beneficial, but a reception by opposition or square is harder, one by sextile or trine is gentler. Two malefics can benefit from reception, but a benefic and malefic won't accept the gift of reception.

Reception will always ameliorate.

If the Lord of the Ascendant or the Moon (whichever is stronger) applies to a benefic in the house of the matter, or even to a malefic in that house that has some dignity, then the desired outcome will occur. Similarly, if the Lord of the matter were to join to something in the Ascendant, then the outcome will be favourable. However, the receiving planet must be in an angular or succedent house, and not in an unfortunate house. Note that if the applying planet won't perfect the aspect to the receiving planet until the following sign, then the dignities it has in the degree at which it perfects should be taken into account.

Roger has already described the fundamental technique of identifying significators and looking at aspects between them, and now he continues with another very important technique called **reception**. This is effectively a combination of aspects and planetary dignities. Roger also mentions reception in the reference material that is included in some manuscripts (and reproduced here in Appendix One), but in a section where he largely just copies Hermann of Carinthia's translation of Abū Ma'šar's *Great Introduction*. However, in that section where he refers to reception, he deviates from Hermann's text, suggesting that reception played a particularly important role for Roger.

He explains the technique in more detail here. Throughout the previous section on intermediaries, the text was concerned with not only identifying the strongest planet, but considering the relationship it has with the planet for whom it is acting as an intermediary – whether it is in a beneficial aspect, whether the two planets are friendly and so on.

The general principle of reception is a relationship between two planets who can provide each other assistance, and is akin to being received as an honoured guest in somebody's house. For reception to occur between two planets, there must be an aspect between them, and one planet must be in a sign where the other has dignity. Some examples will explain this more clearly. If Jupiter is in Taurus and aspects the Sun in Pisces, neither has any particular essential dignity (at least, not by rulership or exaltation). However, Jupiter rules Pisces, and therefore when he "sees" (aspects) the Sun in Pisces that is akin to having a visitor in his home, and he therefore "receives" the Sun.

The text includes two other elements of reception. Firstly, in addition to rulership and exaltation, reception can occur if the other planet is in two other dignities of the host planet. For example, if Venus aspected Jupiter but was not in Pisces, Sagittarius or Cancer (the signs that Jupiter rules or is exalted in), but was in the triplicity of Jupiter and the terms of Jupiter, or the terms of Jupiter and the face of Jupiter, there would still be reception – but Venus would need to be in at least two of Jupiter's dignities for this to work. Secondly, the text defines the roles in reception rigidly – the receiver is always the slower-moving planet and applicant is the faster-moving one. The slower-moving planet is considered superior, like a king being approached by a commoner. The king will receive a commoner, but it would be presumptuous for a commoner to receive the king. However, the gifts can still be two-way; the king might bestow gifts on his guest, but equally the guest might give a token of gratitude to the king.

The text makes the point that reception is always beneficial. A malefic planet like Saturn will be "better behaved" if it is received, and its negative effects reduced. The analogy is that a fighter is more honourable as a soldier in an army, subject to rules and agreements, than as a lone mercenary; reception is equivalent to working in a team. Reception will also work with difficult aspects such as a square or opposition, but the benefits will be harder to come by.

Roger's definition that only the slower-moving planet can be the receiver is quite restrictive. Roger's definition was not the only one, though, and as a result of these differing definitions, the concepts associated with reception seem to have been a source of confusion for later medieval astrologers, and so it is instructive to examine some concepts and compare some terminology used by Arabic authors, to demonstrate that not all Arabic authors defined reception in the restrictive way that Roger did. Hermann's translation of Abū Maʿšar's *Great Introduction* was heavily abbreviated compared to John of Seville's translation, and while John listed twenty-one conditions of the planets, Hermann listed only eighteen. John's version has four categories relating to "pushing" ("pulsatio" in Latin), which Hermann has condensed into a separate section.[22] While two of these categories appear to relate to a faster-moving planet applying to a slower-moving one, two do not. Adelard of Bath's translation of Abū Maʿšar's *Abbreviation to the Introduction* makes this clear; he uses the term "gift" ("donum" in Latin) rather than "pushing":

> The gift of nature is if any planet occupying the house of another applies to it. Hence it is presented with its own nature by that planet, its guest... The gift of power is whenever any of the planets gives its own power to another planet occupying either its house or other dignities. The gift of two natures happens in two ways: one, if any planet situated in a place of its dignity applies to another having a dignity in the same place, the other, whenever a planet applies to a planet, each of which is in its good fortune. The gift of counsel is when in the case in which planets are in application in any place, one

[22] Abū Maʿšar, *Liber Introductorii Maioris ad Scientam Judiciorum Astrorum*, Hermann of Carinthia (trans.), Richard Lemay (ed.), Volume 8 (Napoli: Istituto Universitario Orientale, 1995), VII.3, lines 383-389.

> of them gives counsel to the other. If they are in trine or sextile or together, it is good, but square or opposition it is the reverse.[23]

The first category, the gift of nature, is the unambiguous case where a faster-moving planet applies to a slower-moving one, which receives the nature of the applying planet – which is the case described in Roger's text. The final category, the gift of counsel, allows for either the applying (faster-moving) planet or the slower-moving planet to give its counsel to the other.

Al-Qabisi uses very similar definitions, and also refers to the concept of pushing, saying "When a planet A applies to the Lord B of the sign in which A is, then A pushes its nature onto B.'[24] This makes it clear that al-Qabisi considers the faster-moving planet to be the one doing the pushing, while the slower-moving planet is the receiver.

While Roger's text follows Abū Maʿšar's and al-Qabisi in insisting that only the slower-moving planet can be the receiver, not all Arabic authors used this definition. Māshā'Allāh, for example, in his text *On Reception*, gives an example where Mars in Aries is applying to Saturn in Aries, and states that Mars receives Saturn, but Saturn does not receive Mars.[25] This contradicts Abū Maʿšar's idea that only the slower-moving planet (Saturn, in this case) can be a receiver. Māshā'Allāh's second example is of Mars in Capricorn applying to Saturn in Aries, where he states that they "receive each other mutually in their domiciles".[26] Clearly, this concept of mutual reception would not be possible if only the slower-moving planet is allowed the role of receiver.

Roger, then, is conflating various definitions from different Arabic sources. His opening paragraph states that if the applying planet has dignity in the receiving planet's location OR the receiving planet has dignity in the applying planet's location, then reception occurs. This is particularly interesting, because reception is something of a bone of contention among

---

[23] Abū Maʿšar, *The Abbreviation of the Introduction to Astrology*, Charles Burnett (trans.) (Leiden: Brill, 1994), III.30-34, p.115.

[24] Al-Qabisi, *The Introduction to Astrology*, Charles Burnett, Keiji Yamamoto, and Michio Yano (trans.) (London: Warburg Institute, 2004) III.17, p.99.

[25] Māshā'Allāh, *On Reception* in Dykes, *Sahl and Māshā'Allāh*, pp.439.

[26] Māshā'Allāh, *On Reception* in Dykes, *Sahl and Māshā'Allāh*, pp.440.

contemporary traditional astrologers. Consider the case where Venus is in Sagittarius, applying to Jupiter in Leo; does Jupiter receive Venus? Some contemporary traditional astrologers would say yes, because Jupiter loves any planet in signs that he rules, or where he's exalted – in other words, Jupiter will happily receive any planet in Cancer, Sagittarius or Pisces, provided there's an aspect between them. Thus, since Venus is in a sign that Jupiter rules, Jupiter "likes" Venus so will receive her. Others say no, it's the other way round – Venus doesn't have any major dignity in Leo, so she's not interested in Jupiter, so doesn't want to be received by Jupiter. If she were applying to a planet in Taurus, though, she'd happily be received by that planet. Roger says that either is fine – and you can find an argument to back up either case depending on which Arabic author you choose! In fact, what Roger has done is taken two types of "pushing" from the Arabic texts (the subtle distinction made by Abū Maʿšar's between "pushing nature" and "pushing power"), and said that both constitute "reception".

Finally, Roger's text gives various situations where reception cannot work, and there is a section in the text that identifies each of these briefly, and can be summarised as follows: reception cannot work if one of the planets is impeded, if the two planets have enmity, or if a planet is in a cadent house (third, sixth, ninth or twelfth). In this case, known as the **return of virtue**, the reception will not take place and neither planet will benefit from the other. The exception is that if the aspect doesn't perfect until the following sign then reception can apply if the applying planet has dignity there.

Let's have a look at the example chart in Figure 5.9.

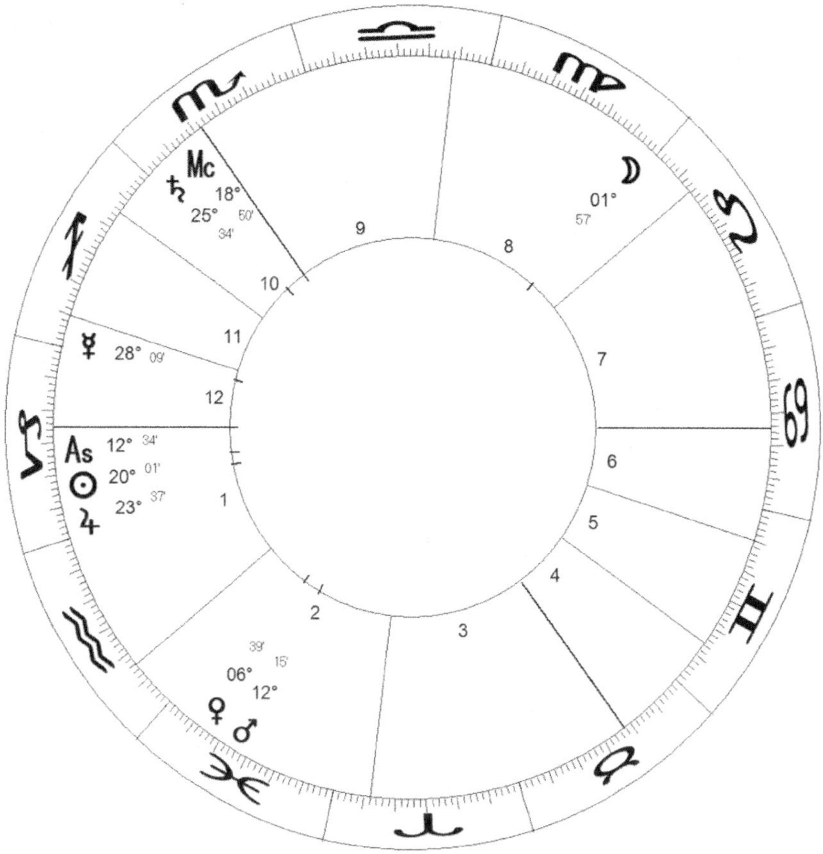

Figure 5.9: Various planets that are candidates for reception.

In this chart, Mars is applying to a trine to Saturn, the Lord of the Ascendant. Saturn is in an angular house, and Mars is in a succedent house. Mars is the faster moving of the two, and has dignity by rulership at 25° Scorpio, the position of Saturn. This fulfils Roger's first criterion and Saturn receives Mars. Venus is also applying to a trine to Saturn, but at first glance it doesn't seem that Venus has any dignity at 25° Scorpio, where she's in detriment – but in fact, Venus is a triplicity ruler of water signs and also the face ruler of the last ten degrees of Scorpio (the triplicity, term, and face rulers are given in the reference material presented here in Appendix One, and the principles are explained in Appendix Two). Although dignity by triplicity alone or face alone wouldn't qualify for reception, having at least two could do, provided that, as Roger specifies, either the receiving or applying planet is in an angle. Saturn is strongly angular in this chart. This looks promising, then, but Roger also tells us that a benefic and a malefic cannot receive one another – so although Saturn could receive Mars as a fellow malefic, he cannot receive Venus as she is a benefic – so there is no reception after all.

Jupiter is also applying to a sextile to Saturn, and is angular. Jupiter has no dignity at 25° Scorpio, but Saturn has dignity at 23° Capricorn, the position of Jupiter, and so Saturn still wishes to receive Jupiter, but as Saturn is malefic he cannot receive benefic Jupiter.

Finally, the Sun is also applying to a sextile with Saturn, and although the Sun has no dignity at 25° Scorpio, Saturn has dignity by rulership at 20° Capricorn, the position of the Sun. Saturn therefore receives the Sun.

Principle of the houses

> After electing the significator a choice of houses to represent the querent and quesited, I always ask the querent if he is asking about his friend or lord or servant, and see how the Lord of the Ascendant of the querent is allotted, to find out the true house of the matter. For example, if the query relates to his master, the first house of the master is the tenth, the second is the eleventh and so on. Hence the associates of the master (which would normally be a third house matter) would be the third from the main and so on, starting from the tenth house.
>
> The matter asked about would then be determined from this new Ascendant. So if the querent is asking on behalf of his master, then the tenth house represents the master. If it concerns a king of a foreign country or someone alien to the querent or another country then for the alien or alien country use the seventh. If the question is about the king, then use the tenth.
>
> Note that if the question relates to returning to one's own homeland, the usual sequence of signs is reversed, so if the first house is Aries, then second house matters would be Pisces, third house matters Aquarius and so on.

As Roger has shown us how to choose significators, the reader now has the basic techniques for making a judgement for a horary question. The text comes to a close with two final techniques that relate to specific kinds of questions. The first is whether the question really does relate to the querent or not; the text says that it is necessary to ask whether the querent is asking a question on behalf of his friend, or master, or servant, as this will change which house is considered to be the "true" Ascendant. The text gives an example: if the query relates to the querent's master, then the first house of the master is the tenth, the second is the eleventh, and so on, and the associates of the master (which would normally be represented by the third house) would be the third from the main, starting from the tenth. The second type of question is very specific – if the question concerns returning to one's home country, the signs are arranged backwards; so if the first house had been Aries, the second would be Pisces, the third Aquarius and so on. This final example is actually very curious – elsewhere in the text, Roger talks about houses and is fairly obviously using quadrant houses, but in this example he appears to be conflating them with signs, so that the whole first house is Aries, the whole second house Pisces (as he says for this specific question the usual sequence is reversed) and so on. Unfortunately, he does not expand on this curious technique, nor give any examples, and there don't appear to be any examples in the Arabic sources that he generally uses. The Arabic astrologer al-Kindi, for example, has an entire section devoted to returning from travel but makes no mention of the reversal that Roger uses.[27]

An example will illustrate the first of these points. Roger's text had already discussed choosing a significator for a question; for example, if a querent asks the astrologer a question on their own behalf, such as "is my brother still alive?", the querent will be represented by the first house, and the brother by the third. However, in some cases, the person visiting the astrologer will not be asking a question on their own behalf, but on somebody else's: their lord, or friend, or servant. In this case, the person is more of a bystander, and the real querent is not the person asking the question, but the other party. So in this case, if the person visiting the astrologer is asking a question on behalf of his master, asking "my master wishes to know if his brother is still alive", then instead of using the first house for the querent and the third for the brother, the astrologer selects the tenth house to represent the master (which Roger called "the true Ascendant"), and the third house from the tenth (the twelfth house) to represent the master's brother. This technique, known as derivative houses, is widely used in traditional astrology, and although it does not appear explicitly in most of the Arabic texts, there are hints of it in works by the ninth-century Persian Jewish astrologer Sahl ibn Bishr. For example, after describing the fourth domicile (house) as relating to real estate, his *Introduction* relates the fifth house to children, and also to "the fruits of

---

[27] Al-Kindi, *The Forty Chapters of al-Kindi*, Ben Dykes (ed., trans.) (Minneapolis: Cazimi Press, 2011), Ch. 8.5 'On returning from travel', p.150.

real estate".[28] This attribution is because the fifth house is the second from the fourth, and the second house represents substance and money, although Sahl did not make this explicit. The earlier Hellenistic author Vettius Valens did make this explicit in *Anthologies*, where for each house he provided examples of meanings in relation to other house. For example, for the third house (whose base meaning is brothers), he said "Concerning the life of brothers. Relative to the IV Place of Parents, it concerns enemies and slaves. Relative to the VII Place of Women it is the IX Place [concerning rank, occupation, and childbearing]."[29] Later authors such as Bonatti also make use of derived houses, giving twelve meanings for each house, such as the eighth house relating not only to death (the base meaning), but "brothers of slaves since it is the third from the sixth; and the infirmities of brothers, because it is the sixth from the third, and the enemies and wives and partners of household intimates, because it is the seventh from the second..."[30]

To illustrate this, consider the chart in Figure 5.10, where the querent asks "is my master's brother still alive?"

---

[28] Sahl, *Introduction* Section 3 in Dykes, *Sahl and Māshā'Allāh*, p.5.

[29] 'The XII Places and Their Relationship to Propitious and Impropitious Times' in Vettius Valens, *Anthologies*, Book IX Mark Riley (trans.) (2010) online at http://www.csus.edu/indiv/r/rileymt/Vettius%20Valens%20entire.pdf.

[30] Guido Bonatti, *Book of Astronomy*, Ben Dykes (trans.) (Golden Valley, Minnesota, 2007), Treatise 2, p.109.

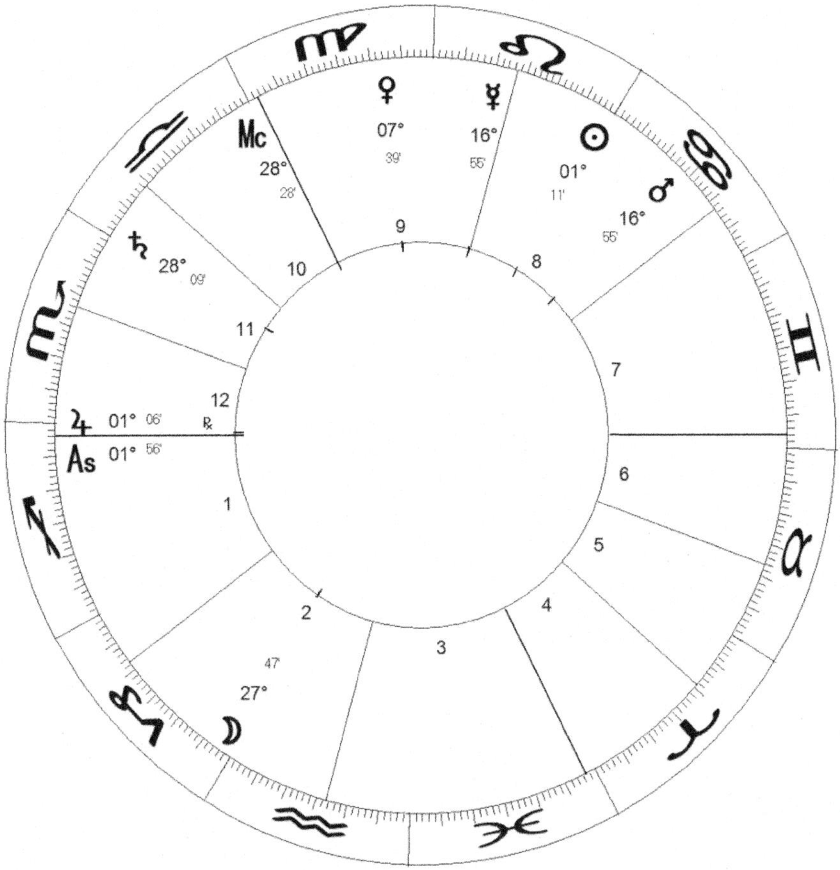

Figure 5.10: "Is my master's brother still alive?"

If you only knew this question was about whether a brother was alive and assumed it was the querent's brother, then you'd look to the ruler of the third house of siblings – the brother would be represented by Saturn. What state is Saturn in? He's exalted in Libra, in the eleventh house of companions. The Moon is applying to him by square, and Saturn has dignity in Capricorn, where the Moon is placed, so receives the Moon. The brother is probably fine, and having a good time with his friends.

However, the querent is asking this question on behalf of his master. His master is the tenth house, so the master's brother is the third house from the tenth – which is the twelfth house. The ruler of the twelfth house – the master's brother – is represented by Mars. What condition is Mars in? He's in fall in Cancer, in the eighth house of death. He is also afflicted by an applying square to Saturn in Libra; Saturn is quite happy in Libra, but Mars has very little dignity there (he's in detriment, and only has dignity by term at 28 Libra), and Saturn has no dignity in Cancer, so Saturn afflicts Mars rather than helping him. The master's brother, then, is in a very poor state in the house of death – and so is probably dead. This demonstrates why understanding the question, and who is asking what about whom, is so vitally important!

CHAPTER SIX: INTENTIONS

Now we'll consider intentions and thoughts, and consider what the querent's intentions and thoughts on the question are.

We still need to consider all aspects of a matter and to understand how the planets and signs harmonise and work in a judgement. We have already seen how planets have dignity in certain places, and how to assess this and choose significators. In addition to the essential dignity of planets, there are accidental dignities. For example, an oriental planet is stronger in an oriental sign, a masculine planet in a masculine sign or degree and so on. Planets can be diurnal or nocturnal, and have a direction associated with them and so are stronger in a sign that shares that quality. Each day of the week is ruled by a planet, as is each hour of the day. If a planet is Lord of the day, that planet is strong. If it is Lord of the hour, its power is even stronger. Planets are also stronger in particular degrees of signs – degrees within signs have characteristics such as lucid, gloomy, smoky, empty, masculine, feminine, full, and otherwise unoccupied of planets; they have faces and terms, degrees of the debility, and degrees that are "wells".

In addition, signs have two other relevant features, novenes and duodenariae. We have said very little about these so far, but have covered the other points in the earlier book [this is in the reference section in Appendix One]. The novenes and duodenariae pertain specifically to the intention, and we haven't said anything about them yet; the other points above have already been discussed, so now we'll consider intentions.

This part of the book is concerned with not simply making a judgement, but finding out what the querent really means. As already seen, the previous section in Roger's book goes into detail about how to choose a planet that will act as the significator for a particular chart, and this section assumes that the significator has already been determined. The text begins with a lengthy recap of planetary dignities, and the ways in which planets are stronger in certain parts of a sign. Some manuscripts include a lengthy reference section that includes all of these features – and this is replicated in Appendix One in this book. After this recap, Roger tells us that there are techniques specifically relating to the client's intentions and thoughts, and that two of these, which he will explain shortly, are novenes and duodenariae.

The concept of making any kind of judgement implies that there is a meeting between the astrologer and the client, the person visiting the astrologer. The client may be asking for general advice about their life, or about a new-born child, in which case a birth chart (called a nativity) would be drawn up, showing the position of the planets at the time of birth; however, the techniques in *Judicial Astrology* imply that the client was asking a specific question about an issue, and instead of drawing up a birth chart, a horary chart would be produced, drawn up for the time the question was asked, which was the topic of the previous chapter.

This section of *Judicial Astrology* is about identifying "the intention" of the questioner. One would presume that the questioner already knows the question, and his or her intention behind asking the question. However, the question the client asks the astrologer might not reflect the client's true intentions; for example, if the client asks whether his father will recover from his illness, that might seem like a straightforward question about health, but the client might secretly be wanting to know when he will get his inheritance. In addition, such a technique could be used to test the astrologer's skill. A letter attributed to one "Argafalau", supposedly written to Alexander the Great and found in a tenth-century Latin compilation, gives an example of using a technique to determine a secret object held in the client's hand, and this technique is covered in detail in a text by Hermann of Carinthia. It's also discussed later in this chapter. Although not related to the issue the client wanted to discuss, presumably if the astrologer is able to tell a client about a secret object on his person prior to the consultation, this would impress the client and give him or her confidence in the astrologer's ability to deal with the question itself.

Roger's text on intentions mentions the use of **novenes** and **duodenariae** in determining the client's intention. These are divisions of a sign into nine and twelve parts respectively, and as there are no standard English terms for these, I'm using the Latin terms that Roger uses (duodenaria is singular, and the plural is duodenariae). His text starts by describing novenes, and then goes on to describe duodenariae, but conceptually it is easier to explain duodenariae so in this chapter, these two brief sections have been swapped.

Duodenariae

Duodenariae divide a sign into twelve equal parts, each part being 150 minutes, or two and a half degrees. The first duodenaria of Aries has the nature of Aries, the second of Taurus, third of Gemini; and the first duodenaria of Taurus has the nature of Taurus, the second of Gemini, and so on in succession. For each sign, the first duodenaria will have the nature of that sign, the second duodenaria has the nature of the following sign and so on.

So if a planet or a point were in the fourth degree of Aries, multiply by 12 to get 48. You give 30 of this to Aries, the remaining stay with Taurus. These degrees of the duodenaria are subject to the nature of Taurus and the Lord of Taurus will rule them, and so on for the others.

Roger defines a **duodenaria** as dividing a sign into twelve equal parts of 150 minutes each, or two and a half degrees. The first duodenaria of Aries has the nature of Aries, the second of Taurus, the third of Gemini and so on, for any sign. He gives an example, which sounds quite clumsy to a modern ear, where a point is in the fourth degree of Aries. He then says you multiply this by 12 to get 48, and "the first thirty are given to Aries". The reason for this clumsy terminology is that attempting to do arithmetic based on the idea of "two and a half degrees" was non-trivial, especially when using Roman numbers, as the earliest manuscript of *Judicial Astrology* does. This method, in effect, maps the two and a half degree segments within a thirty-degree sign onto a full circle by multiplying by twelve. Roger's technique was to multiply the number of degrees by 12 – in his example that gives us 48. He then repeatedly subtracted 30 from this until the result was less than 30; the subtraction only had to be done once in this case, so he counted forwards just one sign – Taurus. Hence this particular duodenaria has the nature of Taurus, and the planet ruling it will be the ruler of Taurus, Venus.

The concept behind duodenariae is a simple one: there are twelve signs of the zodiac of thirty degrees each, traditionally starting from Aries and following a fixed sequence. For the duodenariae in a sign, each sign is divided into twelve equal divisions of two and a half degrees each, with the first division having the nature of the sign itself, the second division having the following sign, and so on. Thus within the sign of Gemini, the first division will have the nature of Gemini, the second division the nature of Cancer, and so on for all twelve divisions. These duodenariae can be thought of as a zodiac within a zodiac. Figure 6.1 illustrates this, showing the duodenariae of Aries and Taurus.

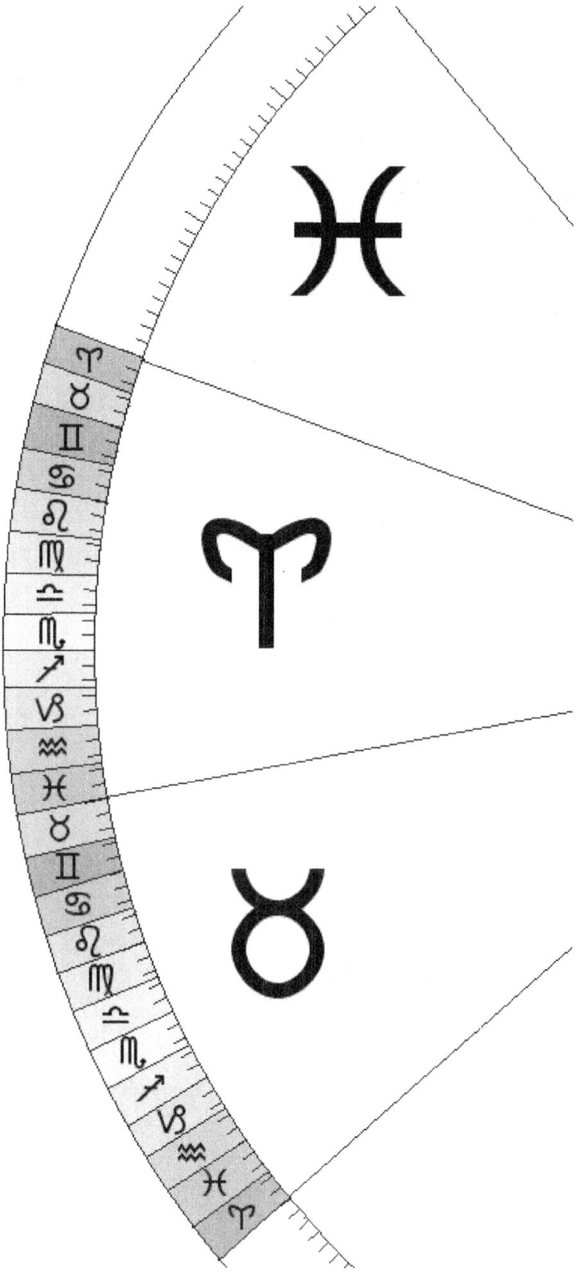

Figure 6.1: Illustration of the duodenariae of Aries and Taurus.

Novenes

Novenes divide each sign into nine parts, each part being 200 minutes, or three and one-third degrees. The first novene of Aries is ruled by the Lord of Aries, being Mars. The second novene is ruled by the Lord of the following sign (Taurus), the third novene by the Lord of the sign following that one.

In the same way, the first and second novenes of the second sign, Taurus, are ruled by Saturn as the signs of these novenes are Capricorn and Aquarius.

Whatever triplicity is examined all triplicities will have a particular cardinal sign, whose Lord starts a new sequence and is said to be the Lord of the first novene, and the Lord of the next sign is the Lord of the second novene and so on.

The text for **novenes** (which is before the text on duodenariae in all manuscripts) starts off with a definition that a novene divides each sign into nine parts of 3°20′. The first novene of Aries is Aries itself, the second novene is Taurus, and so on around the zodiac.

Roger's rather confusing description requires an explanation. Each sign is divided into nine equal divisions of 3°20′. This time, it is not possible to fit an entire mini zodiac into a sign, since there are twelve zodiac signs but only nine divisions. The technique here is that starting with the sign of Aries, the first division of Aries will have the nature of Aries, the second division the nature of Taurus and so on, until the final (ninth) division of Aries will have the nature of the ninth sign, Sagittarius. The next division is within the sign of Taurus, but continues from where it left off, so the first division of Taurus has the nature of the sign following Sagittarius, which is Capricorn. The second division of Taurus has the nature of Aquarius, and so on. This means that the first two novenes of Taurus are Capricorn and Aquarius, and so are both ruled by Saturn.

One manuscript has a table of novenes to make it easy to work out.[31] However, without a table it is still relatively easy to calculate in which novene a planet lies, and Roger provides a useful method by checking the triplicity of the sign. Again, the text is a little clumsy, and an explanation is in order. As explained above, the first novene of Taurus has the nature of Capricorn. The twelve zodiac signs can be divided into four triplicities (or elements) of fire, earth, air, or water, and into three quadruplicities of cardinal, fixed, and mutable. Taurus, for instance, is a fixed earth sign. Roger's method, therefore, is to look at the element of the sign – earth, in the case of Taurus – and ask which sign of the zodiac is the cardinal sign for that element. In the case of earth signs, Capricorn is the cardinal sign. Thus the first novene of Taurus (and indeed of all three earth signs) is Capricorn. This demonstrates Roger's role as a teacher in an environment where mathematics may not have been as natural as to the Arabic authors. Most English documents from the twelfth century use Roman numerals for numbers, while Arabic authors were using Arabic numerals, derived from those used in India, and which were the forerunners of the numbers in use today. An instruction to "consider the degrees and minutes which the planet has moved through its sign… and multiply this by 12", as could be seen for duodenariae, is a lot easier when using Arabic numerals rather than Roman numerals. Roger therefore described the techniques, but gave useful shortcuts for performing the calculations, of which we've seen two examples. Figure 6.2 illustrates novenes, showing the novenes of Aries. The last novene is Sagittarius, which means the following novene, which is the first novene of Taurus, is Capricorn as described above.

The techniques of dividing a sign into nine and twelve parts predate Arabic astrology. The novenes and duodenariae are of Indian and Greek provenance respectively. Contemporary Vedic astrology still uses novenes, although it calls them ninth-parts or "navamsa". Hellenistic astrology made use of duodenariae, calling them "dodecatemoria".

---

[31] Cambridge University Library, GG VI.3, f.150r.

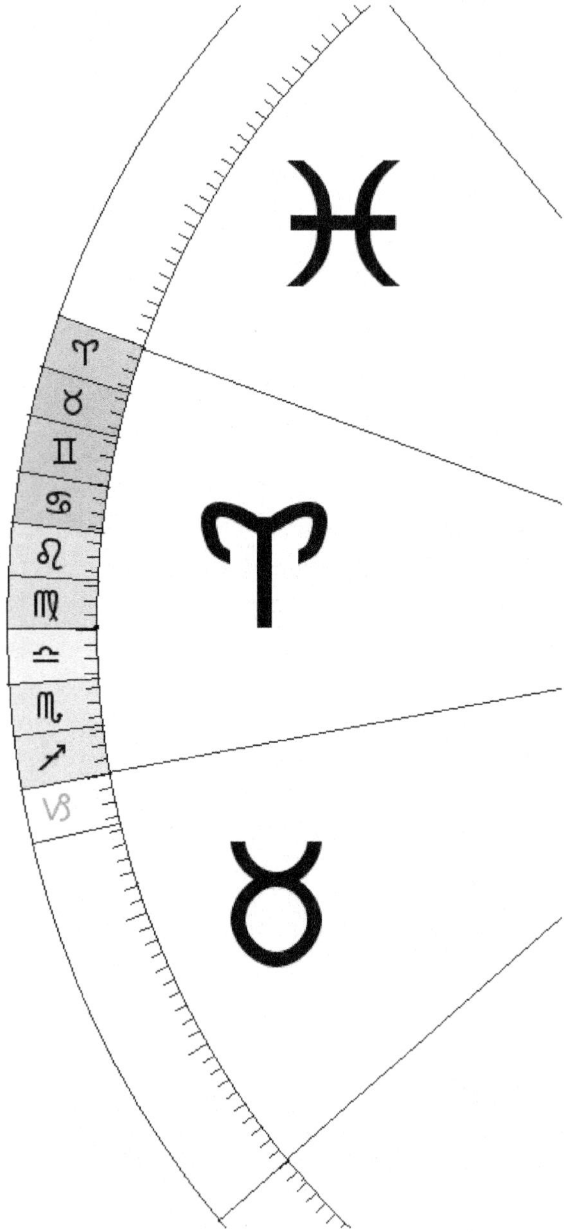

Figure 6.2: Illustration of the novenes of Aries, and the first novene of Taurus.

Trigenariae

> There is another division called the trigenaria, which divides each sign into 30 degrees and the first degree of the sign has the nature of its sign, the second degree the following sign, the third degree the third sign and so on.

The final division, which Roger includes for completeness but does not appear to make use of subsequently, is to divide the sign into thirty degrees and allocate consecutive signs to each degree. This method is also described by Abū Maʿšar, who includes it in the section on duodenariae, attributing it to "Hermes".

So many methods!

Nobody should be surprised that we have so many different ways of approaching a judgement. When we're trying to discern the intention of a thing, there can be all sorts of reasons, and lots of different things can arise, some good, some bad, and each one with a different cause. For this reason, there are different astrological methods from which the planets give different judgements. However, when you take everything into consideration, you will see common themes. For example, one method may show a theme from two planets having a strong reception, some obeying natures of planets and signs, some based on the nature of the planets in their signs and degrees. Whichever of these judgements has the strongest supporting testimony is the one to use.

Roger didn't actually give this section the heading "So many methods!", but it's an appropriate paraphrasing of "Concerning all the varieties of judgements" that he actually used. Imagine you're in Roger's class, and you've now been inundated with different methods for making a judgement. Do you use planetary strength? Reception? Natures of the planets? Duodenariae? Novenes? Trigenariae? It's all a bit overwhelming, and as anyone who has gone through the process of learning astrology of any type knows all too well, learning to integrate a chart and get a coherent story from it is the tricky bit. Roger is telling his students that yes, it is complicated, and there are lots of different methods – just as a judge in a court will hear statements from lots of witnesses, and see which are the most credible, and which seem to agree with each other. If five of your astrological techniques tell you that the client's intention is about an inheritance, and only one says it's about foreign travel, then it's probably about an inheritance!

Finding the intention: duodenariae

> For the intention, look at the nature of the rising sign, and note the rising degree and the duodenaria that contains the ascending degree. Look for the house that is occupied by that sign, and then the house and its Lord to find the intention.
>
> For example, let's say that the sign of the duodenaria is in the fifth house, which is the house of sons, and its Lord is in the fourth, which is the house of heirs, then you'd consider the intention to involve the inheritance of sons.

This example determines the intention from the duodenaria. Figure 6.3 is an illustration based on Roger's example, although Roger did not specify the Ascendant or the degrees of any of the planets. In this hypothetical example, the Ascendant is at 11° Scorpio. The first 2.5° of Scorpio will have a duodenaria of Scorpio, the next 2.5° of Scorpio will have a duodenaria of Sagittarius, and so on through the signs. We can see that 11° Scorpio (shown as a vertical line in this diagram, in Pisces) will fall in the fifth segment, which has a duodenaria of Pisces.

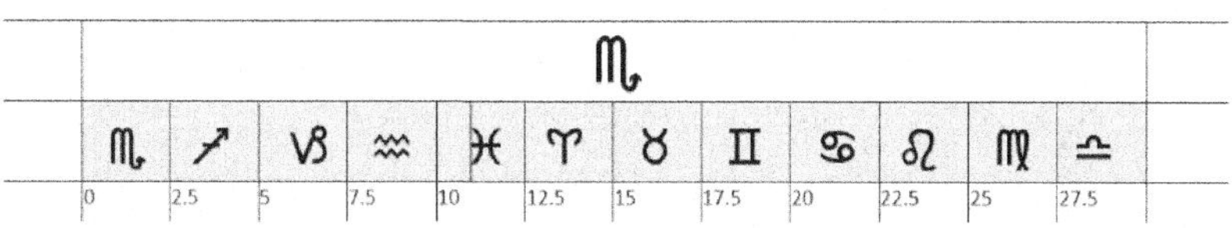

Figure 6.3 – Duodenaria of 11° Scorpio.

The chart in figure 6.4 illustrates one possibility for the example in the text. We can see that Pisces is the sign on the fifth house cusp. The ruler of Pisces is Jupiter, and Jupiter is in the fourth house, the house of heirs. Thus when the client comes to see the astrologer and this is the chart of the meeting, the astrologer can conclude that the question will relate to the inheritance of sons.

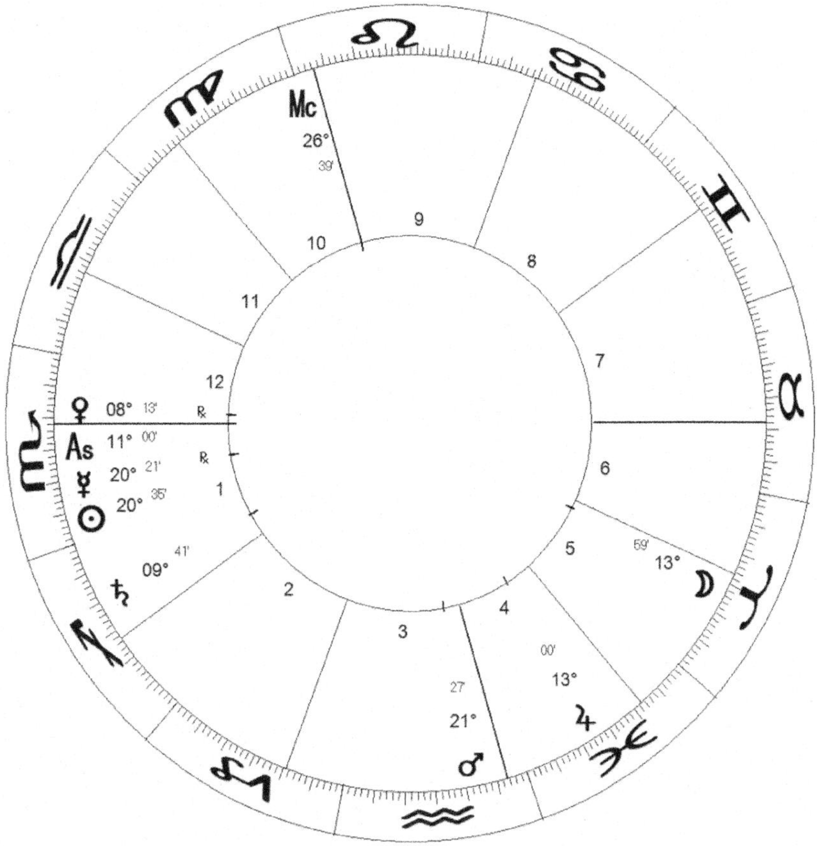

Figure 6.4: Chart illustrating Roger's example of the duodenaria of the Ascendant being in the fifth house, and the ruler of that house being in the fourth house.

Finding the intention: Ascendant

You can also discover the intention from the Lord of the Ascendant and by planets connected to it, looking at their location in the houses and in signs. So if the Lord of the Ascendant is in the eleventh house and is joined with a planet in the seventh house, the intention is to do with the love of women.

Similarly, planets aspecting the degree of the Ascendant are important to determine the intention. So if a planet in the ninth house aspected the degree of the Ascendant, the intention is of ninth house matters.

As Roger was at pains to point out, there is more than one way to determine the intention, and he gives two further examples. One is to see what the Lord of the Ascendant aspects, and the other to see what aspects the Ascendant itself. The former is illustrated in the chart shown in Figure 6.5. The ruler of the Cancer Ascendant is the Moon, which is in the eleventh house in Taurus, and makes a trine (a 120° aspect) to Mars in Capricorn in the seventh house. The chart ruler – the ruler of the Ascending sign – is connected to a planet in the seventh house of marriage and women.

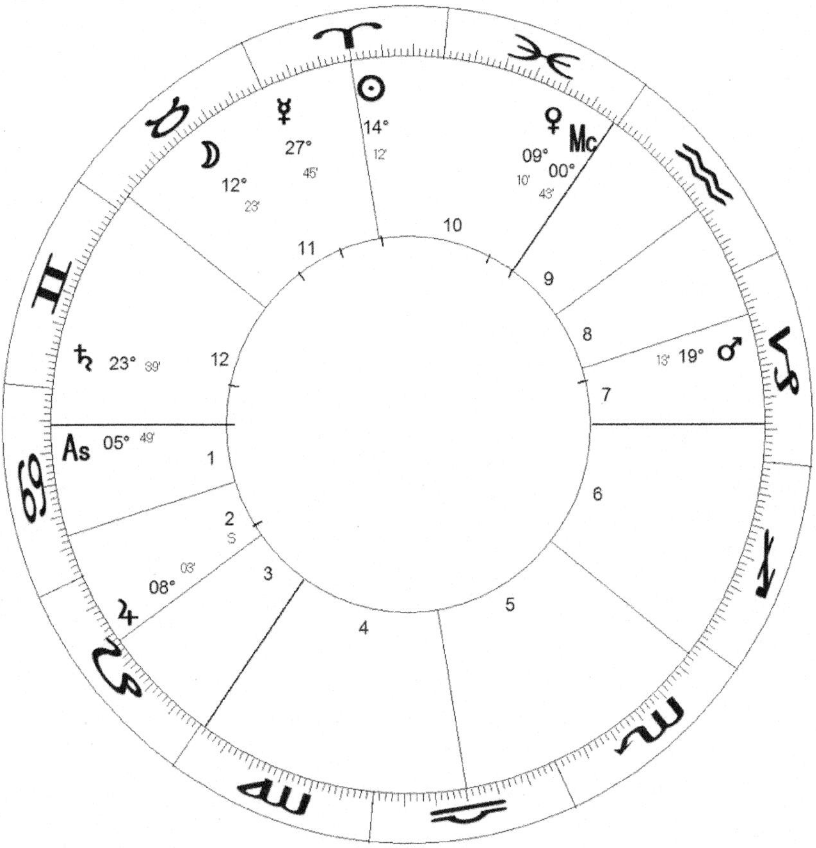

Figure 6.5: Chart illustrating Roger's example of the Lord of the Ascendant aspecting a planet in the seventh house.

Finding the intention: Lord of the Ascendant

The intention can also be determined from the Lord of the Ascendant, provided that planet is in good condition and not impeded. Judgement is then as follows: the first sign and second would not be divided; the third is divided into two, the fourth into three, fifth into four, sixth into two, seventh and eighth into three, ninth into four, tenth, eleventh and twelfth into three.

If therefore the Lord of the Ascendant were to be in the first, the intention concerns the querent himself. If in the second, possessions. If in the first half of the third, it concerns movement within the locality. If in the final half it concerns brothers and sisters. If it is in the first third of the fourth, it concerns the father. If in the second third it concerns the birth, and house and things underground and the building and other inhabitants in the same house. If in the final third, it concerns other great reflections on things that can make one unaware. If it is in the first quarter of the fifth it concerns sons. If in the second it concerns clothes. If in the third, letters (or tidings). If in the final quarter, papers, books and trinkets.[32] In the first half of the sixth house, it concerns the patient and their illness. In the final half, servants, maids, and animals. In the first third of the seventh house, it concerns marriages and wives. In the second third it concerns associates. In the final third, a thief or theft. If in the first third of the eighth house it concerns the querent's death. If in the second third, sharing in possessions. If in the final third, debt. If in the first quarter of the ninth house, it concerns faith. In the second quarter, a journey. In the third quarter, wisdom or civil office or honour bestowed. If in the final quarter, it concerns dreams.

[32] The Latin text states "minoribus", which can mean subordinates or small things. However, most of these descriptions appear to have been copied from Pseudo-Ptolemy's *Iudicia*, and both manuscripts of this text that I have examined (Paris, Bibliothèque nationale de France, lat. 16208, f.62va and Munich, CLM 848, f.46vb) both have the term "novis", meaning novelties or unusual things.

> If it is in the first third of the tenth house it concerns a new master. In the second third, it concerns business. In the final third, the mother. If in the first third of the eleventh house it concerns trade. If in the second third, a rich man. If in the final third, a friend or sweetheart. If in the first third of the twelfth house, it concerns an enemy. If in the second third it concerns deception or a poor man. If in the final third, it concerns animals.
>
> If the Lord of the Ascendant is impeded, then the Moon can be used instead.

The text now gives yet another method – considering the intention from the Lord of the Ascendant. It starts off with a rule – the Lord of the Ascendant must not be impeded; if it is, this technique cannot be used, although Roger states at the end that the Moon could be used as a substitute instead. If the Lord of the Ascendant is not impeded, consider the sign it is in, and which part of the sign. The text then states that each sign may be divided into a number of equal parts. The first and second signs aren't divided, others are divided into two, three, or four parts, and each part represents an intention.

The text is a little confusing here, since in the descriptions themselves, many of the manuscripts of *Judicial Astrology* imply that it is the house that is divided into equal parts, not the sign. However, the opening text does state that signs are divided, although as he's talking about the sign starting from the Ascendant, this does correspond to whole-sign houses, and the meanings he assigns to "the third sign", for example, are clearly third house themes. Normally, Roger clearly does use quadrant houses rather than a whole sign house system (an example that we shall see later, and illustrated in Figure 6.8, can only work in a quadrant system), but here he is copying a text that was incorrectly attributed to Ptolemy called *Iudicia,* which may explain his difference in approach for this section.[33]

---

[33] This is a subtle point that I overlooked when I submitted my thesis on *Judicial Astrology*, which claims that it's the house that's divided.

Roger's rather long-winded paragraph describes all twelve whole-sign houses, and the concept is easier to see visually. Some houses have several meanings – the ninth house, for example, can represent faith, journeys, wisdom, and dreams. In the technique that Roger described here, most houses are divided into two, three, or four equal segments, and each segment has its own meaning. Using the ninth house as an example with the four meanings just referred to, this is divided into four, and the first quarter of the house (the whole sign, using this technique, rather than a quadrant house) relates to faith, the second quarter to journeys, the third to wisdom and the last quarter to dreams.

Figure 6.6 illustrates this concept. In this hypothetical example, the Ascendant is Aquarius, ruled by Saturn. Saturn is at 24°04′ Sagittarius, and although this is in the eighth house (as is the whole of Libra, in fact), Saturn is in the ninth sign. The ninth sign is divided into four equal segments of 7°30′ and so Saturn is in the final quarter of the sign. This means that the intention would relate to dreams. Roger's text is presented more clearly in Table 6.1.

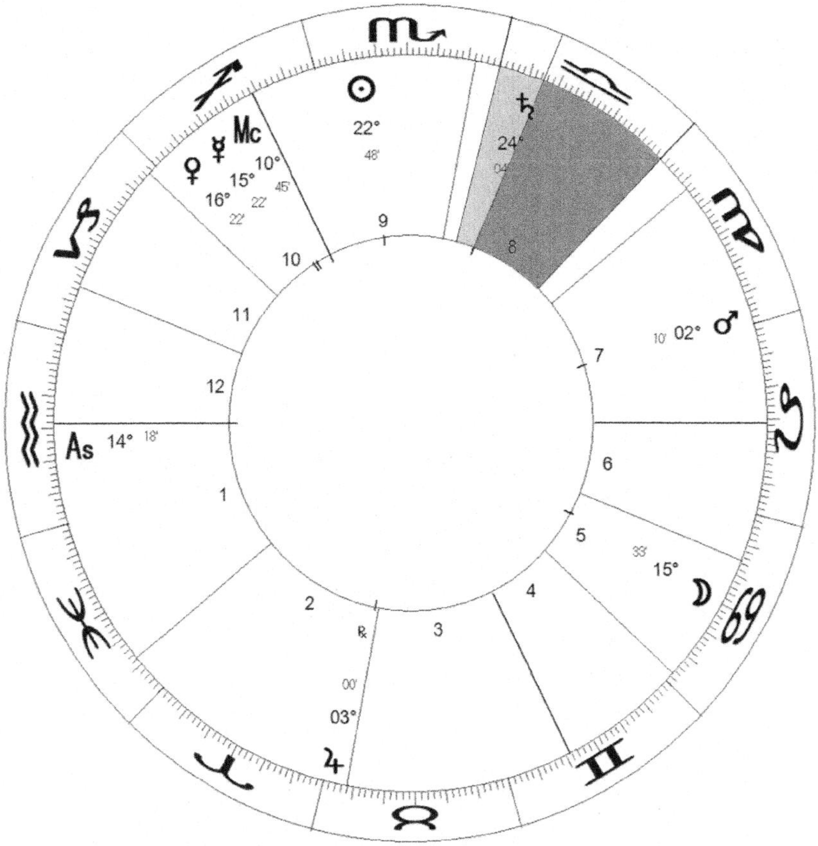

Figure 6.6: House division example for the Lord of the Ascendant.

Sign	Divided into	Segment	Meaning
1st	Not divided		The querent himself / herself
2nd	Not divided		Possessions
3rd	2	First half	Movement within the locality
		Second half	Brothers and sisters
4th	3	First third	Father
		Second third	One's birth, one's home, things underground, the building (and other inhabitants in the same building)
		Final third	Other great meditations on things that can make one ignorant
5th	4	First quarter	Sons
		Second quarter	Clothes
		Third quarter	Letters and tidings
		Final quarter	Writings, books, and trinkets
6th	2	First half	The patient and their illness
		Second half	Servants, maids, and animals
7th	3	First third	Marriage and wives
		Second third	Associates
		Final third	A thief or theft
8th	3	First third	Death
		Second third	Sharing in possessions
		Final third	Debt
9th	4	First quarter	Faith
		Second quarter	A journey
		Third quarter	Wisdom or civil office or honour bestowed by an office
		Final quarter	Dreams
10th	3	First third	New lords
		Second third	Business
		Final third	Mother
11th	3	First third	Trade
		Second third	A rich man
		Final third	A friend or sweetheart
12th	3	First third	An enemy
		Second third	Deception or a poor man
		Final third	Animals

Table 6.1: Intention from the Lord of the Ascendant.

Finding the intention: Lord of the hour

> If the Lord of the Ascendant and the Moon are impeded, see if the Lord of the hour is unencumbered, and judge this as follows: see how many degrees have risen in its sign and multiply this by 12 and project this from the Ascendant. This will tell you about the intention, and you can fall back on this method if everything is impeded.

Roger's text talks about the **Lord of the hour**, which can be used if the previous techniques couldn't be used because the Lord of the Ascendant or the Moon were impeded. Before discussing what Roger means in the above text, let us first look at the concept of the Lord of the hour.

While the modern definition of an hour is one twenty-fourth of a day (from midnight to midnight), there were two definitions of the term "hour" in the twelfth century. The usual definition was that the period from sunrise to sunset was divided into twelve equal **diurnal hours**, and the period from sunset to the following sunrise was divided into twelve equal **nocturnal hours**.

The length of an hour would, then, depend both on the time of year and whether it was day or night. At the summer solstice in Hereford, there are 16 hours and 40 minutes of daytime (between sunrise and sunset), and 7 hours and 20 minutes of night-time (between sunset and sunrise). A diurnal hour at the solstice would, therefore, be 83 minutes and 20 seconds, and a nocturnal hour would be 36 minutes and 40 seconds.

At the equinoxes, daytime and night-time are equal, and the hour is 60 minutes. Thus these hours – the division used today of the day into twenty-four equal hours – were called **equinoctal hours**.

Planetary days and hours were widely used in medieval astrology. The association of planets with days is obvious from the Latin names of days, as shown in Table 6.2:

English	Latin	Planet
Sunday	Dies Solis	Sun
Monday	Dies Lunae	Moon
Tuesday	Dies Martis	Mars
Wednesday	Dies Mercurii	Mercury
Thursday	Dies Iovis	Jupiter
Friday	Dies Veneris	Venus
Saturday	Dies Saturni	Saturn

Table 6.2: Planetary days.

The principle of a planetary hour is that at sunrise on a particular day, the planet ruling the day was also the planet ruling the first diurnal hour. For example, the first diurnal hour of Thursday (Jupiter's day) is ruled by Jupiter. The second hour is ruled by the next planet in the Chaldean order, so for Thursday, the second hour would be ruled by Mars.[34] Table 6.3 shows all the planetary hours for Thursday, and the first two for Friday – as can be seen, the natural Chaldean order means that the final night-time hour of Thursday is ruled by the Sun, so the next planet in the sequence – Venus – is the ruler of the first daytime hour of Friday, as one would expect for *Dies Veneris*.

[34] The Chaldean order is Saturn, Jupiter, Mars, Sun, Venus, Mercury, and Moon in that sequence.

Day	Hour	Day/Night	Lord of the hour
Thursday	1	Day	Jupiter
	2		Mars
	3		Sun
	4		Venus
	5		Mercury
	6		Moon
	7		Saturn
	8		Jupiter
	9		Mars
	10		Sun
	11		Venus
	12		Mercury
	1	Night	Moon
	2		Saturn
	3		Jupiter
	4		Mars
	5		Sun
	6		Venus
	7		Mercury
	8		Moon
	9		Saturn
	10		Jupiter
	11		Mars
	12		Sun
Friday	1	Day	Venus
	2		Mercury

Table 6.3: Planetary Hours for Thursday.

The text itself is brief, and simply says that one should work out the Lord of the hour, see what sign it is in and how far through that sign it is, multiply that by twelve and project from the Ascendant to find the intention. Roger's wording is rather unclear on how to use this technique, but fortunately the earliest manuscript we have of *Judicial Astrology* has a helpful example in the margin, that a later scribe added: "So if the value projected from the Ascendant ends up in the third house, the intention will be a third house matter".[35]

There is no example in the text, but an example here should make the technique clearer. In Figure 6.7 the Ascendant is at almost 10° Libra, and let us assume this chart is for a date and time where the Lord of the hour is Mars. Mars is at 6° Aries. Multiply 6 by 12 to get 72, and then project 72° from the Ascendant (another way of thinking of this in modern terms is to say that Mars is 20% of the way through the sign of Aries, so the distance to project from the Ascendant is 20% of the zodiac, or 72°). Since the Ascendant is at 10° Libra, 72° from this point reaches 22° Sagittarius. In the diagram, the dark shading shows how far Mars is through the sign of Aries, and the thick lined arc from the Ascendant shows this same ratio projected from the Ascendant. This point is in the third house, so the Lord of the hour will relate to third house matters, such as short journeys or siblings (even though the Lord of the hour itself is in the sixth house of illness and servants). A similar technique appears in Māshā'Allāh's *On Hidden Things* as a technique for finding a lost object.[36]

---

[35] Selden Supra 76, f.16v.

[36] Māshā'Allāh, On Hidden Things, in Dykes, Sahl and Māshā'Allāh, p.432.

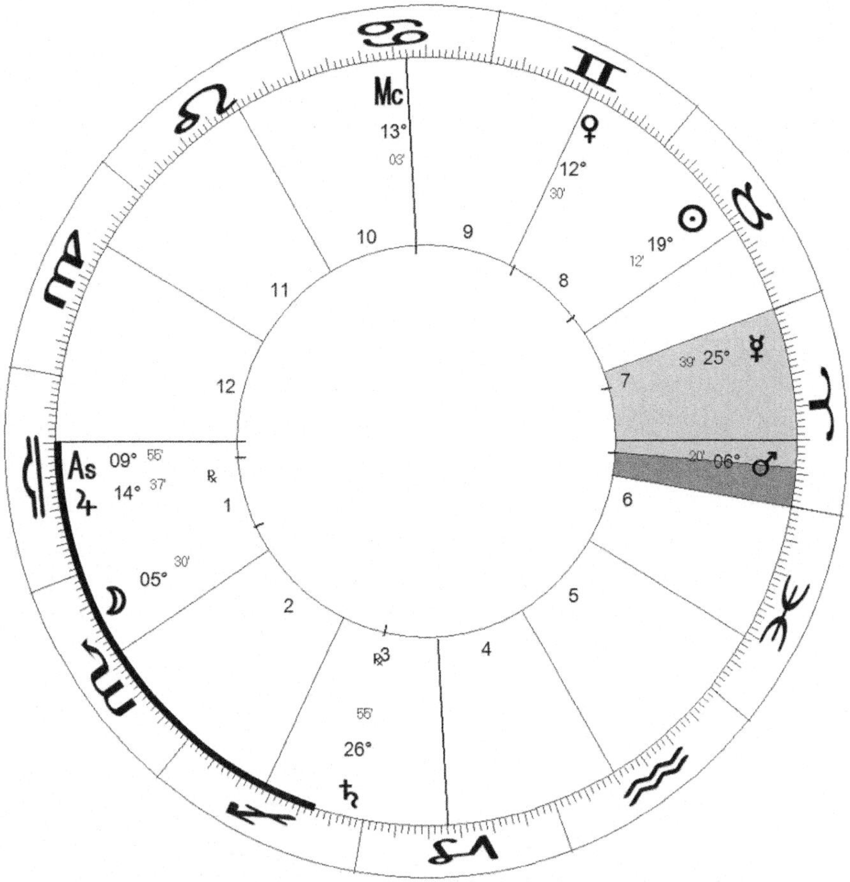

Figure 6.7: Intention from the Lord of the hour (assumed to be Mars in this example).

Hidden objects from the Lord of the hour

The Lord of the hour can also be used in another way to find out the intention and some hidden thing, with all seven planets ruling hours. The hour is divided into three.

If the question is asked in the first part of the hour of the Sun, one looks for oneself or one's associates. The hidden thing will be concerned with food or herbs. If in the second, look for advice concerning war or siege or fortification or fear and panic. The hidden thing will be bones or land or money. If in the last third, look for advice or debate, evil omens and warnings, or avoiding the anger of the powerful. The hidden thing will be white wool or thread or something twisting.

If asked in the first part of the hour of Venus, one looks for advice about one's own deeds, or desiring a woman. The hidden thing is skin or leather, or something flammable. In the second part of the hour, temptation or enchantments, and the hidden thing is something twisting, long, or a useless trifle. In the last third, it concerns a woman or sharing with a companion. The hidden thing is herbs, trees, or things from the seashore.

In the first part of the hour of Mercury one looks for education or the future. The hidden thing is fresh, delicate, of ample form, with short edible roots and outwardly dry, and internally hollow. If in the second part it concerns sickness. The hidden thing is dark edible shoots that grow in the earth. If in the last concerns lost things or a fugitive. The hidden thing is a precious gem of onyx or other pierced jewel.

If in the first part of the hour of the Moon concerns weaknesses of the eyes. The hidden thing is fragrant herbs. If in the second, it concerns imminent foreign travel or concerning lost things. The hidden thing is somewhat dark or obtained from the seashore or water, or is yellow orpiment or dark-coloured jewels. If in the last third, then it relates to lost things. The hidden thing is yellow orpiment [a yellow mineral] or other similar colours.

If in the first part of the hour of Saturn one looks for education and learning, bearing books. The hidden thing is glassy or somewhat green. If in the second, a fighting man or a woman who would give birth. If the hour is in the day it will be masculine, and if in the night it will be feminine. The hidden thing is iron or another metal or anything accustomed to being put in the fire. If in the last it concerns his illness or the illness of his friends, or war or discord and other grief. The hidden thing is the head of a bat or a bird of two colours.

If in the first part of the hour of Jupiter, healing of demonic possession. The hidden thing is a proper thing that is put into fire, or an iron or statue or small trifle sculpted by a carpenter. If in the second it concerns the acquisition of money. The hidden thing is of many colours, or of a white colour or a statue with green gems mixed with red. If in the last part of the hour, then it involves harmony with a like-minded person, and concerning hidden underground treasure that he will discover. The hidden thing is a tin statue, or a leather thong.[37]

If in the first part of the hour of Mars, it concerns the avoidance of threats or treachery. The hidden thing is a staff of gold or other metals. If in the second, it concerns stolen money. This hidden thing is herbs, or something reddish. If in the third part, messengers of enemies, or illness. The hidden thing is wood or something dry.

Another method using the Lord of the hour is described is to find a hidden object. The text states that the planetary hour is divided into three, and each third of the hour relates to an intention, and a hidden object.

This need not relate to the question that the querent will ask the astrologer – the querent may not be asking about something that he has lost, for example – but if the astrologer starts the consultation by telling the querent something

[37] Roger's text has "stagnum" (pool), but I'm reading this as "stannum" (tin) as being more appropriate to Jupiter

about himself that only the querent should know, such as an object that the querent has on his person, it is a demonstration of the astrologer's skill. In this case, the astrologer simply needs to know the time that the querent arrives, to determine what the current planetary hour is, and how far through the hour it is – no mean feat without an accurate clock, of course, although an astrolabe could be used to calculate a reasonably accurate planetary hour, and a footnote in the earliest manuscript of *Judicial Astrology* alludes to this, stating that since the Sun moves 15 degrees in an hour (this would be with respect to the celestial equator, not the ecliptic), "five degrees is a third part of the elevation of the Sun", to determine whether the Sun was in the first, second or third part of the hour.[38]

A simple example, illustrated in Table 6.4, will demonstrate the method. Let us assume that the querent visits the astrologer on Tuesday 6 August 1185 in Hereford at noon. Sunrise was at 04:44, and sunset was at 19:22 (local time, and using the Julian calendar). Hence the day was 14 hours 38 minutes long. Dividing this by 12, each planetary hour was 73 minutes 10 seconds long. Noon was 7 hours 16 minutes after sunrise, or 436 minutes. Since the day was Tuesday, the first planetary hour was Mars, so the sixth planetary hour is Saturn, which started at 10:49, and the seventh planetary hour would be Jupiter, which started at 12:03. Hence, noon is in the final third of the hour of Saturn.

[38] Selden, 16v. footnote.

Hour	Start	Lord of the hour
1	04:44:00	Mars
2	05:57:10	Sun
3	07:10:20	Venus
4	08:23:30	Mercury
5	09:36:40	Moon
6	10:49:50	Saturn
7	12:03:00	Jupiter

1st third	2nd third	3rd third
10:49:50 – 11:14:12	11:14:13 – 11:38:35	11:38:36 – 12:03:00

Table 6.4: List of the first seven planetary hours for Tuesday, showing noon as falling in the sixth hour, and the third part of that hour.

The text for Saturn says that if the time is in the first part of the hour of Saturn one looks for education, or bearing books. The hidden thing is glassy or somewhat green. If in the second, a fighting man, or a woman who would give birth – if placed in the day it will be masculine, if in the night it will be feminine. The hidden thing is iron or another metal or anything accustomed to being put in the fire. If in the last it concerns his illness or his friends' illnesses or war or discord and other grief. The hidden thing is the head of a bat or a bird of two colours.

Hence the astrologer would deduce that this client will be asking a question about illness or war, or some other kind of grief, and may have secreted about his person a head of a bat, or something relating to a bird of two colours – presumably some sort of lucky charm. Table 6.5 summarises Roger's text.

While the idea of recording that a "hidden thing" could be a head of a bat seems very curious, there is a precedent for this. A text that was allegedly a letter to Alexander the Great called the *Letter of Argafalau* contains this same technique, with an explanation that the "hidden thing" is something that the querent has hidden about their person. If the astrologer can identify what this is, then it proves the skill of the astrologer. If you tell your client they have a lucky bat's head in their bag, they should be impressed!

Hour	Third	Intention	Hidden thing
Sun	1st	Oneself or one's associates	Food or herbs
	2nd	War, siege, fortification, fear	Bones, land or money
	3rd	Advice, debate, evil omens or avoiding the anger of the powerful	White wool, a thread from white or dyed wool, something twisted
Venus	1st	One's own deeds or desiring a woman	Skin or leather or something flammable
	2nd	Temptation, enchantments	Twisting, long, harmless trifle
	3rd	A woman or sharing with a companion	Herbs, trees or seashore things
Mercury	1st	Education or the future	Fresh, blooming, delicate of ample form, short edible roots, externally dry and internally hollow
	2nd	Sickness	Dark edible shoots that grow in the earth
	3rd	Lost things or a fugitive	Precious gem of onyx or other pierced jewel
Moon	1st	Weaknesses of the eyes	Fragrant herbs
	2nd	Imminent foreign travel or concerning lost things	Somewhat dark or obtained from the seashore or water, or yellow orpiment [a yellow pigment] or dark-coloured jewels
	3rd	Lost things	Yellow orpiment or similar colours
Saturn	1st	Education, bearing books	Something glassy or somewhat green
	2nd	A fighting man or a woman who would give birth (masculine by day, feminine by night)	Something iron or another metal or anything accustomed to being put in the fire
	3rd	His illness or his friends' illnesses, war or discord and other grief	Head of a bat or a bird of two colours
Jupiter	1st	Healing of demonic possession	Something put into fire, iron or statue or small trifle sculpted by a carpenter
	2nd	Acquisition of money	Something of diverse colours or of a white colour or a statue with green gems mixed with red
	3rd	Agreeing with a like-minded one and concerning hidden underground treasure that he will discover	A tin statue, or a leather thong.
Mars	1st	Avoidance of threats, omens, treachery or attacks	A staff of gold or other metals
	2nd	Stolen money	Herbs or anything red
	3rd	Messengers of enemies or illness	Something wooden, dry

Table 6.5: Intentions and hidden objects from the Lord of the hour

Finding the intention by various other means

> The Part of Fortune and the house it is in will also indicate the intention, so if the Part of Fortune is in the first house, the intention is about first house matters. However, a house can signify many things.
>
> Whichever method we use for determining the intention, consider the nature of the planet signifying the judgement, its house, and its nature. For example, let us say you found a planet in the fifth house, and the Lord of the fifth was Saturn, and Saturn was in the sixth house, in Taurus. Saturn in Taurus signifies the stomach, so the combination of fifth house, sixth house, and Saturn in Taurus suggests you would consider the intention to relate to a sickness of the stomach of a son.

Some of Roger's descriptions are quite basic – for instance, the Part of Fortune might also give a clue to the intention, based on the house it is in. However, he points out that a house can mean many things, and that whatever method we use, we need to consider all interpretations for a significator. As a result, sometimes the clues to the intention can be very detailed. Roger's text gives an example, where the significator is a planet in the fifth house, the house of sons, so the question might involve sons. If the house cusp were in Capricorn or Aquarius, then the fifth house ruler is Saturn, so one observes where Saturn is. Let us say that in this example, Saturn is in the sixth house of illnesses in the sign of Taurus, so the question is to do with the illness of a son. However, Saturn in Taurus relates to the stomach – hence the question will be about a stomach illness in a son. The attribution of the stomach to Saturn in Taurus derives from al-Qabisi's "pains of the planets", and is given in the reference material presented in Appendix One.

In fact, this example, illustrated by the chart in Figure 6.8, is clearly a contrived one. We might ask whether Roger used real client charts in his examples, and this example is clear evidence that he didn't. We don't know exactly who Roger's clients as an astrologer were, but given that he was part of the Bishop of Hereford's household and a teacher of some standing, his clients were likely to be important dignitaries. This makes it unlikely that he would have shared something so personal as a chart with the students in his school. It would therefore be easier and safer to use made up examples. Even today, with our sophisticated software that can draw up a chart in seconds, we astrology teachers still make up random examples on the board: "imagine that there's a New Moon in Pisces, squaring Uranus in Sagittarius and Saturn in Gemini" we might say, as we scribble a diagram on the whiteboard. If we committed that scribble to paper and it was discovered in the future, a twenty-fifth century historian might scratch her head trying to work out what year that chart related to, since that combination did not occur until 2149, but the paper she's analysing looks as though it's from the twenty-first century! Similarly, Roger's example of the fifth house ruler being Saturn and constraining Saturn to be in Taurus in the sixth house is physically impossible in the northern hemisphere. The chart illustrating this example in Figure 6.8 is set for a latitude of 58 degrees south of the equator – and we can be absolutely sure that Roger had no clients near the Antarctic!

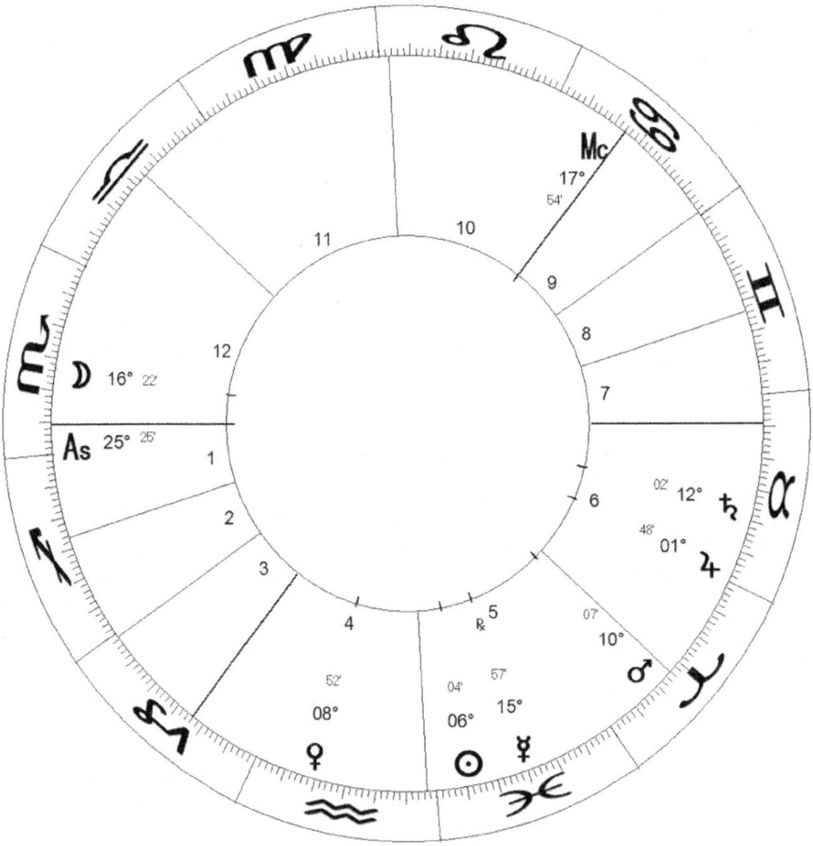

Figure 6.8: Chart illustrating Roger's example of the ruler of the fifth house being Saturn in Taurus in the sixth house.

Finding the intention: summary

There are many ways of finding the intention. The main significator is whatever is strongest in the Ascendant, in the place of the luminaries, and in the syzygy before the spring equinox and prior to the most recent conjunction of Jupiter and Saturn, and whichever is the strongest will signify the intention. If none of these have the requirements but some other planet satisfies the conditions and is free of impediments, then it will share in the judgement.

In particular, pay attention to the planet that the Lord of the Ascendant is separating from, and similarly what the Moon is separating from, and consider the places of the Lord of the Ascendant and the Moon, and what they are aspecting. Also see what is separating from the Lord of the Ascendant.

Finding the intention, then, isn't a simple matter – there are many different ways of doing it. You need to look at each one and find the meaning for each one to build up a fuller picture. This involves not just the techniques outlined here, but looking at the nature of each planet, its house, how strong it is, and what the significance of the placement is.

Roger finishes off with a summary of some of the techniques (although he misses out the ones he gave initially, about duodenariae and novenes), and throws in some new ones, too: the syzygy before the spring equinox, and the next conjunction of Jupiter and Saturn. A syzygy is just a fancy word for a New Moon or a Full Moon, and two very traditional techniques in mundane astrology were to look at the most recent New Moon or Full Moon prior to the spring equinox and to the most recent conjunction of Saturn and Jupiter.

He also gives another technique, whereby you pay attention to whatever the significators are separating from and applying to, which he uses in the worked example that follows in the text.

Worked Example

Assume there is an Ascendant of 15 Libra and an MC of 18 Cancer, the Sun at 29 Sagittarius, Moon at 15 Gemini, Venus 15 Capricorn, Jupiter 20 Cancer, Mars 10 Gemini, Mercury 20 Sagittarius, and Saturn 22 Leo.

Roger has given several partial examples in the text, but without offering a specific chart. This part of the text offers a full chart – a worked example. In common with many medieval texts, the chart isn't drawn up in most manuscripts, but simply spelled out as a set of positions. Roger's text doesn't tell us house cusp positions either, but because he has explained in his reference material (copied here in Appendix One) how to calculate the house cusps given the Ascendant and MC, it is easy enough for us to calculate these – and, indeed, one manuscript does give a drawing of the chart with house cusps given to the nearest degree, which agree with the Alcabitius house system to within a degree or two.[39]

The text that follows does make mention of houses, and it is obvious that some planets close to house cusps have been treated as being in the following house – this was quite a normal practice, although in this worked example it is possible that Roger was using a whole-sign house system. This is unlikely, though, since other examples in his text do depend on a quadrant house system, so I am assuming that he is using the Alcabitius house system here.

To make this chart easy to visualise to our modern eye, Figure 6.9 shows Roger's sample chart in a circular format. Where a planet has been nudged into the following house, this is indicated by an arrow.

Note that this chart does not correspond to any actual date, at least not within several centuries of Roger's period; this is an invented chart, where Roger has made up positions to illustrate his points. We have already seen a contrived

[39] Cambridge University Library, Gg VI.3, f.152r.

example of Roger's in Figure 6.8, which could only work for a southern hemisphere location.

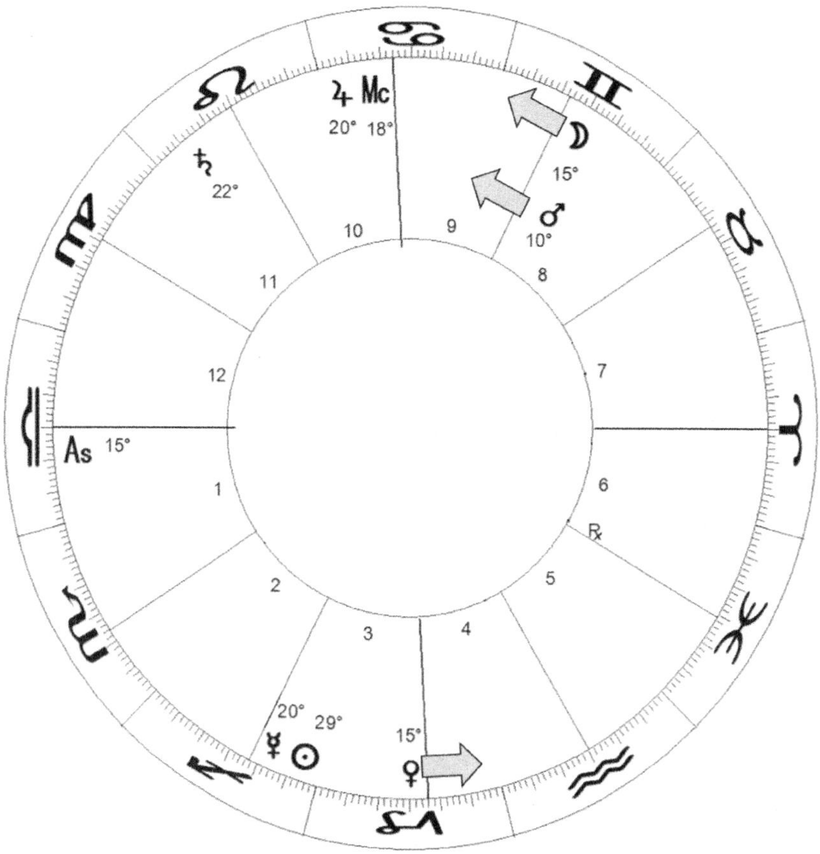

Figure 6.9: Modern representation of Roger of Hereford's example chart.

> First, I would look at the Lord of the Ascendant; this makes a right-angle to the Ascendant.

The Ascendant is Libra, and the planet ruling Libra is Venus, which is exactly 90° from the Ascendant. Planets making aspects to the angles are strengthened, and since this is an exact aspect, and Venus is angular too (very close to the IC, so considered to be a fourth house planet) and has essential dignity in earth signs, this makes Venus very strong in this example and will be used as one of the main significators.

> This is how I would begin. Then I would see from what this is separating; it is separating from the Sun, which is the Lord of the eleventh, and it [Venus] is in the fourth.

The Sun is in late Sagittarius, and the significator, Venus, is in Capricorn, moving away from the Sun. This is said to be **separating**, and the planet that the significator is separating from is also considered important – this was the technique described in Roger's summary. Roger notes that the Sun is the ruler of the eleventh house, and that the significator, Venus, is in the fourth.

> I know, therefore, that the matter concerns some beloved thing that relates to the fourth house; this signifies the father or mother.

Since the Lord of the Ascendant (Venus) is in good condition, she is able to act and does not suffer from the impediments mentioned earlier in the text. Hence it can be used to determine the intention – what the question is likely to involve. The question will concern something beloved (since Venus is linked with all things loved) and will relate to the fourth house of parents. It is rather curious that Roger should link the fourth house with both mother and father, since most Arabic texts give the fourth to father, and tenth to mother; however, Adelard of Bath had translated Abū Maʿšar's *Abbreviation to the Introduction* into Latin in the early twelfth century, and he had explicitly associated the fourth house with both father and mother.[40]

> However, since the Moon is separating from the Lord of the seventh and the seventh is the house of women, it relates to the mother.

Since Roger has determined that the intention is about a parent, he narrows it down to either mother or father. The Moon, provided it is not impeded as described earlier in the text, can act as another indicator of intention by seeing what it is separating from (just as was done for the chart ruler, Venus). In this case, the Moon is separating from Mars, and Mars is the ruler of the seventh house. The seventh house relates to women, so the parent in question must be the mother.

> The Moon is in the house of travel and she aspects Mercury, the Lord of travel, in the other house of travel.

Having determined that the mother is the relevant parent in this question, Roger investigates what else might be involved. The Moon is in the ninth house, which is associated with long-distance travel. The Moon aspects Mercury by opposition, who is the "Lord of travel". This designation could

---

[40] Abū Maʿšar, *Abbreviation* I.112, p.104.

be because Mercury is associated with the image of the messenger, or because it rules the ninth house of long-distance travel in this chart, but in either case the designation makes sense. Roger then looks at the placement of the Lord of travel and notes it is in the third house, which is associated with short-distance travel. Hence there are several testimonies relating to travel in this question, in addition to the querent's mother.

> Since Venus aspects Jupiter in the house of kings, I would say that this relates to a king – and the king is in his exaltation.

Furthermore, Venus – the chart ruler – aspects Jupiter by opposition, and Jupiter is in the tenth house. Both Jupiter and the tenth house relate to kingship, and Jupiter is also in Cancer, where he is exalted. This, therefore, is a very clear signature of a king being involved.

> However, because Jupiter is retrograde and opposite Venus, and Venus is in Jupiter's fall, the king will not be pleased to welcome her.

Roger now points out the pitfalls of what should be a good example of reception. Jupiter is retrograde. This is not explicitly shown in the chart, but any outer planets in the opposite half of the chart to the Sun will always be retrograde, so it is taken for granted that the student would realise this. Venus is in opposition to Jupiter, and in Capricorn, where Jupiter is in fall. This means that the king will not be pleased to see her. Although Roger doesn't labour the point, this is really an example of a sort of "negative reception". If Venus had been applying to Jupiter from a place where Jupiter was dignified – from Pisces, for example – that would be classic reception where Jupiter would be pleased to see Venus. In this case, though, Venus is applying to Jupiter from a place that Jupiter doesn't like at all – Capricorn, where he's in fall. So as a result, Jupiter won't be pleased to meet Venus.

> However, since Jupiter is a benefic, in the sign of his exaltation, strong because he's angular, and free from aspects from evil planets, then the king will listen to her.

Roger is referring to the fact that although Jupiter might seem to reject Venus for the reasons just given, Jupiter is nevertheless in a generous mood as he is a benefic planet, exalted, in an angular house and free of all evil planets, so he will indulge Venus and hear her out.

> Furthermore, the ruler of the Moon receives the Moon, but Mercury is in detriment and ruler of the twelfth house. The twelfth house cusp is in a human sign as is the Moon, which means enmity towards other people.

Finally, Roger looks at another example of reception, discussed earlier in the text, where planets in signs ruled by other planets either benefit or suffer from those rulers (depending upon the condition of the rulers), provided there is an aspect between them. In this example, the Moon is in Gemini, which is ruled by Mercury, and there is an opposition aspect between the Moon and Mercury. However, Mercury is not benefitting the Moon. Mercury is in detriment, and is also the ruler of the twelfth house of hidden enemies, considered to be a malefic house. The twelfth house does have other meanings as well, such as large animals. However, Roger narrows this down by pointing out that the twelfth house is in Virgo, and the Moon is in Gemini, which are both human signs, and therefore the meaning of this is definitely human enemies. The scribe writing the earliest manuscript that we have available emphasises this, too, with a note in the margin: "Concerning the enmity of Mercury: Moon applies to Mercury in detriment – the Lord of the twelfth, in a human sign and Mercury in the sign of its detriment means enmity to other men".[41]

This worked example of Roger's is summed up in sixteen lines of text and a diagram but includes the salient points that he wrote in this chapter on intentions.

[41] Selden, 17v. margin.

Conclusion

The concept of determining an intention as a practice dates back to at least the third-century Indian source, the *Yavanajataka*, and various Arabic sources use the concept of intention, especially Māshā'Allāh's *On Hidden Things*.

Roger's numerous methods of determining the intention seems overwhelming, but we see echoes of this in a text called *Search of the Heart*, translated by the twelfth-century translator Hermann of Carinthia. It appears to be a translation of 'Umar al-Tabari's *Treatise on the discovery of Innermost Thoughts*, and puts Roger's numerous methods into context.[42] This text has a section entitled "Other opinions on identifying the thought", describing three methods: using the Lot of Fortune, and attributed to Dorotheus; the ruler of the Ascendant, attributed to Hermes; and the duodenariae and novenes, attributed to "the Indians".[43] The final opinion is attributed to Māshā'Allāh, who lists numerous methods and combines them just as Roger does. Hermann describes Māshā'Allāh's method:

> The fourth [opinion] is the signification of Māshā'Allāh, generally mixing together all of these from the east: the Lord of the rising sign, the Lord of the sovereignty, Lord of the trigon, the bound,[44] the decan, the ninth-part, the twelfth-part, the star to which the rising degree is bound, the star which occupied the east. Apart from the east, the Lot of Fortune with its Lord, the Lord of the hour, and the Lord of the Sun by day and Lord of the Moon by night. The one which was strongest among all of these, and which many testimonies favoured, that one plainly obtains the signification.[45]

Roger has thrown in plenty of additional techniques too, which makes it quite hard to distinguish between which methods will determine the intention, and which will actually answer the question itself! However, the two concepts are quite closely related.

---

[42] Dykes, *Search of the Heart*, p.4.
[43] Dykes, *Search of the Heart*, Chapter I.9.
[44] Bound is just another word for "term".
[45] Dykes, *Search of the Heart*, p.69.

CHAPTER SEVEN: ELECTIONS

We've already looked at two topics. Now we'll look at a third one, namely the preparation of an election. There are three ways of doing this: using the Lord of the Ascendant itself, or by using the Moon, or by other significators.

These other significators are planets that are chosen because of their relationship to the first house, or the Lord of the Ascendant, or the Lord of the seventh house, but we would give priority to the Lord of the Ascendant.

However, in the preparation of elections, extraordinary care must be taken, so let's cover that first.

The past is looked back upon by the present and the future, and the present is looked back upon by the future. So these may be said to relate to the Lord of the Ascendant.

If the Lord of the Ascendant is in a sign in which it is strong, or has reception, but does not have this in the next sign that it will enter, then choose matters relating to that first sign; if it is strong in the following sign, then choose matters relating to that second sign.

Consider also what the Lord of the Ascendant is separating from, and what planet it is applying to. If the planet it is separating from is in better condition than the planet it is applying to, then choose things relating to the separating planet; if the planet it is applying to, choose things relating to that planet.

In addition, consider who is the stronger out of the Lord of the Ascendant, and the Lord of the seventh, based on strength in the chart and reception.

> Similarly, see who is the stronger out of the Lord of the Ascendant and the Moon, and use the stronger as the judge. The other one will add to or detract from the judgement. If the planet separating from the Lord of the Ascendant is strong, but the planet separating from the Moon is weak, this will reduce the strength of the overall judgement. Do this for all the methods, because looking at all of them will give many good indications and many bad ones – but eventually, one significator must be selected from all the possible outcomes, currently and in the future.

Roger tells us that having covered two topics – judgements and intentions – we can now move on to the topic of electional astrology, which is an extremely short section, and rather confusing to interpret. He points out that the Lord of the Ascendant relates to the current situation and that if it is strong in this sign where it is currently placed, then use matters of that sign, but if it is stronger in the following sign, then use matters of that sign. At first glance, this seems confusing for an election; the technique seems to be offering a choice between just two alternatives, based on a particular chart. The whole point of an election, though, is not to consider two alternatives from an existing chart, but to elect a time to undertake something where the chart is as good as it can be. However, I think what Roger is ultimately telling us to do here is examine a number of possible charts. Then, for each one, work out what the significators are, and whether they're improving or not (so if the Lord of the Ascendant is moving from a sign where he's weak to one where he's strong, then the indication is good). It is, however, open to interpretation, and as this "third book" is so short, there aren't any examples to get a clearer idea of what Roger meant.

CHAPTER EIGHT: THE METHOD OF JUDGING

To bring about the best outcome, the Lord of the Ascendant should be dignified in the sign of the matter being asked about. Also use the Sun and Moon as significators. In a daytime chart, the Sun predominates with the Moon as a lesser significator; in a night-time chart, it is the other way round. Both the Sun and Moon are important; the Sun will always be dominant and carry the light during the day, and the Moon at night, and the distance between the Moon and Sun projected onto the Ascendant (from the Sun to the Moon in the day, and from the Moon to the Sun at night) is called the Part of Fortune. This can be used when neither the Lord of the Ascendant nor the Lord of the matter, nor any usual significator, can be used. Just as the heat of the Sun awakens everything below it as it rises above the horizon, the Moon defines the growth and boundaries from the place of the matter. Thus by calculating the Part of Fortune from the position of the Sun, Moon and Ascendant, it can indicate the outcome of the matter.

The degree of the Sun, then, represents the natural beginning of the matter, the Moon the end of the matter. The Ascendant, though, represents the accidental beginning of the matter, and the Lord of the matter the end. A judgement can also be made from the Lord of the sign in which the Sun is situated, and the Lord of the sign in which the Moon is situated, and the Lord of the Part of Fortune.

In addition, consider planets that are natural significators of the matter, and planets that rule the significators of the matter. Consider also planets that rule the annual revolution (the most recent spring equinox), and the most recent syzygy (New Moon or Full Moon), and planets ruling the last conjunction of Saturn, Jupiter, and Mars, and the planet that is the Lord of the hour.

In practice, you'll find that the significators for the accidental beginnings and endings are more frequently used than the natural ones. However, to reach a judgement you need to examine all natural and accidental significators; the Sun, the Moon, Mercury for knowledge, accidental significators (Lords of various houses), the Part of Fortune, the Lord of the matter, Lord of the Sun, Lord of the Moon. Ideally, you will find three to be able to give a more accurate answer.

There are, then, many methods that you can use. For an election, also cast a chart for the place and time of the querent's birth.

Ensure that you put the Lord of the Ascendant into an angle to be safe. If the main significator is in poor condition, but some other planet receives the Ascendant, then that's a second choice. If something has no reception with the Ascendant but aspects it, then that's the third choice for significator.

In his prologue, Roger promised us four parts to his book, and this is almost certainly the fourth and final part. I say "almost certainly" because this section is very short, and rather disjointed, and most manuscripts don't clearly discriminate between this section and the preceding one on elections. However, one manuscript does clearly label it as the fourth part, and the part is missing from some other manuscripts entirely, suggesting it was intended to stand alone.

Roger starts off in a philosophical tone, first explaining why the Sun and Moon are so important in any chart, and how the Sun awakens things by his heat, and the Moon, with her waxing and waning, builds boundaries, and he likens this to the Sun initiating things, and the Moon finishing things. Since the Part of Fortune is calculated by taking the distance between the Sun and Moon and projecting that onto the Ascendant, Roger sees the Part of Fortune as an important significator, as it combines the qualities of the Sun, Moon and Ascendant.

He distinguishes between the Sun and Moon as being "natural" significators, because they are actual heavenly bodies with a clear location. He then identifies the Ascendant and the Lord of the Matter as "accidental" significators, because they have similar qualities to the Sun and Moon; the Ascendant is the part of the ecliptic rising above the horizon, and it's when the Sun rises that its warmth wakes things up, so the Ascendant can be seen as an analogue of the Sun. The Moon, as it sets boundaries and finishes what the Sun has started, can be seen as representing the matter – the outcome, the judgement; and the Lord of the house representing the matter is therefore an analogue to the Moon.

However, rather than launching into a further explanation of this, there's a distinct sense of Roger running out of steam at this point, and he now throws in a whole list of other things to consider in a judgement: all the significators he's mentioned, Mercury if you want to know about knowledge, the chart for the most recent spring equinox, the most recent syzygy (that's just a Full Moon or New Moon), the most recent conjunction of Saturn, Jupiter, and Mars, and the planet that is Lord of the hour. And if you're doing an election, cast the natal chart of the querent too.

These somewhat throwaway comments suggest that Roger was teaching more than just horary astrology. He mentions casting a natal chart, and also looking at conjunctions of Saturn, Jupiter, and Mars, which is a Persian technique widely used in Arabic astrology for the astrology of world events, a branch called **mundane astrology** – and yet Roger does not touch upon these techniques elsewhere in his book.

Finally, he sums up by pointing out that the more significators you can find that work, the better – three gives you much more accuracy than two – and that (presumably for an election), placing the Lord of the Ascendant in an angle is the safest bet. If the Lord of the Ascendant is in poor condition in general judgements, then find a planet that has dignity in the degree of the Ascendant or receives it as a second choice. If none, then find a planet that at least aspects the Ascendant as your third choice.

And at this point, Roger simply ends. No conclusion, no grand ending!

CHAPTER NINE: CONCLUSION

This, then, concludes Roger's textbook, which he wrote to teach his students the art of astrology. It makes no claims to originality – indeed, Roger tells us that these techniques can be found in a wide range of sources, by which he means Arabic sources that, in Roger's time, had only recently been translated into Latin. We have no idea whether he learned Arabic himself – Hereford Cathedral held an exhibition in 2015 that made a reference to Roger of Hereford, and claimed that he'd travelled to Toledo to learn Arabic. This may or may not have been true, and I'm very grateful to Chris Pullin, the Chancellor of Hereford Cathedral, for pointing me to the source of this claim – which, it turns out, may not be true after all – we simply don't know very much about Roger, the person, at all. We have no idea when he was born – a birth chart for him would be most interesting to have, but he has left us no records. He was sometimes referred to as "Rogerus Infans" (meaning Roger the young), and in a text he wrote in 1176 on computus, he says it may be presumptuous for "one so young" to rewrite some of the rules of computus, leading some scholars to believe that he was a young schoolteacher at that time. However, in that very same text he tells us that he had been "sweating for many years" teaching in the cathedral school, and so his reference to him being "one so young" may simply have been a pun on his part, joking about the fact that his name was "Roger Young". Certainly, since he appears to have been senior enough to have witnessed a charter possibly as early as 1154 he almost certainly wasn't young when he wrote *Judicial Astrology*. We don't know how long he lived, although there do appear to be references to him still being active in Hereford in 1195, and an early thirteenth-century work by Alfred of Shareshill is dedicated to him. Josiah Russell, a scholar writing in 1932, claimed that Roger ended his days as a monk at Bury St. Edmund, but this is heavily disputed.[46]

By a lovely bit of synchronicity, just as I was completing my PhD thesis, I received an email from a professor in the US who claimed to be a descendant of Roger. Naturally, I was somewhat sceptical, but he attached an image from a copy of the 1838 edition of Burke's *Landed Gentry*, which refers to "Roger

---

[46] Josiah Russell, 'Hereford and Arabic Science in England about 1175-1200', *Isis*, 18.1 (1932), p.16.

Hereford, a famous philosopher" who flourished in the 1170s, and provided a genealogy right up to "the present Richard Hereford, esq. of Sufton". Using a genealogy website, I was able to fill in details beyond 1838 and up to the current day, which traced the tentative family tree all the way from Roger of Hereford to Robert James Hereford, who died in 2001. An obituary in the *Herefordshire and Wye Valley Life* in 2012 included an interview with the actor Henry Hereford, an actor who starred in the film *The Girl with the Dragon Tattoo* in 2011, as well as a number of more recent TV appearances. In the interview, Henry Hereford claimed that his "ancestors have resided at Sufton Court in Mordiford near Hereford since 1120". While such oral histories are not conclusive evidence, it does nevertheless suggest quite a strong link – Roger of Hereford did indeed own lands in Mordiford, which is a tiny village where the current Hereford family still owns Sufton Court.

However, interesting as this aside is, it still doesn't tell us very much about Roger of Hereford himself. At first sight, the fact that most astrologers have never heard of him shouldn't come as a surprise; the big stars of the twelfth-century astrology world were translators like Adelard of Bath, Hermann of Carinthia and John of Seville, who learned Arabic, travelled to Islamic regions, and spent years translating astrological texts, making them available to Christian Latin-speaking scholars for the first time. By comparison, a provincial schoolteacher who read these texts and compiled a textbook to teach schoolkids doesn't seem particularly significant. Only a handful of academic texts even mention Roger of Hereford, and the most detailed of these is the excellent MPhil dissertation by Nicholas Whyte, written in 1991, which gives a good summary of the text but focuses on the potential significance of one particular chart in the text, and doesn't attempt to provide a translation or full analysis of the techniques.

However, this viewpoint underestimates the role of teachers. Astrological texts weren't a curious sideline of Arabic scientific texts – they constituted over half of all the Arabic scientific texts translated. These texts initiated a twelfth-century renaissance of science and philosophy, which led to astrology being taught in universities across Europe from that point onwards, right up to the end of the seventeenth century. Neither was Hereford a provincial backwater; its cathedral school was the forerunner of the universities (Oxford University became a full-blown university a few decades after Roger's textbook), it was renowned for being a centre of learning for science and astrology, and even earlier than Roger it had the patronage of the king of England himself, Henry I.

Seen in this light, Roger's writing of *Judicial Astrology* was a seminal event. For the first time, students in cathedral schools could be taught astrology. The book was considered important enough to be copied across Europe for the next few centuries. As astrologers, we're now lucky enough to have access to good translations of Arabic texts on astrology into English, but until now we haven't known how this material was transmitted and taught.

As we saw above, we don't know very much about Roger of Hereford himself; he has been in the shadows. We do, however, now know what he wrote, and what he taught. Let us return to the Prelude that began this book; at some point in the 1170s, a schoolteacher walked into his class at Hereford Cathedral School, and began teaching the students in that class the principles of horary astrology. Until now, we didn't know what he told them or how he taught astrology. We didn't even realise that he was the first person in England to do such a thing – his seminal book hadn't been translated or published in full.

I hope, then, that this book goes some way to filling that gap. The twelfth-century revolution that saw horoscopic astrology taught for five centuries in major centres of learning across Europe began with teachers like Roger of Hereford. It is now time for Roger to come out of the shadows, so that after eight centuries we can once again hear his voice and read his work.

APPENDIX ONE: ROGER'S REFERENCE MATERIAL

Roger's textbook survives in 22 existing manuscripts, spread across Europe. Unfortunately, none of them are from the twelfth century, which means we haven't found Roger's original version, which he would have written in the 1170s; the earliest manuscript we have is one in the Bodleian Library at Oxford, and is in a volume labelled Selden Supra 76, dating from the thirteenth century, probably between 1240 and 1250.[47] The other problem with these manuscripts is that most of them are now in university libraries, but in general that isn't where they were originally written. In the case of the Selden manuscript, we can tell from a list of monks given on one sheet (not part of Roger's text, of course) that by the sixteenth century this manuscript was housed in Winchester. Medieval monastic libraries collated all sorts of texts, so the volume (called a **codex**, plural **codices**) that a particular text is bound in contains a number of texts, often from different periods. After the dissolution of the monasteries in England by Henry VIII in the sixteenth century, the manuscripts in monastic libraries were either lost, or distributed to collectors or universities, where they may have been separated and rebound into different codices.

This means that when you look at, say, Selden Supra 76 today, it looks like a coherent collection of astrological, astronomical, and magical texts. It starts with Roger's *Judicial Astrology*, but also includes astronomical tables from the ninth-century Persian polymath al-Khwarizmi, a text on the construction of an astrolabe, al-Kindi's *On the Stellar Rays*, and two texts on alchemy. However, when Roger's text was in a volume sitting on the shelves of the Benedictine cathedral priory of St Peter, St Paul, and St Swithun in Winchester in the early sixteenth century, it was bound with a different set of texts – including sermons, two texts by al-Ghazali, al-Kindi's treatise on the

---

[47] The catalogue in the Bodleian Library merely gives a date of "thirteenth century", but when I analysed the handwriting, I tentatively dated it to the first half of the thirteenth century. I'm extremely grateful to Professor Erik Kwakkel at the University of British Columbia, a palaeography specialist, who very generously looked at some of my analyses and confirmed my dating and narrowed it down further, as he found features normally only seen after 1240, but lacking features normally found after 1250.

intellect, and William of Malmesbury's book on the kings of England. We know this because some medieval library catalogues still survive.

Roger's *Judicial Astrology* has several sections to it, but seeing what order those sections are in today in existing codices doesn't necessarily mean that Roger intended them to be read in that order. Roger clearly starts off with a prologue, covered here in Chapter Four, in which he tells us that his book is in four parts, and names them (simple judgements, intentions, elections, and the method of judging), which I've described in separate chapters of this book (Chapter Five to Chapter Eight). However, in many of the manuscripts, Roger's prologue runs straight into a lengthy section of reference material before he starts with the section on simple judgements. Some manuscripts miss this section out entirely, implying that the reference material was meant to be a stand-alone section that would have been useful to students, but not needed by those already practising astrology.

The other feature of the reference material is that while we can hear Roger's voice in the main part of his text, telling students how to build up from simple principles, the reference material is, by and large, simply material copied directly from his Arabic sources. In many cases, Roger's text is almost identical to the text in various Latin translations of these Arabic works, which had been translated by other twelfth-century translators such as John of Seville, Hermann of Carinthia, and Adelard of Bath. Roger would have had access to these texts, translated a few decades before he wrote his book, and so the material would have been relatively novel, and worth providing to his students.

Because of its stand-alone nature and because, frankly, it's a fairly boring set of lists and tables that are available in various Arabic sources, I've separated it from the rest of Roger's book, so as not to detract from the flow of Roger's own words. Some of what Roger says in his main book does assume that his students know this reference material – there's an example in Chapter Six where he refers to Saturn in Taurus relating to a sickness of the stomach. This attribution isn't obvious from the material he covered in the book, but is part of the reference material covered here.

The reference material starts by defining the zodiac, and how to use both an astrolabe and a table to draw up house cusps of a chart, before launching into true reference material about attributes of signs, planets, and houses, and definitions of various ways that planets can relate to each other and how they can be impeded.

The two zodiacs

In any judgement, we need to identify houses in the chart, but first we need to note that there are two zodiacs that can be used. One has the zodiac starting at the intersection of the ecliptic and the celestial equator at the equinox, the other according to the constellation signs.

In both cases, the sky is divided into two equal halves with two points (on the ecliptic) opposite each other, one ascending, one descending. In one method, the ecliptic is divided into twelve equal signs starting from the point where the ecliptic crosses the celestial equator and begins to descend to the opposite northern point where it begins to ascend. These two equinoctial points form the basis of fixed divisions in the sky, and this method is used for making astrolabes, and producing tables of chords and arcs, and many other uses.

The other method is to use the constellations after which the signs of the zodiac are named and is used for astrological judgements and tables. These signs are equal in size and are named after the constellations – Aries, Taurus and so on.

The motion of the ecliptic against the fixed stars moves one degree in 100 years, and hence the position of a planet measured against the fixed stars as opposed to the position in the ecliptic would move one degree in 100 years. The difference between the two methods now differs by 8 degrees, so that a planet measured in the first degree of Aries in the method using fixed stars would appear to be in the ninth degree of Aries under the method using the ecliptic.

Roger begins by explaining that there are two zodiacs, both of which involve dividing the ecliptic into twelve equal segments. The first method he describes is what we now call the **tropical zodiac**, where the zodiac begins at the point where the **celestial equator** crosses the **ecliptic**. The celestial equator is the projection of the Earth's equator into space. In the solar system, most of the planets, including Earth, lie on a flat plane. Because the Earth is tilted at about 23.4° this flat plane is tilted (from Earth's perspective) by the same amount with respect to the celestial equator. We can draw a circle corresponding to this flat plane, and the Sun appears to move along this path, as do most of the planets. This path is called the ecliptic, as illustrated in Figure A1.1. The ecliptic and the celestial equator intersect at two points, and if you imagine the Sun travelling (from our perspective on Earth) around the ecliptic, then when it is at one of those intersection points, it is the spring or autumn equinox. The tropical zodiac is considered to begin at the intersection point where the Sun is at the spring equinox – this is 0° Aries, and the ecliptic is divided into twelve equal segments from this point, representing the twelve signs.

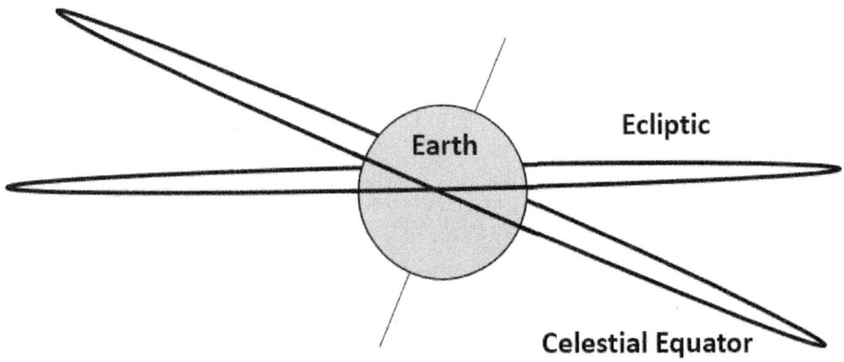

Figure A1.1: Diagram showing the celestial equator and the ecliptic.

Roger mentions a second system, which is to use the constellations after which the signs are named, and that these signs are also 30-degree segments. Since the Sun, Moon, and planets all move roughly along the ecliptic (although they can deviate by a few degrees), the constellations that lie on this path are very useful ways of indicating the positions of planets. In Roger's time, there were twelve such constellations that lay on the ecliptic, given names such as Aries the ram, Taurus the bull and so on. These are the familiar zodiac constellations. Rather than using the intersection of the ecliptic and the celestial equator, Roger tells us that this second method simply allocates 30-degree segments to the ecliptic based on the constellation that lies in each segment. This method is what we now call the **sidereal zodiac**.

When zodiac terminology was being developed, centuries before Roger's time, these two zodiacs more or less coincided. However, these two zodiacs drift apart over time. Roger tells us that they shift by a degree every 100 years, and that by Roger's time in the twelfth century they differed by eight degrees. Although Roger's value of eight degrees was correct, Roger was incorrect in thinking that they drifted by one degree every 100 years, a figure he would have got from Ptolemy, as the actual slippage is about one degree every 72 years. This slippage means that if one person noted that, say, Mars was in the first degree of Aries using constellations, Mars would actually be in the ninth degree using the ecliptic method.

In fact, the two zodiacs are not as clear-cut as Roger implies. Constellations are patterns of stars, and the zodiac constellations do not all lie directly along the ecliptic – although they are close to the ecliptic, their angles vary; some do lie along the ecliptic, but others straddle it. Neither are they all 30 degrees wide. This means identifying the location of a planet simply by observing which constellation it is in doesn't give a reliable value. Indian astrologers – both in Roger's time and today – do use a sidereal zodiac loosely based upon constellations, but they too use precise 30-degree segments with a defined starting point. This is illustrated in Figure A1.2, which shows what is, in effect, three zodiacs: the tropical zodiac, the sidereal zodiac, and the constellational zodiac. This diagram is set for the twenty-first century, not Roger's time, as the discrepancy between the tropical and sidereal zodiac is now much more pronounced, with a difference of about 23 degrees.

In this diagram, the tropical zodiac is shown as the inner wheel, and the sideral as the outer wheel. You can see that each sign is precisely 30 degrees, but the two zodiacs are offset by 23 degrees. The constellations are drawn in, too, and while you can see that Taurus lies roughly along the ecliptic, and does indeed take up almost all of the 30-degree segment of sidereal Taurus, Scorpio is more vertical, and while it crosses the sidereal Scorpio, its start and end do not take up the entire segment, and part of Scorpio nudges into the sidereal sign of Sagittarius.

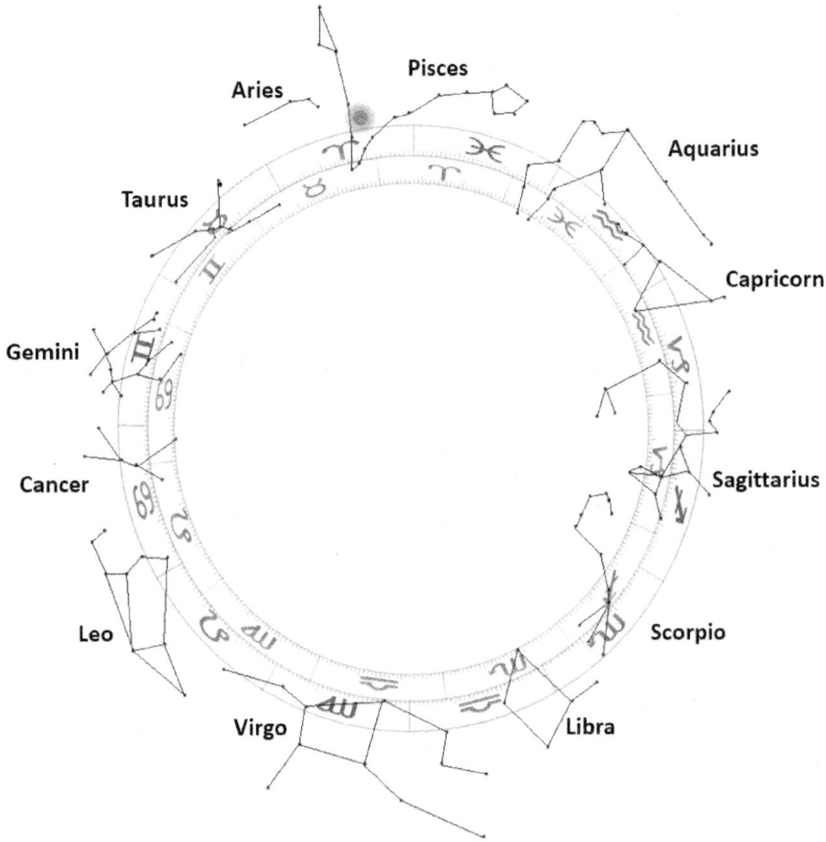

Figure A1.2: Diagram showing the tropical zodiac (inner) wheel, sidereal zodiac (outer wheel), and the zodiac constellations.

The constellations of Capricorn and Aquarius overlap somewhat, making it very hard to judge whether a particular planet is "in" Capricorn or Aquarius. Pisces in particular sprawls across two signs, and so if you saw a planet in the sky where the grey dot is in this diagram, that planet would be clearly in the constellation of Pisces, in the sidereal sign of Aries, and in the tropical sign of Taurus. Constellations and zodiacs aren't that clear-cut!

House calculation: using an astrolabe

Having discussed the two methods of defining the zodiac, we should move onto the distinction between the houses. Just as there are two ways of defining the zodiac, there are two ways of defining the division of houses – one using an astrolabe, the other using the hours.

Roger now explains that there are two methods of defining the division of **houses**. A house is another division of the ecliptic into twelve, but instead of starting at the point where the ecliptic crosses the celestial equator, the first house begins at the point of the ecliptic rising over the observer's horizon – this point is called the **Ascendant**. The point opposite the Ascendant is called the **Descendant**; the point of the ecliptic that is culminating (at its highest point) is called the **Midheaven** (usually abbreviated to MC); and the point opposite the MC is called the **Imum Coeli** (usually abbreviated to IC).

In Hellenistic astrology, a whole sign house system was often used. In this system, the sign that the Ascendant was in defined the entire first house; the Ascendant might be at 1° Gemini, or 15° Gemini, or 29° Gemini – in that case, the entire sign of Gemini was the first house, the entire sign of Cancer was the second house and so on. The MC might not be in the tenth sign – it could be in Aquarius, for example, with Gemini as the Ascendant, even though Aquarius would be the ninth sign, and not the tenth. However, some later Hellenistic authors developed systems to divide the chart into four **quadrants** based on the Ascendant/Descendant axis, and the MC/IC axis, and these were developed even further by Arabic astrologers. When these texts came into the Latin-speaking West in the twelfth century, such as Roger's *Judicial Astrology*, quadrant house systems were generally adopted.

Because the MC is not always at right-angles to the Ascendant, in quadrant house systems, houses vary in size and so are not always 30 degrees in extent. Roger's text provides two methods of calculating houses, one using an astrolabe, and the other using a table of hours.

For example, Figure A1.3 below shows a hypothetical example (not in Roger's text) to illustrate this – it is a chart drawn up for the latitude of Hereford, for 6 April 1175 at 07:30 LMT. This chart has an Ascendant of 17° Gemini, and an MC of 11° Aquarius (for any given latitude, a particular Ascendant will always have the same corresponding MC – so although the time of day when 17° Gemini is rising will vary through the year at Hereford, when it is rising, 11° Aquarius will always be culminating and be the MC). It can be seen that the quadrant from the IC to the Descendant has three houses, which are far bigger than the houses in the quadrant from the Ascendant to the IC. The method of house division was based on various ways of dividing the celestial sphere.

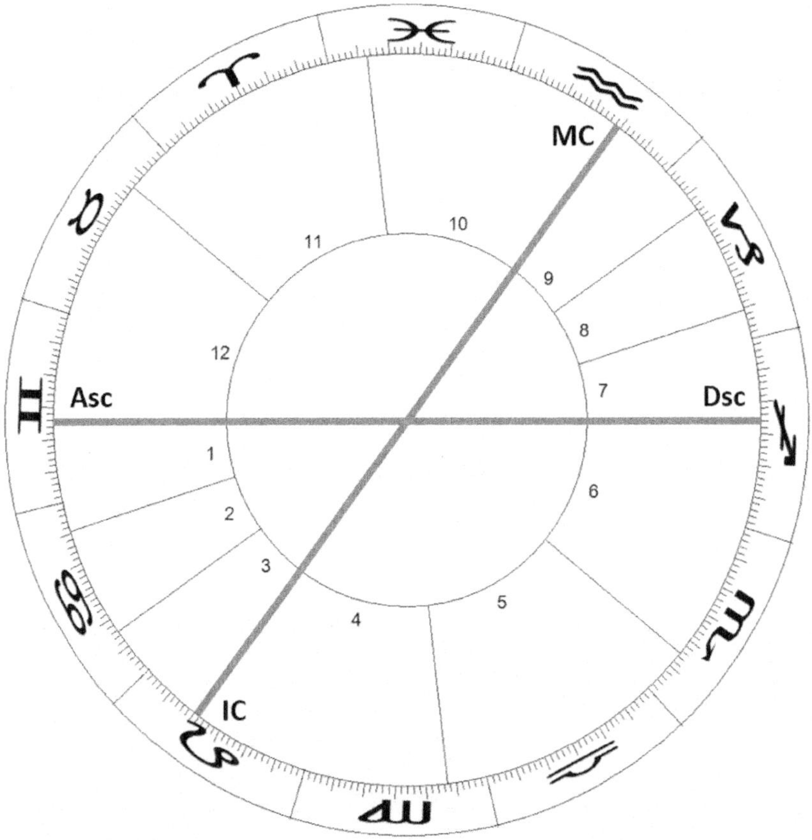

Figure A1.3: Quadrant house system: Alcabitius.

Using the astrolabe, align the degree of the Sun (in the zodiac) on the ecliptic circle, with the position in the almucantar corresponding to its altitude (as measured by the alidade), and the degree of the Ascendant can be seen immediately as the degree rising over the first almucantar.

Roger's text cannot be understood without a working knowledge of the **astrolabe**, which represents a projection of the sky for a particular latitude onto a fixed plate, usually made of brass. This plate is overlaid by a movable disc that is cut away so the underlying plate is visible. This movable disc is called a **rete** with representations of key fixed stars on it. On top of this is a moveable ruler, called the **alidade**, which could be used to measure the elevation of stars and planets, or the Sun. The back of the plate has a variety of useful calendrical scales on it, and charts for determining where the Sun is on any given date. An astrolabe can be used for determining the time, finding directions (for example, the direction to Mecca) and as it is a model of the sky it can also be used to work out where various circles on the celestial sphere intersect, and so can be used to calculate key points on an astrological chart such as the Ascendant, MC, and house cusps. Since the plate is specific to a particular latitude, the plates are designed to be easy to remove. Historically, astrolabes came with a range of plates allowing a traveller to insert the plate relevant to their own latitude. An example is shown in Figure A1.4, which shows an early ninth-century Arabic astrolabe from Syria. By the twelfth century, astrolabes were being made in Latin-speaking Europe, too, of a virtually identical design.

Front view of astrolabe

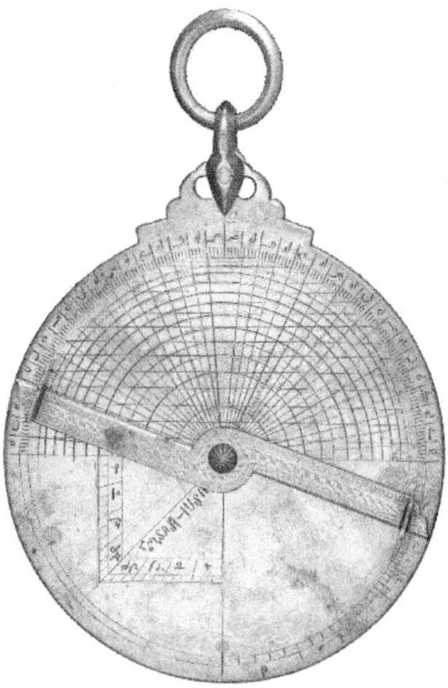

Back view of Astrolabe

Figure A1.4: Late ninth-century brass astrolabe from Syria.

The Ascendant is found by finding out the position of the Sun in the zodiac from the table on the back of the astrolabe, visually measuring its altitude with the alidade (the ruler), and then aligning the rete such that the degree of the zodiac lines up with the circle representing the altitude. The Ascendant can then be read off the rete. As an example, consider the chart that we have already seen in Figure A1.3, set for 6 April 1175. The astrolabe would be equipped with the latitude plate for 52°, the latitude of Hereford. Figure A1.5 shows a photograph of a latitude plate for 52°, from a brass astrolabe made in the thirteenth century in Spain. The arcs at the top of the plate are the altitude lines, and the arcs at the bottom are the hour lines, used for house calculations, which we'll cover shortly.

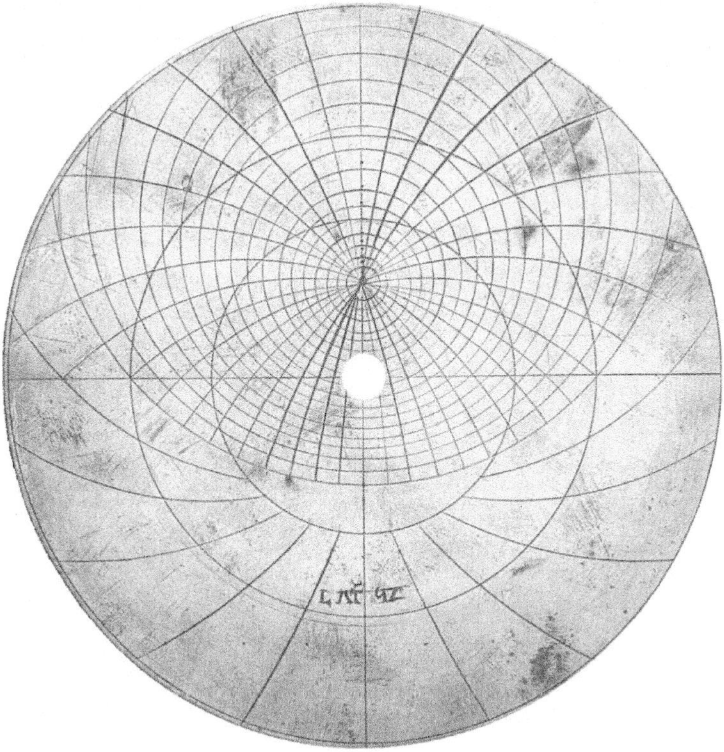

Figure A1.5: Latitude plate for 52° North, from a thirteenth-century Spanish astrolabe.

Figure A1.6 shows a diagram of the astrolabe, following Roger's instructions, which tell us to "align the degree of the Sun on the ecliptic circle with the position in the almucantar corresponding to its altitude (as measured by the alidade)". In this case, Roger would know that the Sun was at 22° Aries on 6 April 1175 (either by using the guide on the back of the astrolabe, or from tables). He would then go outside and observe the height of the Sun above the horizon visually at 07:30 LMT, using the alidade to measure how high up in the sky it was; at that time, he would see that the Sun was at an altitude of 20°. The altitude line representing 20° is marked as a thick black line on the diagram, and 22° Aries is shown as a large dot at the end of that arc. The rete is movable, so we adjust the rete so that 22° Aries is on the 20° altitude line as shown. The degree rising on the 0° altitude line, called the **almucantar**, is the Ascendant, shown by a large dot on the inner grey wheel. This is about 17° Gemini.

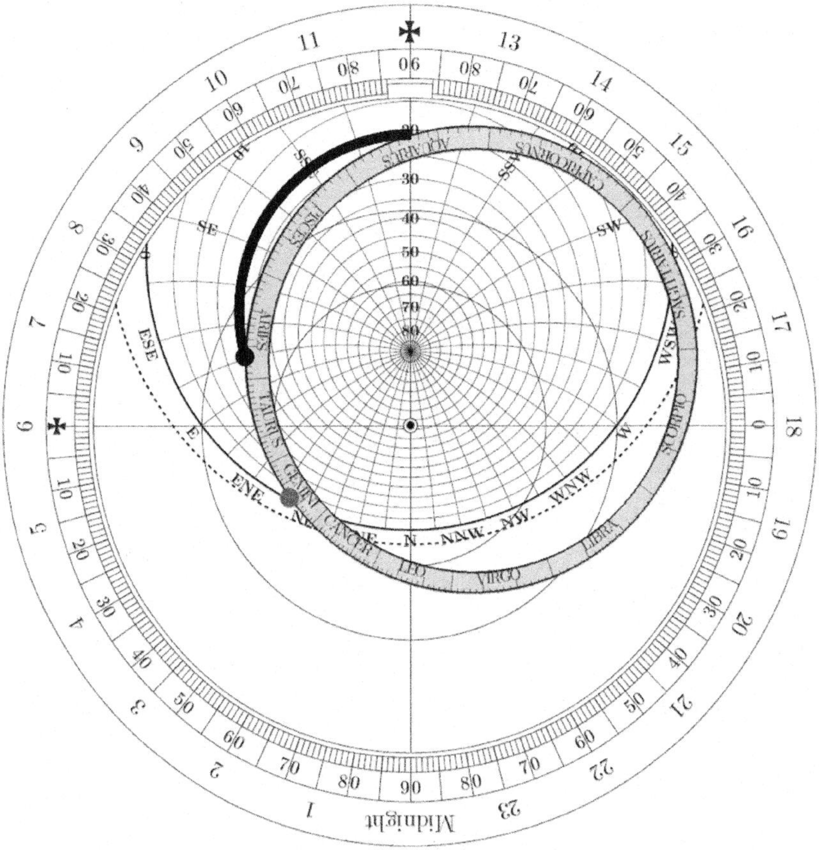

Figure A1.6: Calculating the Ascendant using an astrolabe.

Credit: Template image used by permission of the Master and Fellows of St John's College, Cambridge, and is copyright Dominic Ford and Katie Birkwood.

> To construct an astrological chart from this, first add eight degrees to the degree of the Sun before placing that degree on the relevant altitude on the almucantar. Then the degree shown on the first almucantar (the eastern horizon) is the Ascendant, but this only works if you remember to add those eight degrees (to the Sun's longitude). Hence it is necessary to take care in casting an astrological chart for judgements.

For a modern astrolabe, no adjustment is necessary, but Roger is clearly using an astrolabe where the table on the back is giving the position of the Sun in sidereal co-ordinates. This appears to have been a common practice – a manuscript in the British Library attributed to Roger gives a set of readings, presumably done by astrolabe, of the noon altitude of the Sun as it enters each zodiac sign.[48] However, the dates in that manuscript also show Roger was giving those positions in the sidereal zodiac. For example, the entry for Sagittarius says "xvi", meaning 16 degrees. Using a rough year for when Roger was working, the Sun entered the tropical sign of Sagittarius on 15 November 1175 (the Julian calendar was in use then, which is why this date differs from the modern date when the Sun enters Sagittarius). However, when the Sun was at its highest point on that day, modern software shows that it was at an altitude of 17°45′, not the 16° in the manuscript. However, 8 days later, on 23 November when the Sun was at 8° Sagittarius in the tropical zodiac, the altitude of the Sun at true noon was indeed 16°13′, matching Roger's figures.

In the example given above, I said that Roger would have known that the Sun was at 22° Aries on 6 April 1175. That's not quite true; if Roger used a table similar to the one in the British Library manuscript, or the table on the back of the astrolabe was calibrated the same way, then it would tell him that the Sun was at 14° Aries on 6 April 1175, since that was the sidereal position. Roger is telling us that since the astrolabe is used for drawing up charts, the

[48] London, British Library, Arundel 377, f.86v.

first things we need to do is add 8° to that value to get the correct tropical position of 22° Aries.

> By moving the rete so that the degree of the Ascendant moves across two hour lines in the eastern part of the astrolabe, the degree shown on the middle hour line is the start of the third house.

We have already ascertained that the Ascendant is 17° Gemini, so this point, indicated by the large dot, is moved to the second **hour line** (shown as thick black arcs in the bottom half of the diagram). The middle hour line then shows the cusp of the third house, indicated by a large dot at about 25° Cancer shown in Figure A1.7.

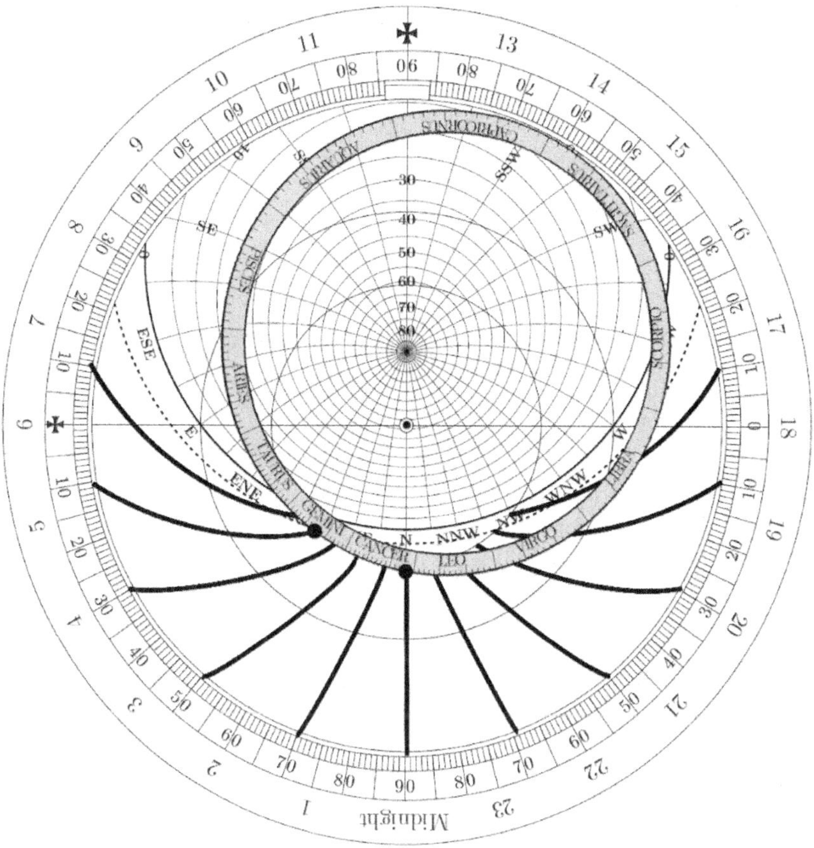

Figure A1.7: Calculating the third house using an astrolabe.

Credit: Template image used by permission of the Master and Fellows of St John's College, Cambridge, and is copyright Dominic Ford and Katie Birkwood.

> Moving the Ascendant across a further two hour lines will give the position of the start of the second house.

Now we move the rete so that 17° Gemini is on the fourth hour line. The middle hour line then shows the cusp of the second house, indicated by a large dot at about 5° Cancer as shown in Figure A1.8.

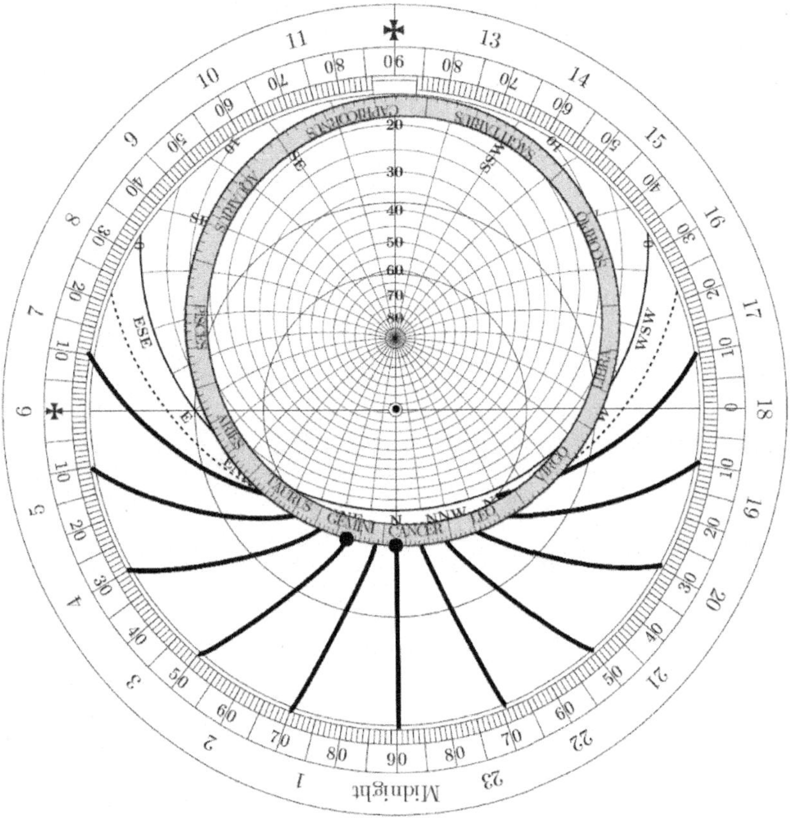

Figure A1.8: Calculating the second house using an astrolabe.

Credit: Template image used by permission of the Master and Fellows of St John's College, Cambridge, and is copyright Dominic Ford and Katie Birkwood.

Placing the degree of the Ascendant back on the first almucantar (the eastern horizon), the middle hour line shows the fourth house, and the last almucantar (the western horizon) shows the seventh house, which is opposite the degree of the Ascendant.

Now we move the rete backwards so that 17° Gemini is on the almucantar. The middle hour line then shows the cusp of the fourth house, indicated by a large dot at about 11° Leo as shown in Figure A1.9. In fact, since the Ascendant was on the almucantar when we first calculated it, we could have read both the fourth house position and also derived the seventh house cusp immediately then (see Figure A1.6 above).

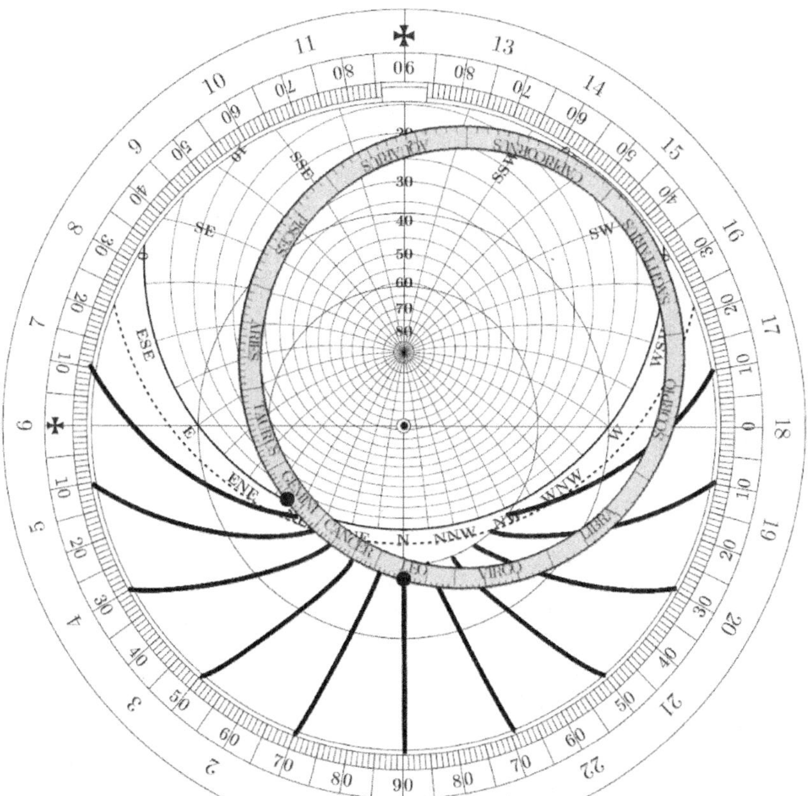

Figure A1.9: Calculating the fourth and seventh houses using an astrolabe.

Credit: Template image used by permission of the Master and Fellows of St John's College, Cambridge, and is copyright Dominic Ford and Katie Birkwood.

Similarly, moving the degree of the seventh house by two hour lines gives the start of the fifth house, and moving it a further two hour lines yields the sixth house. Thus three houses are determined by the degree of the Ascendant, and three by its nadir (the opposite point).

The Ascendant is 17° Gemini so the seventh house cusp is opposite that, at 17° Sagittarius. By moving this point two hour lines from the seventh house (the almucantar on the right hand side of the astrolabe), the middle line shows the cusp of the fifth house, at about 23° Virgo, and moving it a further two hour lines shows the cusp of the sixth house at about 7° Scorpio. These are shown in Figures A1.10 and A1.11, with the large dots showing the cusp.

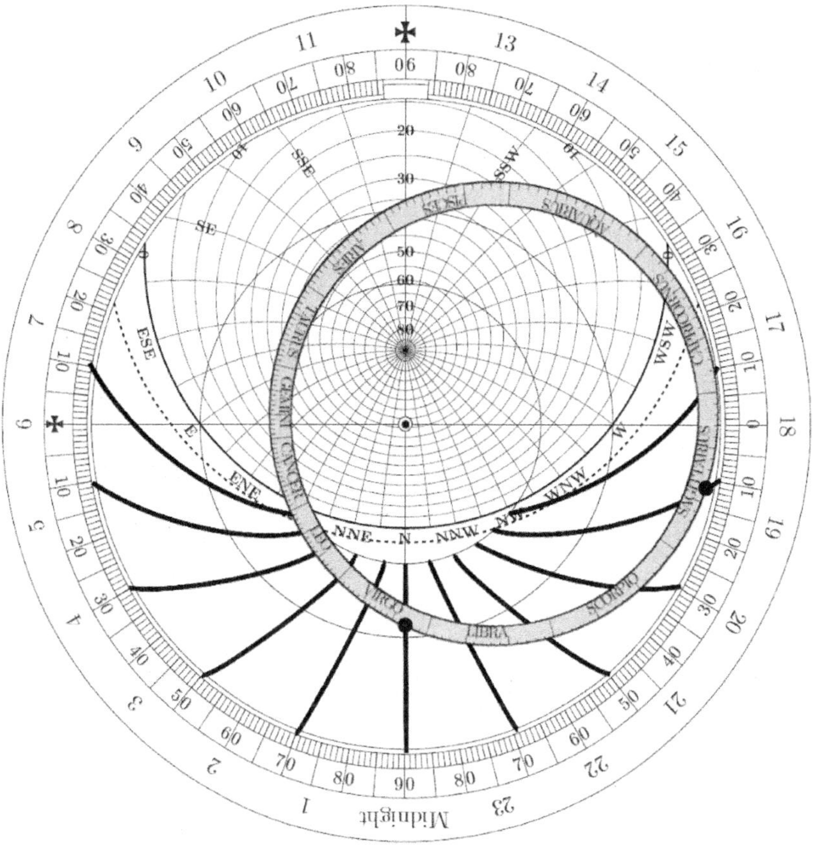

Figure A1.10: Calculating the fifth house using an astrolabe.

Credit: Template image used by permission of the Master and Fellows of St John's College, Cambridge, and is copyright Dominic Ford and Katie Birkwood.

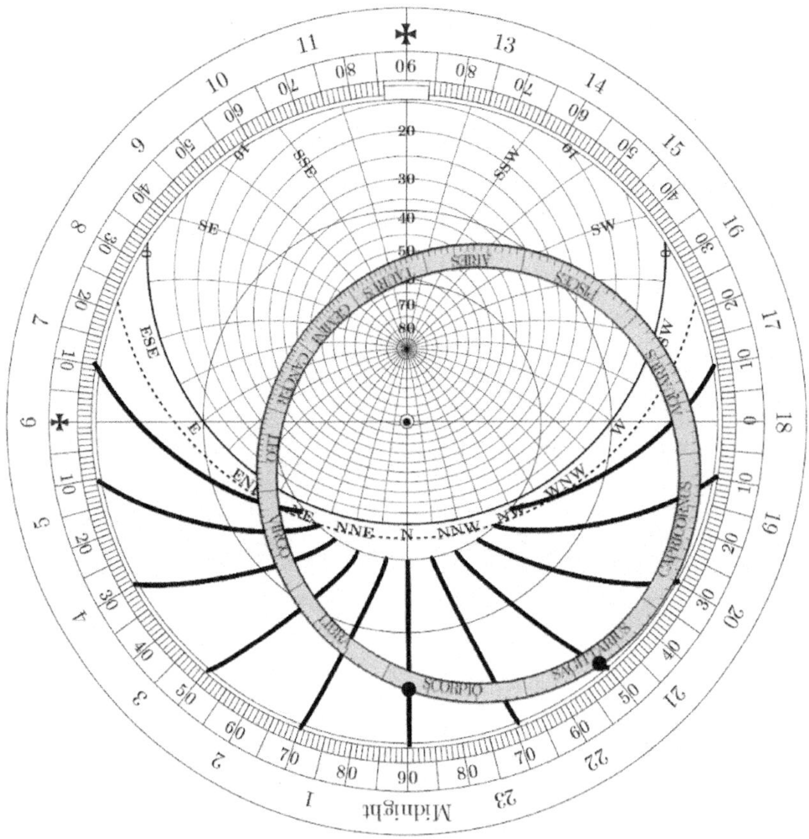

Figure A1.11: Calculating the sixth house using an astrolabe.

Credit: Template image used by permission of the Master and Fellows of St John's College, Cambridge, and is copyright Dominic Ford and Katie Birkwood.

Following these instructions has now given us the first six houses, and the remaining six house cusps are simply opposite the first six. This method yields a quadrant house system that is equivalent to the Alcabitius house system, named after the Arabic astrologer al-Qabisi. The original chart drawn up in Figure A1.3 was calculated with Alcabitius houses, showing that the astrolabe method matches this quite closely.

House calculation: using tables

The second method of calculating houses is by using the hours. Using the table below, use the degree of the Ascendant to look up the length of two nocturnal hours. This will be the distance between the first and second house, the second and third, and the third and fourth. In the same way, use the length of two diurnal hours to make the distance between the fourth and fifth house, the fifth and sixth, and the sixth and seventh. It can be seen that this is no different to the previous description, since the degree of the Ascendant – when the Sun is in that position – gives us its nocturnal hours and its opposite point the diurnal hours.

From the degree of the Ascendant, we can immediately derive six houses. The other six can then be derived from their opposites: the first house gives the cusp of the seventh, the second house the eighth, the third house the ninth, the fourth house the tenth, the fifth house the eleventh and the sixth house the twelfth.

For those without an astrolabe, Roger provides a set of **tables of hours**. As we saw in Chapter Six in the section on determining the intention from the Lord of the hour, a distinction was made between diurnal (daytime) and nocturnal (night-time) hours. In the summer, for example, diurnal hours are longer than nocturnal hours – taking the example we saw in Chapter Six at the solstice in Hereford, a diurnal hour would be 83 minutes and 20 seconds while a nocturnal hour was 36 minutes and 40 seconds.

At the spring equinox, anywhere in the world, the Sun rises at 06:00, culminates at 12:00 and sets at 18:00 (all times are approximate Local Mean Time as measured by a sundial). A sunrise chart for the equinox would have 0° Aries as the Ascendant, 0° Capricorn as the MC, 0° Libra as the Descendant, and 0° Cancer as the IC. Each quadrant would be 90°. At the summer solstice at Hereford, the Sun rises at 03:44, culminates at 12:00 and sets at 20:16. A sunrise chart for the summer solstice would have 0° Cancer as the Ascendant, 23°40′ Aquarius as the MC, 0° Capricorn as the Descendant and 23°40′ Leo as the IC. In this case, the quadrant from the Ascendant to the IC (houses 1 to 3) only occupies 53°40′, while the quadrant from the IC to the Descendant occupies 126°20′. That example is for a sunrise chart, but in fact even in mid-winter there will be a time of day when 0° Cancer is rising (at the winter solstice, for example, that will happen at sunset), and when that happens, the MC will always be 23°40′ Aquarius. This is illustrated in the two charts (not in Roger's manuscript) shown earlier in Figures 5.3 and 5.5.

For this reason, Roger's "table of hours" does not provide the length of each diurnal and nocturnal hour for a given date, but instead gives a nominal number of degrees that describes distances between houses for any given Ascendant. For example, looking up 30° Gemini in the table gives a value of 20°50′ (this really means 0° Cancer, but there is no number zero in the table). Since Gemini appears at the top, labelled "Diurnal hours", the value in the table gives us the diurnal hour degrees. Multiplying this figure by six gives us the distance from the Ascendant to the MC, namely 125°. Multiplying it by two gives us the distance between the fourth and fifth houses.

Several manuscripts give Roger's table, but as they are all handwritten, some copyist errors have crept in. Table A1.1 shows this table, and the errors are highlighted in grey.

The table has only six columns; it is not necessary to have two sets of tables, one for diurnal hours and one for nocturnal, nor to make the table for all twelve signs. This is because the year is symmetric – the number of daytime hours on the longest day (the summer solstice) is the same as the number of night-time hours on the shortest day, and for any date the number of nocturnal hours will always be the number of diurnal hours subtracted from 24 hours.[49] When converted to arcs of the circle, as this table is, the length of a nocturnal hour is the length of the diurnal hour in degrees subtracted from 30 degrees.

[49] The terms "daytime" and "night-time" are used in the astronomical sense of the Sun being above or below the horizon, respectively – dawn and twilight are considered to be night if the Sun is below the horizon, even if it is light.

DIURNAL HOURS																		
°	Aries			Taurus			Gemini			Cancer			Leo			Virgo		
1	15	7	30	17	59	20	19	54	45	20	49	56	19	48	30	17	50	40
2	15	15	0	18	3	40	19	57	50	20	48	52	19	45	20	17	46	20
3	15	23	30	18	8	0	20	0	55	20	47	28	19	41	10	17	42	0
4	15	30	0	18	12	20	20	4	0	20	46	44	19	38	0	17	37	40
5	15	38	30	18	16	40	20	7	5	20	45	40	19	35	50	17	23	20
6	15	45	0	18	21	0	20	10	10	20	44	36	19	32	40	17	29	0
7	15	52	30	18	25	20	20	13	15	20	43	32	19	29	30	17	23	40
8	16	0	0	18	29	40	20	16	20	20	42	28	19	26	20	17	20	20
9	16	7	30	18	34	0	20	19	25	20	41	28	19	23	10	17	16	0
10	16	15	0	18	38	20	20	22	30	20	40	20	19	20	0	17	11	40
11	16	20	40	18	42	30	20	25	35	20	39	15	19	15	50	17	6	0
12	16	26	20	18	46	40	20	27	40	20	38	10	19	11	40	17	0	20
13	16	32	0	18	50	50	20	29	45	20	37	5	19	7	30	16	54	40
14	16	37	40	18	55	0	20	31	50	20	36	0	19	3	20	16	49	0
15	16	43	20	18	59	10	20	33	55	20	33	55	18	59	10	16	43	20
16	16	49	0	19	3	20	20	35	0	20	31	50	18	55	0	16	37	40
17	16	54	40	19	7	30	20	37	5	20	28	45	18	50	50	16	32	0
18	17	0	20	19	11	40	20	38	10	20	27	40	18	46	40	16	26	20
19	17	7	0	19	15	50	20	39	15	20	25	35	18	42	30	16	20	40
20	17	11	40	19	20	0	20	40	20	20	22	30	18	38	20	16	15	0
21	17	16	0	19	23	10	20	41	24	20	18	25	18	34	10	16	7	30
22	17	20	20	19	26	20	20	42	28	20	16	20	18	29	0	16	0	0
23	17	24	40	19	29	30	20	43	32	20	13	15	18	25	40	15	52	30
24	17	29	0	19	32	40	20	44	35	20	10	10	18	21	20	15	45	0
25	17	33	20	19	35	50	20	45	40	20	7	5	18	15	0	15	38	30
26	17	37	40	19	38	0	20	46	44	20	4	0	18	12	40	15	30	0
27	17	42	0	19	41	10	20	47	48	20	0	55	18	8	20	15	23	30
28	17	46	20	19	41	20	20	48	52	20	57	50	18	3	0	15	15	0
29	17	50	40	19	48	30	20	49	56	20	54	45	17	59	40	15	7	30
30	17	55	0	19	51	40	20	50	0	20	51	40	17	55	0	15	0	0
	Libra			Scorpio			Sagittarius			Capricorn			Aquarius			Pisces		
NOCTURNAL HOURS																		

Table A1.1: Representation of Roger's table of hours. Copyist errors are shown in grey.

In this example, using the chart that was examined in the section on using the astrolabe to calculate house cusps, it can be seen in that example (which was set for 07:30 local time on 6 April 1175) that the Ascendant was just over 17° of Gemini. Since the concept of the number zero was novel in the twelfth century and not widely used, tables generally started from one rather than zero, and one would say that the Ascendant was in the eighteenth degree of Gemini. Looking for Gemini in Table A1.1, one can see that is in the list of signs at the top, by the heading "diurnal hours", so the degrees of arc will represent the size of houses based on diurnal hours. Looking at the entry for the eighteenth degree of Gemini, one can see the diurnal hour length is 20°38′10″ of arc, so the nocturnal house length is this value subtracted from 30°, or 9°21′50″.

Roger's instruction is to find the length of two nocturnal hours and to use this as the distance between the first and second house, the second and third, and the third and fourth houses. Since we've ascertained that one nocturnal hour in this example is 9°21′50″, two nocturnal hours are twice this value, namely 18°43′40″ of arc. Thus, since the Ascendant is at 17° Gemini, the second house cusp will be 18° beyond this (minutes and seconds shall be ignored for this example), or 5° Cancer, the third house cusp a further 18°, namely 23° Cancer, and the fourth house cusp a further 18° at 11° Leo. The Ascendant has already been calculated before applying this method, and the house cusps for the second, third and fourth houses have now been derived by this method. By definition, this means positions of the opposing eighth, ninth and tenth houses are also known. The same method can be used for the diurnal hours, again following Roger's instructions to use the length of two diurnal hours to make the distance between the fourth and fifth house, the fifth and sixth, and the sixth and seventh houses. The length of the diurnal hour in the previous example was 20°38′10″ of arc, so the distance between the cusps of the fourth and fifth, the fifth and sixth, and the sixth and seventh houses will be twice this, or about 41° each, and the same for the opposing houses (tenth, eleventh and twelfth).

This method of using tables is only approximate and can be a couple of degrees out, but nevertheless it can be seen that this matches the results calculated by the astrolabe quite closely. Roger tells us that this is the same as the previous method, using the astrolabe, but this isn't quite correct. The table method, by definition, yields identically sized houses within each quadrant, while the Alcabitius system derived from the astrolabe often yields houses within quadrants of slightly different sizes (although since the difference is usually only a degree or two, it's quite possible that Roger didn't notice this). In fact, what Roger is describing with the table method is what we now know as the Porphyry house system.

Reasoning behind the table

This is the reasoning behind the table. The maximum hours of daylight in Hereford exceeds the minimum by 11 degrees and 40 minutes, so the average is 5 degrees and 50 minutes. That is to say that the maximum exceeds the average by 350 minutes and exceeds the minimum by 700 minutes. Thus a quarter of this is 175 minutes, a sixth 116 minutes and 40 seconds, and a twelfth 58 minutes and 20 seconds. Following Ptolemy, in the first month, while the Sun is in Aries, a quarter is added, and this is the amount of the diurnal hour. In the second month, when the Sun is in Taurus, a sixth is added. In the third month, when the Sun is in Gemini, a twelfth is added. And in the following three months, these reverse amounts are subtracted: so in the following month a twelfth, then a sixth, then a quarter. The remaining six months may be counted in the same way, with the figures being nocturnal hours.

Roger describes the methodology behind his table of hours. As described above, the longest arc of a diurnal hour, at the summer solstice, is 20°50′. This is 5°50′ more than the equinoctal hour of 15°, so the difference between the maximum and minimum will be twice this value, namely 11°40′ or 700 minutes of arc. Near the equinoxes, the amount of daylight hours increases or decreases rapidly and is noticeable on a day-by-day basis, while near the solstices there is barely any noticeable difference in the number of hours of daylight from one day to the next. A graph of the number of hours of daylight for any given latitude plotted against the date will yield a sine curve, but as trigonometry was not widely known in the twelfth century, Roger explains how this can be approximated. Figure A1.12 shows just how close this simple approximation is to a sine curve. Roger makes explicit reference to "Tholomeum" (Ptolemy), so is calculating his table in accordance with the rules set out in Ptolemy's *Almagest*, which had been translated into Latin by the time Roger was writing his book. However, Ptolemy's rules, using chords rather than trigonometry, are general for any latitude, and the handy approximation Roger uses appears to be his own. However, despite his simple description of adding a quarter, a sixth or a twelfth part to approximate this curve, a close examination of Roger's table shows that he was actually using ten increments to create it rather than three.

This section completes the part of Roger's text that covers what today would be called astronomy rather than astrology. The text then continues with a reference guide to astrological principles.

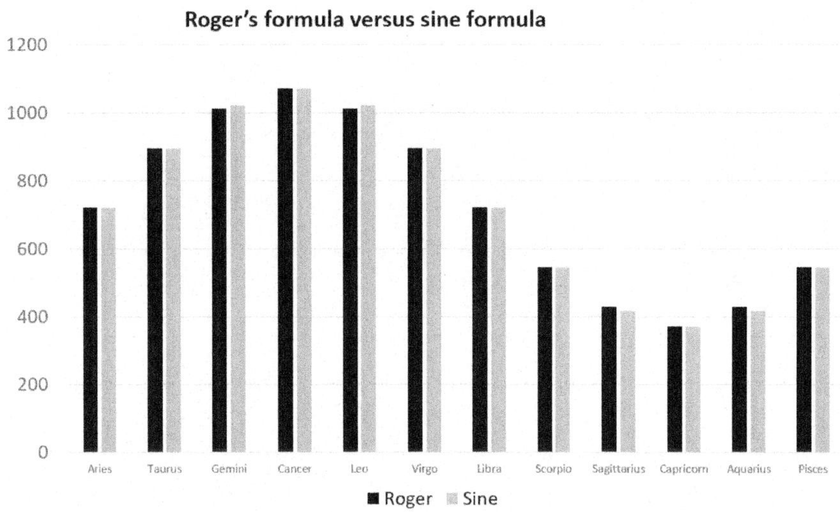

Figure A1.12: Roger's approximation to a sine curve from Ptolemy.

The nature of the twelve signs

ARIES: The nature of Aries is fiery, bitter-tasting, oriental, stretched-out, of two colours, of double form, domesticated, aggressive, defective, few offspring, luxurious, bleating, bellowing, angry, of half a voice.

Of places, the lands of Babylon, Persia, and Palestine; of cultivated pastureland, places of construction, furnaces, baths, and wooden forts. It is associated with the east wind.

In a person, it represents the head and face. When Saturn is in it, it represents the breast, Jupiter the stomach, Mars the head, Sun the thighs, Venus the feet, Mercury the legs, and the Moon the knees.

In appearance, much hair, and a short person with a long face, heavy eyes, ears that point forwards, and a long neck.

Roger describes each of the twelve signs, but before moving on to the others, let's consider the first sign, Aries, and break down what he says. His descriptions are somewhat formulaic, and don't correspond to what we think of as characteristics of the signs in modern astrology.

Unlike modern astrology, where we tend to place a lot of emphasis on keywords for signs, medieval astrology saw planets as the active agents, and the signs in which they are placed tells us how strong a planet is – see Appendix Two for a summary of how this works. However, medieval astrology did consider signs as having characteristics, particularly relating to weather forecasting, diagnosing illnesses, geographical locations, and for describing someone's physical appearance.

Some characteristics relate purely to the animal that the sign represents – so Aries, the ram, is domesticated since it is a sheep, aggressive as rams are wont to be, bleating and bellowing, and having "half a voice"; this term is used for creatures that can make a noise but can't talk. Only human signs have a full voice, and water signs have no voice at all.

Other characteristics relate to the element of the sign – all fire signs are considered hot and dry, and are linked to the east, and to the east wind. Each element also relates to one of four **humours** used in medicine; the humour that fire signs are associated with is yellow bile, and is therefore bitter-tasting.

Some relate to the astronomical appearance of the constellation after which the sign is named. Figure A1.13 shows the constellation of Aries rising above the horizon, together with some constellation art depicting the ram.

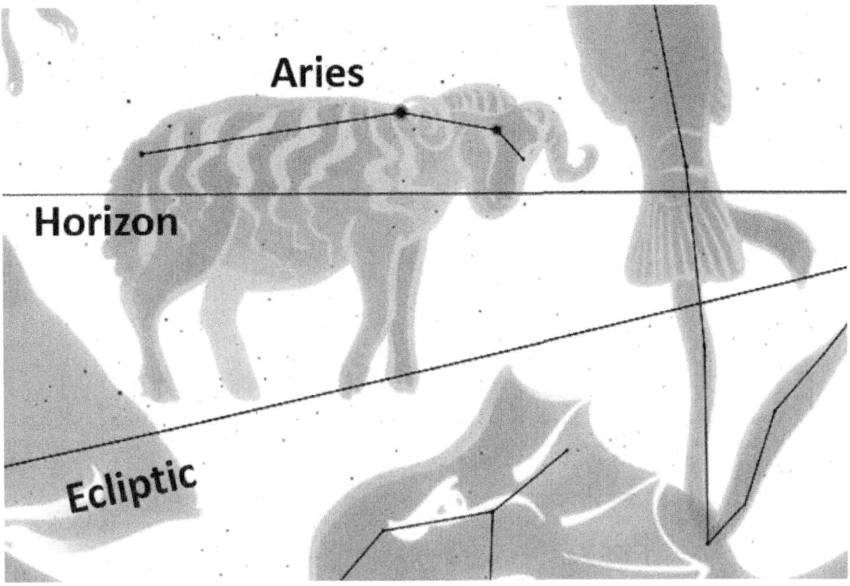

Figure A1.13: Aries the ram rising above the horizon.

Roger tells us that Aries is stretched-out, of two colours, of double form, and defective, descriptions that aren't at all obvious, but do in fact relate to the astronomical appearance. In the northern hemisphere, Aries is a sign that rises quickly; in contrast, Libra rises very slowly. This is particularly noticeable at higher latitudes such as Hereford – the sign of Aries rises in about 50 minutes, while Libra takes nearly three hours to rise. This is because the ecliptic section that is the sign of Aries is, while not quite parallel to the horizon, fairly horizontal, while the section of the ecliptic that is Libra is approaching the vertical. Signs that are nearer to the vertical are called **straight**, and ones nearer to the horizontal are called **crooked** (as they appear to be bent over), and as they are more horizontal they rise much more quickly than straight signs. It is even more obvious with the constellation of Aries, which as it rises over the horizon is almost horizontal. Roger refers to this as "stretched-out" (he uses the Latin term "porrectus"). Calling Aries "defective" also seems odd, but this is because the constellation doesn't include the legs of the ram, as can be seen in Figure A1.13 – so the ram has been "cut off". Roger doesn't explain why Aries is "of two colours and of double form", although the twelfth-century astrologer and rabbi Abraham ibn Ezra has a somewhat throwaway line in which he explains that "They also said that it indicates two colours and two shapes because of its instability" straight after saying that Aries is cut off; no further information is given about why this should give the sign two colours and two forms, however![50]

Roger's association of signs with countries and types of places are very similar to those found in Arabic sources, although Roger omits them for some signs presumably because many places familiar to the Arabs would not have been familiar to Roger, and even various Arabic authors disagreed about the allocation of certain signs. For example, Abū Maʿšar allocates Leo to "the land of the Turks to the end of the inhabited world", which is vague to say the least,[51] while the eleventh-century al-Biruni associated it with "Gog and Magog and ruined cities there" which is even harder to identify.[52]

The association of signs with parts of the body is well-known in medieval texts and later illustrations of "Zodiac man", such as the early fifteenth-century example shown in Figure A1.14, where Aries is on the person's head,

---

[50] Abraham ibn Ezra, *Book of Reasons*, Shlomo Sela (ed., trans.) (Leiden: Brill, 2007) I, 2.2.6, p.39.

[51] Abū Maʿšar *Great Introduction*, 6.9.7 p.637.

[52] Al-Biruni, *The Book of Instruction in the Elements of the Art of Astrology*, R. Ramsay Wright (ed.) (London: Luzac & Co, 1934), 365 p.220. This is given as an example of differences of Arabic opinion – there is no evidence that Roger had access to al-Biruni's text, although he certainly had access to a Latin translation of Abū Maʿšar. The "land of the Turks" is not modern-day Turkey, which was Greek-speaking Byzantium in Roger's time, but refers to Turkmenistan and the steppes to the east. One Arabic manuscript of Abū Maʿšar also gives Leo to Mesopotamia, which found its way into the Latin translation as "Persia, Media, Babylon, and Palestine", which Roger also used.

Taurus on the neck, and so on down to Pisces on the feet. However, in addition to allocating Aries to the head and face, Roger also gives a list of planets in each sign, and allocates them to a body part; thus Saturn in Aries represents the breast, Jupiter in Aries the stomach, and so on. These are derived from another Arabic source, this time al-Qabisi's *Introduction to Astrology*, where he lists the "pains of the planets in the signs".[53] An example of this usage was given in Chapter Six, "Finding the intention by various other means", where an example is given of Saturn in Taurus relating to a "sickness of the stomach".

The physical description of a person describes someone who has Aries characteristics – for example, somebody with Aries rising. These descriptions are taken directly from a text called *Iudicia,* which was attributed to Ptolemy in Roger's time, although the author is actually unknown (and is usually referred to as "Pseudo-Ptolemy").[54]

Roger continues, in a similar formulaic vein, for the other signs.

[53] Al-Qabisi, *Introduction* I.37, pp.37-41.

[54] Pseudo-Ptolemy, *Iudicia*, Paris, Bibliothèque nationale de France, Lat 16208, f.59va.

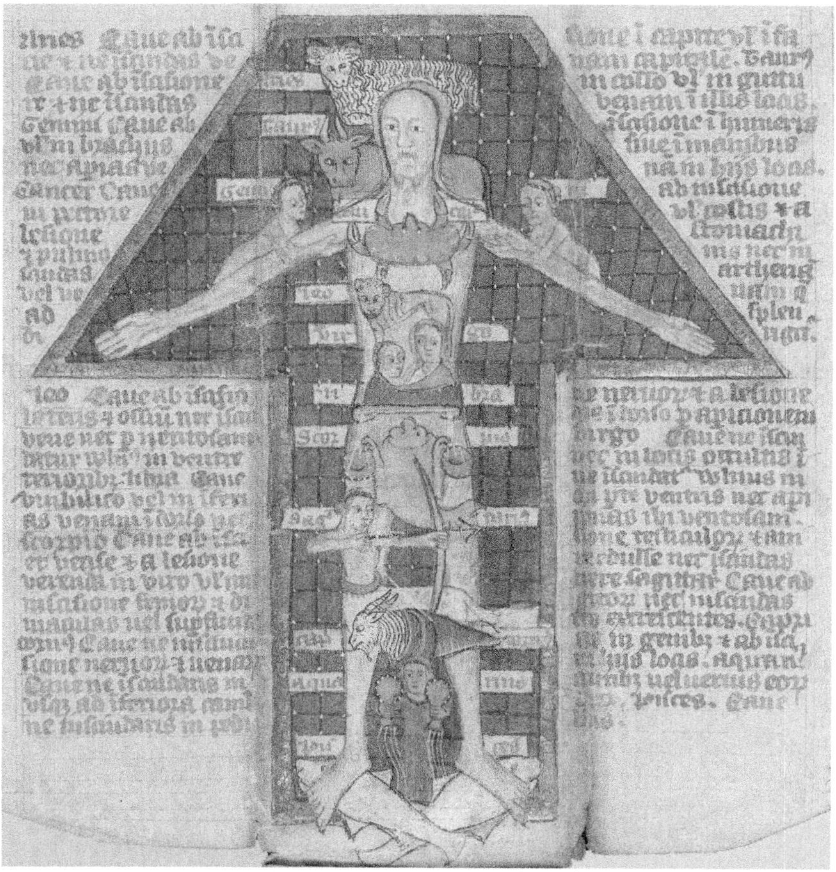

Figure A1.14: Zodiac Man with zodiac sign imagery relating to parts of the body.

Credit: Wellcome Collection MS 8932 folio 5, CC BY 4.0.

TAURUS: The nature of Taurus is earthy, dry, bitter, southern, domesticated, wild, with few offspring, luxurious, having a loudly crying bleating half voice, and melancholic.

Of trees, it represents seedlings.

Of places, mountain caves, dry fields, pastureland, and woods and wooded places.

In a person, it represents the neck and throat. When Saturn is in it, it represents the stomach, Jupiter the back, Mars the neck, Sun the knees, Venus the head, Mercury the feet, and the Moon the legs.

It is associated with someone of illegitimate parentage.

In appearance, a large forehead with a long nose, large nostrils, heavy eyes, a high hairline, thick and abundant hair, honest, and vain.

GEMINI: The nature of Gemini is airy, sweet, the colour of the sky, upright, western, rational, with a beautiful voice, and barren.

Of places, it has Armenia, Egypt, Cappadocia (modern-day Turkey), deserts, wooded glades, and amphitheatres.

Of character it shows generosity and kind-heartedness.

In a person, it represents the shoulders, arms, and the hands. When Saturn is in it, it represents the stomach, Jupiter the genitals and lower regions, Mars the breast, Sun the legs and ankles, Venus the neck, Mercury the head, and the Moon the thighs and ankles.

In appearance, tall and handsome.

CANCER: The nature of Cancer is watery, salty, wild, many offspring, and northern.

Of places, it has Armenia Minor and Balkh, underwater shores, and shrubby rocks. It is associated with the north wind.

In a person, it represents the chest, heart, stomach, side, spleen, lungs and all defects of these. When Saturn is in it, it represents the genitals and lower parts, Jupiter the thighs, Mars the chest, Sun the feet, Venus the arms and upper arm (humerus), Mercury the eyes, and the Moon the head.

In appearance, a person with a large body, delicate skin, fierce teeth and small eyes.

LEO: The nature of Leo is fiery, choleric, luxurious, oriental, of medium voice, cunning, vicious, very brave, and venerable.

Of places, it has Mesopotamia, valleys with fast-flowing streams or rivers, places of mines and quarries, royal palaces, and fortified towns with caves.

In a person, it represents the stomach, heart, side, and back. When Saturn is in it, it represents the private parts, Jupiter the thighs and knees, Mars the belly, Sun the head, Venus the heart, Mercury the shoulder and throat, and the Moon the neck. Someone who has knowledge of treatment.

In appearance, superior, excessively large, with long and slender legs.

VIRGO: The nature of Virgo is earthy, divided into two parts, three-formed, southern, with a sweet voice and good soul, and barren.

Of places, it has Judea, Galilee, Spain, and the Euphrates.

In a person, it represents the belly, diaphragm, and the intestines. When Saturn is in it, it represents the feet, Jupiter the knees and below, Mars the belly, Sun the neck, Venus the stomach, Mercury the heart, and the Moon the shoulders.

In appearance, a beautiful character, benign with beautiful eyes and a beautiful countenance.

LIBRA: The nature of Libra is sanguine, of two forms, upright, western, rational, with a beautiful voice, generous personality, and good.

Of places, it has Greece, Italy, Africa, cultivated places, and wild places of hawks, and poisonous things lying in ambush. It is associated with tall trees.

In a person, it represents the loins, lower back, heart, navel, breast, private parts, and the side of the body from the hips to the groin, and nostrils. When Saturn is in it, it represents the knees and below, Jupiter the eyes, Mars the private parts, Sun the shoulders, Venus the head, Mercury the belly, and the Moon the heart.

SCORPIO: The nature of Scorpio is phlegmatic, northern, many offspring, defective, mute, and having a good generous soul.

Of places, it has Arabia, and Asuria, vineyards, prisons, and places with snakes.

In a person, it represents the private parts, testicles, bladder, anus, and thighs. When Saturn is in it, it represents the ankles, Jupiter the feet, Mars the head, arms, and thighs, Sun the heart, Venus the private parts, Mercury the back, and the Moon the belly.

In appearance, a beautiful countenance with much hair, small eyes, a small face, long legs, deceitful and angry, and with long feet.

SAGITTARIUS: The nature of Sagittarius is fiery, of two colours, choleric, cut-off, oriental, few offspring, of mediocre voice. Its first half is rational and the second half quadruped and mute.

Of places, it has Ethiopia and India, mountainous places, and similar terrains, rocky plains, and places of cows and bulls.

In a person, it represents the thighs. When Saturn is in it, it represents the feet, Jupiter the legs and head, Mars the feet and hands, Sun the belly, Venus the thighs and arms, Mercury the private parts and below, and the Moon the back.

In appearance, large or thick legs, a long face and an ample chin and fine hair, and a clever and shrewd person.

CAPRICORN: The nature of Capricorn is earthy, round, imperfect, of two forms, southern, luxurious, deformed, with a low bellowing voice, domesticated, few offspring, angry, and very gloomy.

Of places, it has Ethiopia's eastern parts, Greece, and Italy, forts with gates and water wheels, pools, pits, coasts, and banks where ships land, places of dogs, foxes, serpents, wild animals, strangers, poor people's dwellings, and fire terraces. It is associated with the south wind.

In a person when Saturn is in it, it represents the head and feet, Jupiter the knees and eyes, Mars legs and shoulders, Sun the back, Venus the thighs and heart, Mercury the private parts, and the Moon thighs and the private parts.

In appearance, slender legs, a dry body, a face like a he-goat, and lots of hair.

AQUARIUS: The nature of Aquarius is airy, occidental, with few offspring.

Of places, it has Egypt and Ethiopia, places overflowing with rivers and canals, wells, the open sea, lonely places, and places supporting vines and vessels. It is also associated with the west wind.

In a person, it represents the lower legs and lower ankles. When Saturn is in it, it represents the head and the neck, Jupiter the shoulders, Mars the ankles and heart, Sun the private parts, Venus the knees, Mercury the thighs, and the Moon the heart and the private parts.

In appearance, one leg thicker than the other, a beautiful appearance and colour, of noble knowledge, spending much, and holding to high ideals.

PISCES: The nature of Pisces is double, aquatic, northern, many offspring, gluttonous, mixed with many colours, sluggish, and mute.

Of places, coastal basins and pools with shores and fish, with temples and rituals. It also has the north wind.

In a person, it represents the feet. When Saturn is in it, it represents the shoulders, arms, and neck, Jupiter the heart and head, Mars the ankles and belly, Sun the thighs, Venus the neck and back, Mercury the legs and private parts, and the Moon the thighs.

In appearance, a large chest, small head, a magnificent beard in the middle of the face that is big, white, and full.

The times of the signs

Sign	Years	Months	Days	Hours	Days	Hours	Points
Aries	15	15	37	12	3	0	20
Taurus	8	8	20		1	16	0
Gemini	20	20	50		4	0	15
Cancer	25	25	62	12	5	5	0
Leo	19	19	47	12	3	23	0
Virgo	20	20	50		4	0	15
Libra	8	8	20		1	16	0
Scorpio	15	15	37	12	3	0	20
Sagittarius	12	12	30		2	12	0
Capricorn	27	27	67	12	5	15	0
Aquarius	30	30	75		6	6	0
Pisces	12	12	30		2	12	0

Table A1.2: The times of the signs.

Roger now provides a table showing "the times of the signs", reproduced here in Table A1.2, without any explanation. It is very similar to one given in Abū Maʿšar's *Great Introduction*, and is used in various techniques in medieval astrology relating to periods of a person's life. However, Roger makes no use of these in the main body of his text.[55]

[55] Abū Maʿšar, *Great Introduction*, 6.8, pp.631-633.

The nature of the seven planets

SATURN has a cold and dry nature, and can be dark, secret, damp, severe, weighed down, stinking, devouring, retentive and clinging, much given to thinking, holding fast to the powerful, while considering other people to be small or unimportant.

Saturn is associated with agriculture and habitations that are earthy and watery and heavy, masons, those who dig the ground, cartwrights, the destitute, ships, long journeys, outcasts, evil attacks, fraud, wickedness, solitude and loneliness, deliberation, determined speech, establishing a nest, kings, consults, chains, prisons, obligations, hatred of the good, spite, fear, solemnness, sorrow, penitence, suffering, error and deception, punishment and retribution, funerals, hatred, lamentations, widows, inheritances, old things, fathers, grandfathers, slaves, mercenaries, eunuchs, the notorious, and criminals.

Associated with Saturn is study, infrequent conversation, and inexhaustible knowledge. It is associated with the right ear and the spleen. Saturn is melancholy, masculine, evil, and diurnal.

Saturn's characteristics in a person: a beard with few hairs, unattractive, serious, dull, gloomy, having cracks in his heel, a grey complexion, slim, coarse hair, dressed in stinking black clothes, and appearing to be an evil person.

Roger provides keywords and associations for each of the planets. These are more involved than the keywords for signs, since medieval astrology is usually concerned with finding planets that signify something, rather than signs. For each planet, Roger provides a summary of its nature, jobs and tasks associated with the planet, the type of people associated with it, and – just as for the signs of the zodiac – physical characteristics of a person associated with the planet.

Like most medieval texts, Roger's starts with the outermost planet, Saturn, and works its way inwards to the Moon. Most of his attributions come directly from Abū Maʿšar's *Great Introduction*, with some from al-Qabisi's *Introduction to Astrology*. Roger's keywords are heavily abbreviated from his Arabic sources. For example, Roger simply lists keywords for Saturn without distinction (most of them negative, as can be seen above), while al-Qabisi makes a clear distinction between Saturn in good condition and poor condition astrologically. For example, al-Qabisi tells us that "of professions it has noble activities involving water, like cultivation and management of lands and rivers when it is fortunate; but vile activities when it is harmed".[56]

JUPITER is handsome, diurnal, warm, humid, sweet, and with a temperate nature.

Jupiter is associated with leading offspring, laws, temples, festivals, sometimes ill-advised by being reckless and unthinking, with dignified victory, expectation of supremacy, joy, elegance, generosity, skill, judgement, eloquence, grandeur, magnanimity, light-heartedness, eroticism, charm, indulgent, good, desiring prophetic speech, and health. It is associated with the left ear.

Jupiter's characteristics in a person: a round beard, and beautiful voice. His two upper teeth are large and separated. He also has beautiful red robes mixed with white and brown. A beautiful mind and soul, and long and beautiful hair.

---

[56] Al-Qabisi, *Introduction* II.2, p.63.

MARS is masculine, nocturnal, malevolent, cunning, dry, sharp, violent or vigorous, and fierce. He is associated with adolescence, power, the liver with Jupiter and the nostrils with Venus, ignitabula (an ignitabulum is a steel used for producing sparks to light a fire), destruction by fire, hasty or unexpected outcomes, tyranny, evil, malice, the military, forts, protection, unfairness, battles, audacity, fighting, love of glory, sedition, sexual passion, robbers, stonemasons, wounds, immodest speech, unguarded affairs, terror, deceit, indecency, spiteful, anything contaminated or polluted, swift, shameless, defiled, illegitimate, siege engines, abortions or anything premature, vulgar, protection of sheep, injuries, wounds, surgery, mortal sin, trades of death, and calamity. Mars is stronger when participating with Saturn.

Mars' characteristics in a person: red mixed with brown in the face, sparse red hair in the beard like a eunuch's, small eyes, and a great sower of discord.

SUN is strong in good aspect and bad by conjunction in a single sign, fiery, tempered. The Sun is associated with all things bright and shining, the source of life and animate soul, the right eye, the middle of the habitable zone,[57] leaders, advisors, strength, victory, honesty, splendour, greatness, good reputation and fame, ambition, desire of gold, and eloquent speech. On the other hand, when in harmful condition it represents things that are sometimes convenient, sometimes inconvenient, sometimes raising, sometimes bringing down. Laws, judges, magistrates, intelligence, fathers, brothers, never refusing a request, strong vengeance against evil, imperial rule, and meditations on the divine.

The Sun's characteristics in a person: a plump body, and beautiful face with big eyes. White complexion, mixed with citrus, a beautiful beard full of long hair.

---

[57] This doesn't really make sense, but seems to be derived from a single Arabic manuscript that uses this phrase; most use the phrase "the middle part of life", which makes more sense. See Abū Maʿšar, *Great Introduction* VII.9.6a fn. 336, p.809.

VENUS is cold, wet, and temperate. Venus is associated with women, birth, younger sisters, clothes, ornaments, gold, and silver. Frequenters of bath houses and ablution. Beauty, aptitude, wit, love of music, joy, jokes, melodies, betrothals, weddings, the marriage bed and conjugal unions, perfumes, leisure, wantonness, sweet speech, effeminacy, indignity, falsehoods, wines, pleasant and sweet things, luxuries and all things of that nature. Illegitimate children, delight in one's children, mutual respect, piety, credulity, a full or voluptuous figure tending towards fat, seeking pleasure, creative arts, markets selling sweet-smelling things, temples, observing the law, and fair justice.

Venus' characteristics in a person: beautiful eyes and eyebrows, sweetly spoken, and a slim body of medium stature.

MERCURY is mixed, its nature easily adapting to the planets with which it is mixing.[58] Mercury is associated with childhood, younger brothers, love of boys, divinity, faith, prophecy, eloquence, teachers with students, tricks, reasoning and perception, observation, high knowledge, and all study, especially mathematics and divination. Full understanding, use and practice of critical examination of novelties, and hidden secrets. Little joy and pleasure, prophetic advice, reputation, rumours, ambition with glory, payment of taxes, apothecaries, complaints with great costs, participation, business, deception, fraud, malevolence, laziness, fear, variable mood, and meek obedience. Devoted love of brothers, driving off evil, speaking the truth, pleasant voice, aptitude in all crafts, perfection with confidence in all professions, sewing, shearing, combing [of wool], and aptitude with the hands. It represents bubbling springs, fountains, flowing rivers, irrigation.

Mercury's characteristics in a person: slim body, wise, literate, a complete person, gaining many friends and gaining good fortune from them, one having a beautiful but sparse beard, thin lips, and a slender nose.

Mercury is masculine when conjunct masculine planets and oriental when in front of the Sun, and feminine when conjunct feminine planets and occidental if before the Sun.[59]

---

[58] All manuscripts of *Judicial Astrology* have "ascensum", meaning ascending, but this is almost certainly an error from an early copy; Hermann of Carinthia's translation, from whom Roger copied most of this text, has "omnem commixtionis assensum facilis" meaning that Mercury can "assent", or easily go along with whatever other planets are doing; for example, Mercury can be seen as male or female, diurnal or nocturnal, according to its relationship with other planets.

[59] In front of the Sun means rising before the Sun, and therefore appearing as a morning star; before the Sun means setting after the Sun, and therefore appearing as an evening star.

MOON is cold, with accidental heat as its light is from elsewhere (the Sun). Light in weight, desiring fame and joy. It indicates the beginning of activities, kings, nobles, resources and provisions, acquiring goodwill, knowledge, laws, and other contemplations. The power of rituals, the study of earth and water and their measurement, weakness of memory. Married women, pregnancy, suckling, grandmothers, older sisters, messengers, mandates, fugitives, falsehoods. Accusations and flattery. Greedy, little love-making.

The Moon's characteristics in a person: no violence nor roving, gentle, with a round face, medium height, one eye larger than the other.

Table of the planetary years

At this point in the text, most manuscripts show a table, with the heading "table of the years of the planets".

Roger gives us no explanation on what its purpose is, or how to use it, although they in fact relate to predictive techniques relating to stages of a native's life, and the length of life. Very similar tables appear in Abū Ma'šar, and it's clear that this is meant to be a direct copy of the table. It was clearly a source of confusion in the twelfth century – there were two Latin translations of Abū Ma'šar's *Great Introduction* available, one by John of Seville, and one by Hermann of Carinthia, and there are a few discrepancies between each author's figures.

Later copyists seemed even more confused – six of the existing manuscripts of Roger's *Judicial Astrology* include this table, and they all have copyist errors in, making it impossible to reproduce a definitive table. Table A1.3 shows the table in Hermann of Carinthia's translation of Abū Ma'šar's *Great Introduction*, which is presumably what Roger was trying to recreate.

Planet	Firdaria	Greater	Major	Medium	Minor
Sun	10	1461	120	39½	19
Venus	8	1151	72	45	8
Mercury	13	480	76	48	20
Moon	9	520	108	39½	25
Saturn	11	265	57	43½	30
Jupiter	12	427	79	45½	12
Mars	8	284	66	40½	15
North Node	3				
South Node	2				

Table A1.3: Years of the planets according to Abū Ma'šar.

The houses

First house: life, body, soul and the beginning of all undertakings and motions, manner of speech, and reputation. It signifies the start of life.

Second house: substance or wealth, the quest for money, possessions, things to be lent and taken, nourishment, aides, knights and soldiers, and deputies and accomplices. It signifies the end of youth.

Third house: brothers, sisters, neighbours, legal discussions, trials, controversies, short journeys, orders, messengers, dreams, movement, favourites or kinsmen, and religious faith. It signifies the state of life before death.

Fourth house: father, parents, ancestors, water sources, fields, farms, citizens, forts, buildings, secrets, subterranean places, treasure troves, the end of the matter, death and remains and what happens to the remains after death, and signifies the end, prisons, and heirs. It signifies what follows death.

Fifth house: children, messengers, suitors, pleasure, fun, enjoyment or reward, honours, friendship, hopes and the rewards of inheritance and trust.

Sixth house: illnesses and their causes, status and condition, servants, maids, wickedness, injustice, local movement, and small animals that are not ridden. It signifies events before old age.

Seventh house: women, marriage, weddings and their participants, adversaries, disputes, participating in dealings with opponents and all complaints, thieves, lost goods, and the place for which a journey is undertaken, all contentions, and loss. It signifies the middle of the end of life towards old age.

Eighth house: death, poisons, fear and all irrecuperable lost things, sloth, idleness, fraud, ignorance, frenzy, desperation, anger and inheritances of the deceased, labour, sadness, wars, and signifies servants and helpers of adversaries. It signifies the last years of life after old age.

Ninth house: journeys, exiles, honour, justice, truth, virtue, religion, laws, temples, ceremonies, philosophy, all sciences, writings, messages, visions, rumours, stories, faith, the past, and men reduced in rank. It signifies the middle of life.

Tenth house: worth or rank, sovereignty, rule, judges, eloquence, expression, craftsmen, works, mothers, covenants with kings, glory and all majesty, and plundered goods. It signifies the middle of life.

Eleventh house: good fortune, friendship, favours, support, patronage of the king, tributes and possessions of the king, his soldiers and auxiliaries, commendations, and men who follow the king. It signifies the end of the years of the first half of life, and the start of the second half of life.

Twelfth house: enemies, grief, toil, restriction, penalty, envy, slander, treachery, prisons, captives, calamities, degradation, disgrace, ruination, mules, animals that are ridden, and mutterings. It signifies the end of life.

Roger gives a brief listing on meanings of the houses. Most of these have been taken directly from Abū Maʿšar's *Great Introduction,* while the short sentence about what stage of life it represents comes from al-Qabisi's *Introduction to Astrology*. This is absent for the fifth house, although al-Qabisi does give it as one's reputation after death.[60]

---

60 Al-Qabisi, *Introduction* I.61, p.53.

Debilities of the planets

> The debilities of the planets are: fall, cadent, detriment, applying to an unfortunate planet, in the first station, retrograde, under the rays, in dark degrees, peregrine, out of sect, descending to the south or being south and still descending, slow-moving, in the via combusta between 20 Libra and 3 Scorpio, in a square or opposition aspect to the Sun or a malefic where there is no reception, conjunct the head or tail within 12 degrees, besieged by malefics.

This very short section describes the ways in which planets can become unfortunate in a chart. It is a very brief list with no explanation in the text, so the following summary explains what this means. Roger's brief text is taken almost verbatim from Hermann of Carinthia's translation of Abū Maʿšar's *Great Introduction.*[61]

Fall: a planet that is in the opposite sign to its exaltation, and so is greatly weakened.

Cadent: in the third, sixth, ninth or twelfth house. Houses following an angle (Ascendant, MC, Descendant, and IC) are called angular and are considered strong, the subsequent houses (second, fifth, eighth, and eleventh) are called succedent and are moderate, and the houses following them are considered weak.

Detriment: a planet in the opposite sign to the one it rules.

Applying to an unfortunate planet: a faster-moving planet moving towards a slower-moving planet is said to be "applying to it". If that planet is unfortunate – retrograde, cadent, or otherwise afflicted – this will also affect the planet applying to it.

---

61 Abū Maʿšar, *Liber Introductorii Maioris* (Hermann) VII.6 lines 496-504, p.140.

In the first station: planets generally move forwards around the zodiac, but (with the exception of the Sun and Moon) periodically slow down, stop and start moving backwards (this is known as going retrograde). Then they slow down and stop again, and start moving forwards again. The first time they stop, just before going backwards, is said to be the first station.

Retrograde: the planet is moving backwards.

Under the rays: the planet is within 17° of the Sun and cannot easily be seen.

In dark degrees: each sign has a number of degrees that are listed as dark or smoky. The origin is not known but may relate to an earlier sidereal tradition of parts of the zodiac constellation that have hazy stars.

Peregrine: a planet that has no essential dignity (by rulership, exaltation, triplicity, term or face).

Out of sect: a diurnal planet (Jupiter, Saturn, or Sun) is stronger in a daytime chart, and a nocturnal planet (Moon, Venus, or Mars) in a night-time chart. Similarly, a diurnal planet is stronger in a diurnal sign (Aries, Gemini, Leo, Libra, Sagittarius, or Aquarius) and a nocturnal planet in a nocturnal sign (Taurus, Cancer, Virgo, Scorpio, Capricorn, or Pisces). Finally, a diurnal planet is stronger if it is in the same half (upper or lower) as the Sun, and a nocturnal planet if it is in the opposite half to the Sun. If all three of these criteria are met, a planet is said to be **in hayyiz**, which is very positive. If none of these three are met, a planet is out of sect.

Descending to the south or being south and still descending: as well as having longitude (its position in the zodiac), a planet will also be higher or lower than the ecliptic (only by a few degrees since all planets are close to the ecliptic). If it is dipping down towards the ecliptic, or has dipped down below it and is still descending, this is considered negative.

Slow-moving: a planet that is moving in its daily motion at less than its average daily motion.

In the via combusta between 20° Libra and 3° Scorpio: this section of the zodiac is considered unfortunate, and planets here are weakened.

In a square or opposition aspect to the Sun or a malefic, where there is no reception: squares and oppositions are considered unfortunate if they are to a malefic planet (Mars or Saturn), or to the Sun. However, if they are in a sign ruled by the Sun or malefic, they are said to be received by the Sun or malefic (as described in Chapter Five), which neutralises the negative effects.

Conjunct the head or tail within 12 degrees: the different manuscripts and sources disagree about what this means. The "head or tail" usually refers to the Moon's northern and southern nodes respectively, which are the two points where the Moon's orbit crosses the ecliptic. However, each planet also has its own two nodes, where its orbit crosses the ecliptic. Although Roger's text (which he took directly from Hermann of Carinthia's translation) doesn't say which applies here, John of Seville's translation explicitly states that it can be either the planet's own nodes or the Moon's nodes.[62]

Besieged by a malefic: a planet trapped between the two malefics (Mars and Saturn), either in the same sign, or by aspect.

[62] Abū Maʿšar *Liber introductorii maioris ad scientam judiciorum astrorum*, John of Seville (trans.), Richard Lemay (ed.), Volume 5 (Napoli: Istituto Universitario Orientale, 1995), VII.6 lines 1227-1228, p.306.

Debilities of the Moon

The Moon can be damaged in 12 ways:[63] eclipsed, under the rays, opposite the Sun within 12 degrees, conjunct an unfortunate planet, in the duodenaria of Saturn or Mars, in fall or detriment, within 12 degrees of the node, descending in the south, in the via combusta, at the end of a sign, being slow of movement, in the ninth house from the Ascendant.

This section is also very short, and describes the ways in which the Moon can become unfortunate in a chart. Some of these are similar to the impediments of the planets in the previous description.

Eclipsed: a lunar eclipse occurs during a Full Moon when the Sun is directly opposite both in longitude and latitude, so the shadow of the Earth is cast on the Moon, dimming it or turning it red. Astrologically, this is indicated if the Moon is opposite the Sun and conjunct one of the Moon's nodes.

In the duodenaria of Saturn or Mars: the duodenariae are explained in Chapter Six and are 2.5° segments of a sign, each ruled by a planet. If the Moon is in a segment ruled by Mars or Saturn, this is weak as those planets are malefics.

At the end of a sign: this is an unfortunate position, since the last few degrees of a sign have term rulers of Mars or Saturn.

In the ninth house from the Ascendant: each planet has one particular house known as its **joy**. For the Moon, this is the third house, so being in the ninth house is unfortunate as it is opposite the house of the Moon's joy.

[63] Some manuscripts say 11 ways, which may be because both Latin translations of Abū Maʿšar's *Great Introduction* say 11, although Roger does indeed list 12.

Conditions of the planets

Roger now lists various way in which planets can relate to each other, and he's largely copied the definitions from Hermann of Carinthia's twelfth-century Latin translation of Abū Maʿšar's *Great Introduction,* with the exception of reception where Roger goes into much more detail. However, while Hermann explains what each term means after giving the definition, Roger doesn't, which makes for a very confusing read! Roger was clearly identifying this for reference purposes only, so I have started this section by giving Roger's text, and then providing an explanation of these relationships after the text to make it clear what is meant.

There are 18 conditions of the planets: aspect, application, separation, equality, solitude, alienation, translation, collection, collation, prohibition, returning, contradiction, impediment, evasion, interception, compassion, remuneration, reception.

Aspect: when a planet is at the same degree as another planet by conjunction, or by sextile, square, trine or opposition.

Application: when an aspecting planet approaches another.

Separation: when an aspecting planet moves away from another.

Equality: when the degrees of a sign have an equal rising time, or equal daylight. For example, the first degree of Aries connects to the last degree of Pisces.

Solitude: when a planet does not apply to anything else within that sign after it has separated from another planet.

Alienation: when a planet is not aspected from any sign. This most often happens with the Moon. Its application then is given to the Lords of the terms in which the planet it is in. This method is sometimes used with a planet in solitude.

Translation: this is from one planet to another and there are two kinds. One is that one planet separates from another and applies to another heavier planet. The other is the heavier planet applies to an even heavier planet and transfers the lighter planet's nature to the heaviest planet.

Collection: when two or more planets apply to one planet.

Collation: this is of two kinds, one is like collection, the other translation. One is where two planets are in aversion to each other but both aspect or apply to a planet, and that planet aspects a place on the zodiac. The other is that the Lords of the Ascendant and the matter do not aspect each other or are separating, but another planet between them can receive the light from one planet and transfer it on the other.

Prohibition: this is in two ways. One is when three or more planets are in the same sign but different degrees, and the heavy planet has the most degrees. Then the middle planet prevents the other planet from applying to the heavy planet until it passes it. The other way is by aspect, when two planets are in the same sign and one applies to the other, and another planet applies to the later one but with fewer degrees or the same degrees, then the earlier planet in the sign prevents the application, until the applying planet has passed the one blocking it. By that I mean to say that if the middle planet crosses over the heavier one, then the lighter one will apply to the heavier one.

Returning: this is in two ways. One is that a planet under the rays is applied to by another, or is retrograde. The planet applied to returns what it would have received. The returning is sometimes beneficial, sometimes negative. Beneficial returning is of three kinds. The first is when the planet applied to receives the one applying to it. The second is when both are in an angular or succedent house and the applying planet is direct. The third is when the receiving planet is remote, and the applying one is in an angular or succedent house. The negative returning is when both are remote or combust or retrograde. That will result in the matter being denied.

Contradiction: when a planet applies to another planet, but before it reaches it the planet goes retrograde and its application is prevented.

Impediment: when there are three planets where the heavy planet has a certain number of degrees, the lighter one a greater number of degrees, and the lightest planet (even lighter than the light one) is applying to the heavy planet, until the former goes retrograde and passes over the heavy planet. Then the application to the heavy planet is impeded.

Evasion: when a planet applies to another planet, but before reaching it, the planet it is applying to moves to another sign, where another planet is closer to the planet that has just changed sign. The application is nullified.

Interception: this is in three ways. The first is when a planet is applying to another planet, and another planet is in the second sign from the planet and goes retrograde, before the application is perfected, and the light to the applying planet is cut off. The second is when a light planet applies to a heavy one, which is applying to an even heavier one, and before perfecting the application the heavy planet passes the heavier one. This signifies that the quesited thing will become something else. The third is when a planet applies to a planet with an equivalent Lord rather than the intended one.

Compassion: when a planet is in its fall or in a well and a friendly planet having dignities in its place applies to it.

Remuneration: when it is next in the vicinity of the friendly planet and the opposite can happen.

Reception: when a planet applies to another planet, and one planet has dignity in the place of the other planet. This is stronger when it is in rulership or exaltation, and weaker if it is in other dignities unless it is in several of them at the same time, namely triplicity and term, triplicity and face, term and face, or in joy. However, we must see whether the particular power of the application will be prohibited by a third planet, so a wider analysis must be considered. In general, each judgement will only come about when the application perfects by degree, either by conjunction or in aspect. The first way such prohibition can happen is when there are three planets in the same sign, the lighter first, the heavier second, and the heaviest third. The planet in the middle prohibits a conjunction with the last planet. If the middle planet crosses over the last planet before the first one reaches it, then the matter is denied. However, if the first planet and the last were to make a judgement and the middle planet hasn't crossed the heavier one by the time the lighter one reaches it, it is said that the matter is given by the translation of light. The second is if two planets are in the same sign, and a third applies by aspect to the heaviest if it has fewer degrees than the lighter of the two is prohibited by the lighter. However, if it has more degrees then the judgement can be made, as neither of the two prohibits. Also, in aspect the nearer prohibits the further. This is stronger in conjunctions than in aspects. The third is if two lighter planets in different signs (and not aspecting each other) applied to one heavier planet and the nearest prohibits the other, or if one of the two were to apply to the one to whom the earlier one applied at the time. The fourth is when some planet is with a heavier planet in one sign and applies to another in another sign, whereby it approaches it hoping to be able to make a judgement. However, it is with another planet in the same sign. In all these cases, it is to be noted whether it will come to be a translation of light, or whether there is a conjunction of light.

Let's break each of these eighteen conditions down. Roger didn't provide an explanation, but Abū Maʿšar did, so we can shed further light on some of these very confusing definitions.

Aspect, application, and separation are very simple concepts. An **aspect** is simply one of the five Ptolemaic aspects: conjunction, sextile, square, trine, or opposition. Roger uses the word "degree", but he's not implying that the aspect has to be exact by degree, but simply within an orb. Earlier Hellenistic texts tended to aspect by sign, so a planet at 1° Sagittarius would trine a planet at 29° Leo as the start of the signs of Sagittarius and Leo are 120° apart. By Roger's time, aspects as we use them today were the norm, and so those two planets would not be trine as they are not in orb of a 120° angle. Aspects are not static, however. Consider the case where the Moon is at 15° Leo and Jupiter is at 18° Sagittarius. They are 123° apart, which is within orb of being a trine aspect (a trine being 120°), but since the Moon moves faster than Jupiter, she will soon catch up and be at 18° Leo, at which point she will have perfected the aspect (this is a term used in horary astrology and covered in Chapter Five, but is not a term that Roger used) – this is known as an **applying** aspect. Then she will move past the aspect and be **separating**. This is a key feature in Roger's description – in general, applying aspects represent things coming to fruition, while separating aspects represent things that have already happened. To determine whether an aspect is applying or separating, you need to know which of the two planets is the faster. As a general rule, the **Chaldean order** of planets, which is Saturn, Jupiter, Mars, Sun, Venus, Mercury, and Moon, is in order of speed from slowest to fastest. However, it is not always that straightforward – if a planet is about to go retrograde it will be very slow, so Mercury on a particular day may be slower than the Sun, and of course a faster planet that is retrograde is moving away from a slower planet in later degrees than itself, rather than applying to it. Roger refers to the faster planet as the "lighter" and the slower planet as the "heavier" in these descriptions.

Figure A1.15 demonstrates these concepts. Both Mars and the Moon are sextile to Jupiter, who is at 8° Pisces. Both move faster than Jupiter. The Moon, at 5° Taurus, will soon catch up with Jupiter and perfect the aspect, so she is applying to Jupiter. Mars, however, at 10° Capricorn would already have perfected the aspect and is now moving further and further away from a sextile, so he is separating from Jupiter.

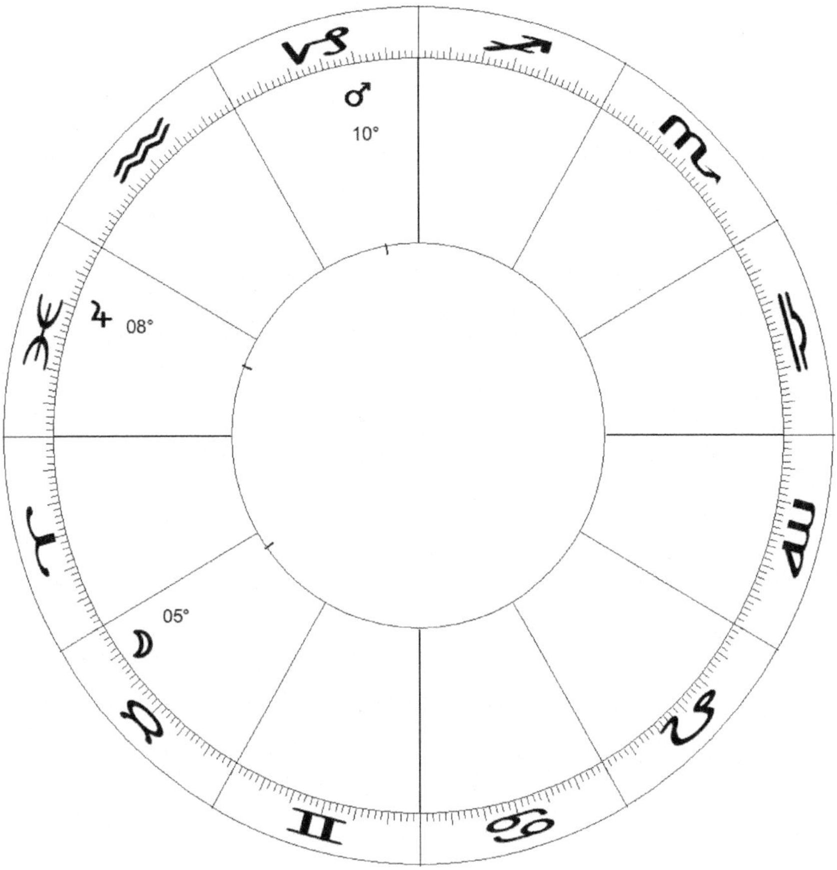

Figure A1.15: Moon applying to a sextile with Jupiter, Mars separating from a sextile to Jupiter.

Equality is a rather loose translation of the term that Roger used, which was "paralitas", and in fact Roger's term doesn't fully reflect Hermann's text. If we think of aspects as points on the zodiac that relate to each other – so that when two planets are there they take on that relationship – there are also points on the zodiac that pair up based on timings. One of these relates to how long a segment of the zodiac takes to rise. At the latitude of Hereford, where Roger was writing, Aries takes about 50 minutes to rise, while Libra takes 170 minutes. We can be even more precise than this – there isn't a sharp boundary between signs when it comes to rising times; the first degree of Aries rises in 95 seconds, and each degree in Aries takes a little longer to rise, and the final degree of Aries takes 109 seconds to rise. There is a symmetry here – the first degree of Aries takes the same time to rise as the last degree of Pisces (95 seconds in Hereford); 10° Pisces takes the same time to rise as 20° Aries (104 seconds); and 5° Aquarius takes the same time to rise as 25° Taurus (153 seconds). Thus there is a symmetry of equal rising times reflected along the 0° Aries / 0° Libra axis, as shown in the left hand diagram in Figure A1.16.

However, Roger's text is a little confused, as he simply says that this equality is between "degrees of a sign of equal rising, or of equal daylight" without expanding on what he means by "equal daylight". Abū Maʿšar does expand on this, and although the concept is similar, the definition is different. When the Sun is at 0° Cancer, it is the summer solstice and the longest day of the year. In Hereford, there are 16 hours and 40 minutes of daylight (defining "daylight" as when the Sun is above the horizon) on that day, as Roger has already told us earlier when he described how his tables for house calculation worked. The number of hours of daylight at, say, 40 days before the solstice is the same as the number of hours of daylight 40 days after the solstice, so there is a symmetry of daylight hours. This means that any point on the zodiac will have a corresponding point, reflected in the 0° Cancer / 0° Capricorn axis. When the Sun is at either of these points, the number of hours of daylight will be the same. For example, when the Sun is at 25° Taurus, and is therefore 35° away from 0° Cancer, there are 15 hours and 30 minutes of daylight. When the Sun is 35° past 0° Cancer, at 5° Leo, there are also 15 hours and 30 minutes of daylight. This means that 25° Taurus and 5° Leo are linked. We already saw above that 25° Taurus is also linked to 5° Aquarius, so each point on the zodiac has two types of "paralitas" – one is the point with which it shares the same rising time, the other is the point with which it shares the same number of daylight hours. These two types of "paralitas", which Abū Maʿšar spells out, are shown in Figure A1.16.

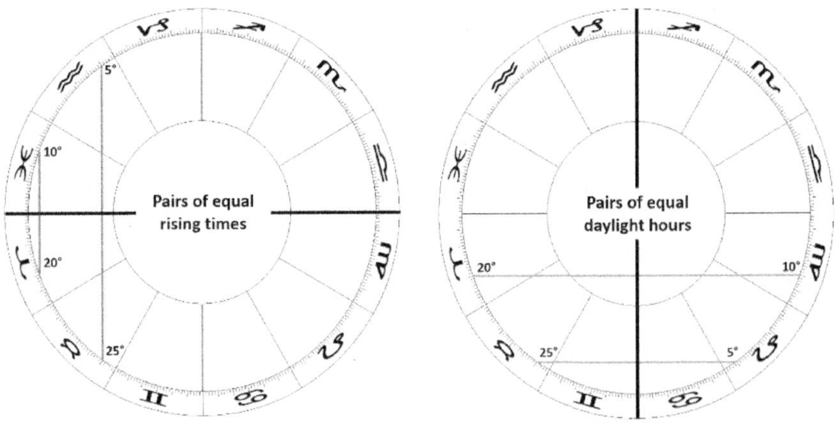

Figure A1.16: Equal rising times and equal daylight hours.

This technique was widely referred to in Hellenistic sources, and is used in contemporary horary astrology, too. The method of pairing planets with equal amounts of daylight is called **antiscia**, and the pairing with equal rising times is called **contra-antiscia**, although these are not terms used by Roger.

Figure A1.17 shows a practical example of both. In this example, the Moon is at 2° Leo. Its reflection along the Cancer/Capricorn axis is 28° Taurus, which is where Mercury is. Thus, although these two planets don't traditionally aspect each other, there is a connection between them as they have the same number of hours of daylight. Jupiter is at 18° Gemini. Its reflection along the Aries/Libra axis is 12° Capricorn, where Saturn is. Therefore, there is a connection between Jupiter and Saturn, as the degrees they are in take the same time to rise, even though there is no traditional aspect between them.

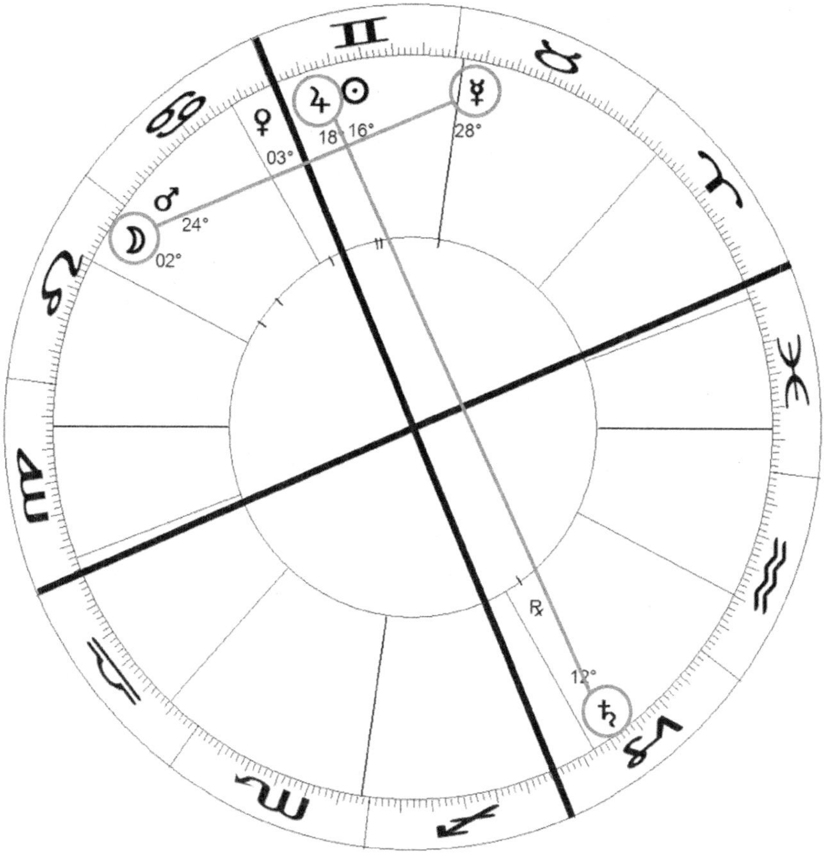

Figure A1.17: Two types of equality.

Roger's definition of **solitude** is quite straightforward, and is often referred to as being **void of course** in later texts. It usually happens when a planet is in the late degrees of a sign, and is not applying to any other planet. Related to this is **alienation** where a planet is in a sign, but all the other planets are in signs that don't aspect that sign; for example, if Jupiter is in Gemini, any planet in Taurus, Cancer, Capricorn, or Scorpio can't make a traditional aspect to him. If all of the other planets are in those signs, then Jupiter is in alienation, also known as being "peregrine". Roger points out that this happens most often in the case of the Moon. However, when a planet is peregrine, it is considered to be in a relationship with the Lord of the term in which it is placed.

The concept of **translation** and **collection** was covered in Chapter Five in the section on using intermediaries. The general principle is that if two planets don't make a direct connection themselves, then another planet can act as an intermediary, and Roger adds a third type here, **collation**, which specifies that not only are the main two planets not aspecting each other because the aspect is separating, but that they are in signs that don't aspect each other. As he says, collation is just another example of translation or collection in this case. Roger does add that the collecting planet aspects "a place on the zodiac", implying that collection can also assist with matters of other houses. For example, in Figure A1.18, a horary question is posed: "Will my long journey be profitable?"

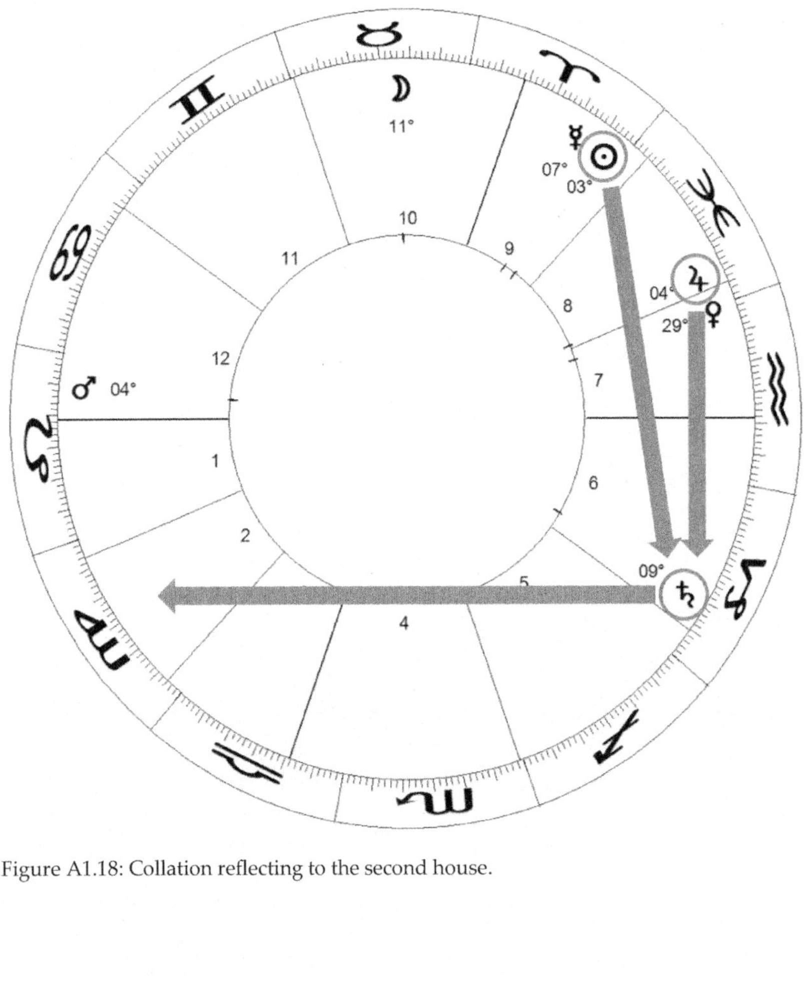

Figure A1.18: Collation reflecting to the second house.

The querent is represented by the ruler of the Ascendant, the Sun. The journey is the ruler of the ninth house, Jupiter. The Sun and Jupiter do not aspect each other. However, the Sun and Jupiter are both applying to Saturn, who will collect the light from both. It can then reflect that light to another part of the chart – for example, by trine to the second house. This means that the second house theme of making money looks promising in this case.

As a general rule in a question on horary, we work out which planet represents the person asking the question (the querent), and which planet represents the matter itself (the quesited), and see if there is a connection between the two. Sometimes there is an apparent connection, but that connection is blocked by a third planet. This is called **prohibition**.

In Figure A1.19, a horary question is asked: "Will I get the job?" The ruler of the Ascendant, Mars, represents the querent, and Saturn, the ruler of the tenth house, represents the job. Mars is applying to Saturn, and both are in good condition, so this looks promising. However, Mars is currently blocked from reaching Saturn as Jupiter is in the way, and so prohibits the desired outcome from taking place until Mars has overtaken Jupiter. Roger's example is somewhat laboured – he first gives the case when all three planets are in the same sign as they are here, and then gives the case where the applying planet (Mars, in this example) is in a different sign and applying by aspect – but the principle is exactly the same.

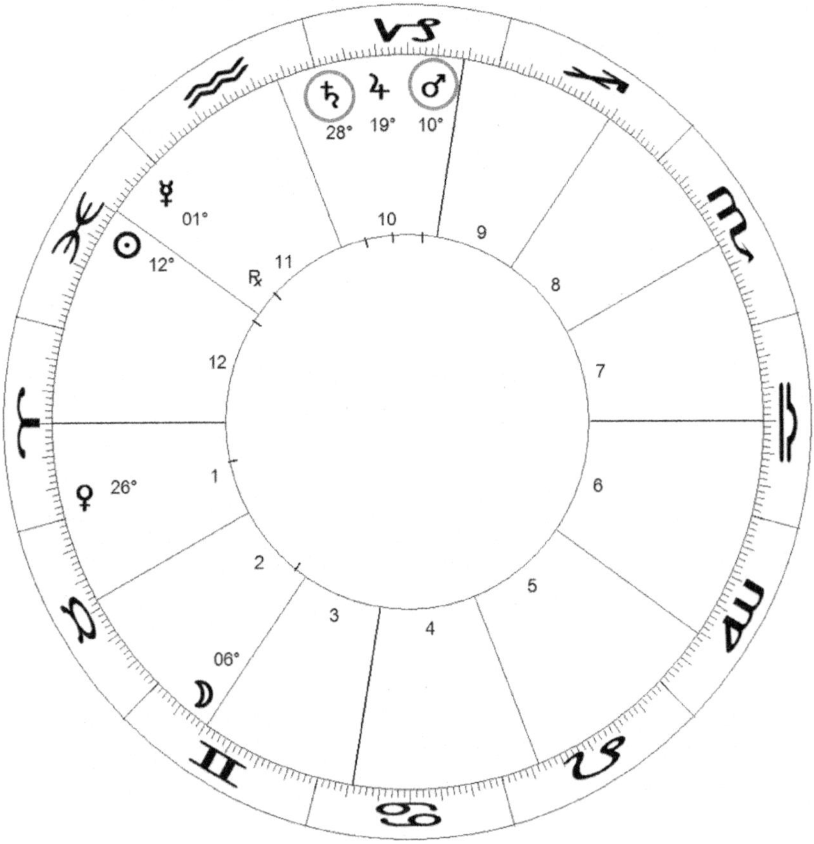

Figure A1.19: Mars applies to Saturn, but Jupiter prohibits.

In Chapter Five, Roger discussed finding significators when the planets that would usually be chosen are "impeded", and he gives a number of rules for choosing different ones. As a general rule, planets are considered in poor condition if they are too close to the Sun or retrograde, but according to Abū Maʿšar, this doesn't have to be a show-stopper. Although Roger's text doesn't go into detail explicitly, Abū Maʿšar sees planets as "managing" the affair in question, and that a planet applying to another is "handing over" the management to that planet. If that planet is in poor condition, then it can't take on the management, so it **returns** it to the first planet. This can sometimes be beneficial, and sometimes not. The text says that sometimes the planet being applied to is "under the rays", meaning close enough to the Sun that the planet isn't visible (this generally means within about 17° of the Sun) or retrograde, and in this case the planet cannot take on the management. However, if the planet has reception with the applying planet (Roger's use of reception is covered in the relevant section in Chapter Five, and is also mentioned later in this Appendix) then the management remains with the applying planet, but the outcome is still beneficial. In the same way, if the applying planet is direct and not in a cadent house (third, sixth, ninth, or twelfth house) the outcome will be beneficial. Abū Maʿšar's text rather confusingly makes the latter condition into two conditions: the first being that both planets are in a non-cadent house, and the second being that the applying planet is in a non-cadent house but the planet being applied to is in a cadent house. Clearly, those conditions can be more simply expressed as the applying planet being non-cadent, and therefore able to take on the management. Roger follows Abū Maʿšar's text by spelling out three conditions. If both the applying planet and the one being applied to are retrograde, combust or cadent, then that results in the matter not coming to fruition.

In addition to prohibition, mentioned above, there are other conditions that can prevent an application of one planet to another being met. All of these involve one planet applying to another, but being thwarted. **Contradiction** is when it seems that a planet is applying to another one, but then goes retrograde so the application doesn't perfect. **Impediment** is when a planet is applying to another, but a third planet suddenly goes retrograde and ends up between the two planets, blocking the first one. **Evasion** is when a planet is applying to another one, but the planet it is applying to moves into the next sign. If there is another planet in that sign, it can end up blocking the applying planet.

This is illustrated in Figure A1.20, Venus in Cancer is applying to the Sun, also in Cancer, as shown in the left-hand image. However, before she reaches the Sun, the Sun moves into the next sign, where Saturn is situated at 7° Leo. The right-hand image, which is the situation ten days later, shows that the Sun has moved past Saturn before Venus reaches the Sun, and so now Saturn is blocking the application of Venus to the Sun.

Figure A1.20: Evasion: Venus applies to the Sun, but is blocked by Saturn in the next sign.

Roger's definition of **interception** is also when an application is frustrated by another planet. He tells us this can happen in three different ways, but Roger's text is a little confusing so some examples will help here.

The first way is a similar concept to evasion, but instead of the planet that is being applied to "escaping" into the following sign, a planet already in the following sign goes retrograde and moves back into the current sign, blocking the application. For example, using the left-hand illustration in Figure A1.20, if Mercury were retrograde, he might move back into Cancer and come between Venus and the Sun before Venus had perfected the application.

The second way is illustrated in Figure A1.21, where the question is "will I be able to attend my favourite conference this year?" The querent is represented by Venus, the ruler of the Ascendant, and the conference is represented by the ruler of the eleventh house, the Sun. Saturn is beyond both of these, so doesn't appear to play a role. At first glance, it seems that this aspect will perfect, but in a couple of days the Sun overtakes Saturn, so that Venus is now applying to Saturn, not the Sun. Roger says this means the quesited thing will change to something else, and the original intention is frustrated. Since Saturn is the ruler of both the fourth and fifth houses, perhaps this indicates that instead of going to the conference, the querent will be sidetracked by family matters involving the father or children instead. Roger's third method seems to be very similar to prohibition – a planet wants to apply to another one representing the quesited matter, but instead applies to a planet blocking it, which represents something else.

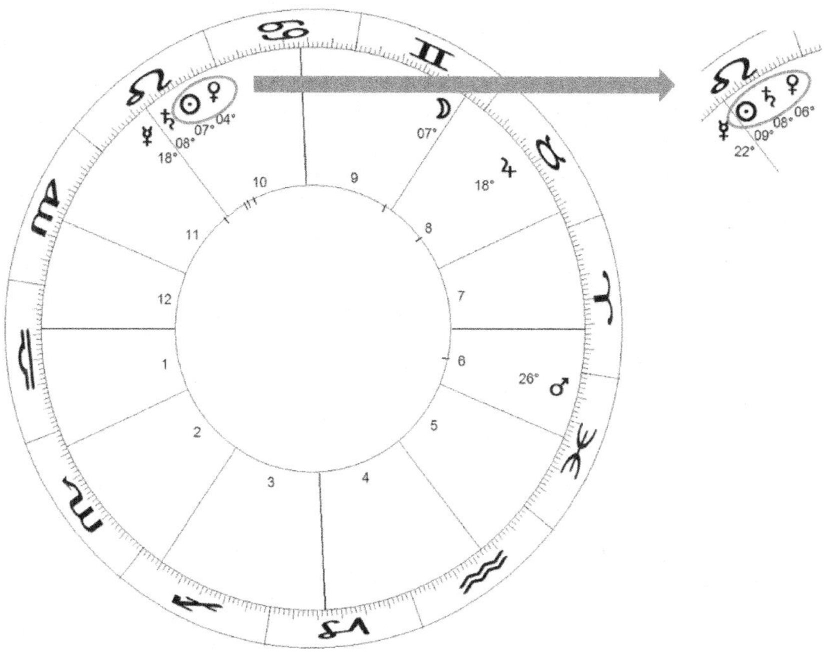

Figure A1.21: Interception: Venus applies to the Sun, but is intercepted by Saturn when the Sun overtakes Saturn.

Roger's text then gives two complementary attributes. Sometimes a planet is in a poor condition, because it is in its fall, or in a **well**. Roger doesn't give any information about wells, but it is in Abū Ma'šar[64] and represents specific degrees that are considered unfortunate. **Compassion** is when a planet is in this unfortunate situation, but a friendly planet is applying to it, and helping it. **Remuneration** is when that unfortunate planet finds itself able to return the favour later on, when it has moved into better circumstances, and the planet that helped him is now in need of aid.

Reception is a topic that Roger has covered in some detail in his book, and was covered in Chapter Five. In that chapter, Roger stressed that the definition of reception was that the receiving planet is always the slower moving planet. However, in this reference section, he is simply citing Abū Ma'šar, who has a looser definition – he merely says that reception occurs when one planet has dignity in the place of the other planet, without mentioning speed. The section includes various ways that reception can be blocked by another planet prohibiting it, but this largely repeats what has been said above about various ways by which an application of a planet can be frustrated.

---

64 Abū Ma'šar, *Liber Introductorii Maioris* (Hermann) V.21, p.91.

Table of parts

The next section of the text simply gives a list, without any explanation, headed "Table of parts". The concept of parts is Hellenistic, where they were called **lots**, although as Western scholars such as Roger got the information from Arabic texts, they were generally known as **Arabic parts**, hence Roger's title.

The concept behind a lot, or part, is that it is a calculated point on the chart that represents something. The thing it represents may be some kind of quality (fortune, morality and so on) or it may relate to a particular issue such as siblings or marriage. Arabic astrologers extended the range of Hellenistic lots greatly, and invented new ones for various purposes such as agriculture – there is, for example, a part of watermelons which can be used to determine the state of your watermelon crop for the coming year! The principle behind a lot is that it combines the qualities of two planets, and manifests them by projecting them onto the Ascendant.

The best-known of the Arabic parts is the Part of Fortune. It is calculated in a daytime chart by taking the distance from the Sun to the Moon in degrees, and then moving that same number of degrees from the Ascendant to arrive at the Part of Fortune. Figure A1.22 illustrates this. In the daytime chart on the left, the Sun is at 18° Virgo, and the Moon is at 5° Scorpio. To get from the Sun to the Moon, we need to travel 47° along the zodiac. If we now travel 47° from the Ascendant, we arrive at 9° Aquarius, which is the Part of Fortune. For the night-time chart on the right, we reverse the formula – instead of going from the Sun to the Moon, we go from the Moon to the Sun. In this chart, the Sun is at 26° Virgo, and the Moon is at 0° Pisces. To get from the Moon to the Sun, we travel 206° around the chart, and doing the same from the Ascendant brings us to the Part of Fortune at 0° Capricorn.

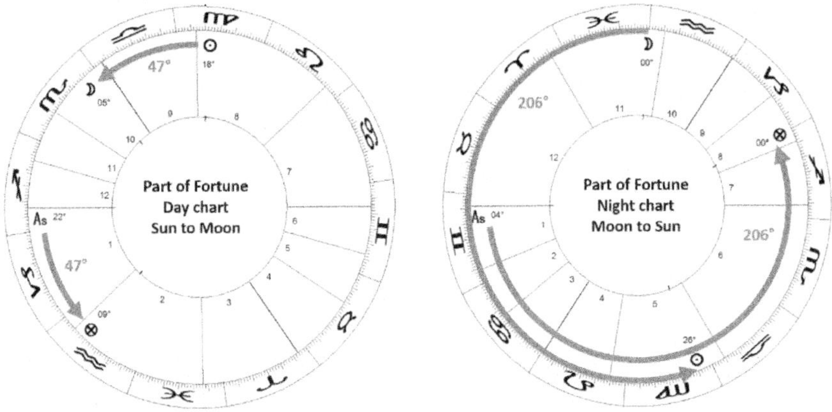

Figure A1.22: Part of Fortune.

The Part of Fortune is one of the **planetary parts**, and is associated with the Moon. The other planets also have their parts, so there are seven planetary parts in all. Abū Maʿšar then gives a list of 80 parts that are associated with the houses, although Roger misses a few of these out as seven of them have exactly the same formula as some of the other parts. For example, the part of sexual intercourse and adultery is given as the Sun to Venus projected from the Ascendant, but the part of adultery of men is also given as the Sun to Venus projected onto the Ascendant; Roger has understandably not included some of these duplicates in his table. He does appear to have made one error – or perhaps a later scribe did – in completely missing out the rather important part of kings, which should be Mars to the Moon projected onto the Ascendant. Thus although several manuscripts have a line before this table explaining that there are 80 parts associated with the houses, in fact Roger only has 72. Finally, Abū Maʿšar lists ten parts that are not associated directly with either planets or houses; curiously, Roger adds an eleventh, the part of truth, which is not in Abū Maʿšar's list. Sometimes Roger duplicates an entry, simply writing "eiusdem" ("the same") without explanation. Abū Maʿšar's text does clarify that these are different traditions, for example according to Hermes, or according to the Persians, but Roger does not identify the source.

While most of the parts are calculated by taking the distance between two planets and project that onto the Ascendant, that isn't always the case. Sometimes a part is between two other parts, and sometimes the distance is projected onto the location of another planet instead.

Table A1.4 shows Roger's list of parts.

	Name of part	From	To	Projected
Planets				
Moon	Fortune	Sun	Moon	Asc
Sun	Future	Moon	Sun	Asc
Saturn	Habits	Saturn	Pt Fortune	Asc
Jupiter	Morality[65]	Pt Future	Jupiter	Asc
Mars	Vigour	Mars	Pt Fortune	Asc
Venus	Love	Pt Fortune	Pt Future	Asc
Mercury	Cleverness	Pt Future	Pt Fortune	Asc
Houses				
1st	Life	Jupiter	Saturn	Asc
	Sustenance	Pt Fortune	Pt Future	Asc
	Reason	Mercury	Mars	Asc
2nd	Works	Lord 2	Cusp 2	Asc
	Exchange	Saturn	Mercury	Asc
	Discovery	Mercury	Venus	Asc
3rd	Brothers	Saturn	Jupiter	Asc
	Number of brothers	Mercury	Saturn	Asc
	Death of brothers	Sun	Cusp 10	Asc
4th	Fathers	Sun	Saturn	Asc
	Death of fathers	Saturn	Jupiter	Asc
	Grandfathers	Sun	Saturn	Asc
	Lineage	Saturn	Mars	Mercury
	Terrain	Saturn	Moon	Asc
	Terrain	Mercury	Jupiter	Asc
	Agriculture	Venus	Saturn	Asc
	End of the matter	Saturn	Lord Syzygy	Asc
5th	Children	Jupiter	Saturn	Asc
	Time and no of children	Mars	Jupiter	Asc
	Male children	Moon	Jupiter	Saturn
	Female children	Moon	Venus	Asc
	Sex of child (in womb)	Lord Moon	Moon	Asc

[65] Most manuscripts incorrectly give "mortality", but "morality" is correct, and is in one manuscript of *Judicial Astrology*.

	Name of part	From	To	Projected
6th	Suffering	Saturn	Mars	Asc
	Sickness	Mercury	Mars	Asc
	Slaves	Mercury	Pt Fortune	Asc
	Captivity	Lord Sun	Sun	Asc
7th	Betrothal	Saturn	Venus	Asc
	Intercourse and adultery	Sun	Venus	Asc
	Intercourse and adultery	Moon	Mars	Asc
	Chastity of women	Moon	Venus	Asc
	Marriage	Venus	Cusp 7	Asc
	Hour of marriage	Sun	Moon	Asc
	Deception of women	Sun	Moon	Asc
	Father's descendants[66]	Saturn	Venus	Asc
	Controversy	Mars	Jupiter	Asc
8th	Death	Moon	Cusp 8	Saturn
	Killing planet	Lord 1	Moon	Asc
	Year of fear	Saturn	Mars	Asc
	Place of fear	Saturn	Lord Syzygy	Asc
	Anguish	Saturn	Mercury	Asc
9th	Journeys	Lord 9	Cusp 9	Asc
	Travel by water	Saturn	15 Cancer	Asc
	Religion	Moon	Mercury	Asc
	Providence or foresight	Saturn	Moon	Asc
	Knowledge	Saturn	Jupiter	Asc
	Reputation and history	Sun	Jupiter	Asc
	Rumours[67]	Mercury	Moon	Asc

[66] Roger uses the Latin term "pars agnatorum", which has connotations of children born after the father has made a will, and therefore who may not inherit.
[67] Roger just has "rumours", but Hermann's translation is more specific: it's whether a rumour is true or false.

	Name of part	From	To	Projected
10th	Leadership	Light	Exalt Light[68]	Asc
	King's advisors	Mercury	Mars	Asc
	Kings and nobles	Sun	Saturn	Asc
	Sudden rising in station	Saturn	Pt Fortune	Asc
	Authority	Mercury	Sun	Asc
	King's court	Mars	Saturn	Asc
	Of the king and births	Saturn	Moon	Asc
	Merchants, merchandise	Mercury	Venus	Asc
	Unavoidable works	Sun	Jupiter	Asc
	Mothers	Venus	Moon	Asc
	Merchants	Pt Sun	Pt Fortune	Asc
11th	Riches	Pt Fortune	Pt Future[69]	Asc
	Grace and affection	Pt Fortune	Pt Future	Asc
	Reverence	Pt Fortune	Sun	Asc
	Deliberation	Pt Fortune	Jupiter	Asc
	Delights	Pt Fortune	Pt Future	Asc
	Hope	Saturn	Venus	Asc
	Friendship	Moon	Mercury	Asc
	Necessity	Pt Future	Mercury	Asc
	Abundance	Moon	Mercury	Asc
	Nobility of the soul	Mercury	Sun	Asc
	Familiarity	Jupiter	Venus	Asc
12th	Enemies	Saturn	Mars	Asc
	Enemies	Lord 12	Cusp 12	Asc
	Hardship, punishment	Pt Future	Pt Fortune	Asc
General				
	Hyleg	Syzygy	Moon	Asc
	Corruption	Pt Fortune	Mars	Asc
	Military	Saturn	Moon	Asc
	Ferocity	Lord 1	Moon	Asc
	Cunning	Mercury	Pt Future	Asc
	Troubled places	Saturn	Mars	Asc
	Obstacles and injury	Mars	Pt Brothers	Asc
	Obstacles and injury	Pt Love	Mercury	Asc
	Repayment	Mars	Sun	Asc
	Truthful works	Mercury	Mars	Asc
	Truth[70]	Mercury	Venus	Asc

Table A1.4: Table of parts.

---

[68] By day, Sun to 19 Aries, by night, Moon to 3 Taurus (exaltation degrees).

[69] Roger uses the term "Pars boni", but a reading of Abū Maʿšar's text shows that this is in fact the solar part, the Part of the Future.

[70] This is missing from Abū Maʿšar and only appears in *Judicial Astrology*.

Virtues of the planets in the signs

Each sign is given a very brief summary. The earliest copy of the manuscript has this in a neat tabular format, while other manuscripts simply list them. In addition, there are various scribal errors, which means that there is no definitive version within *Judicial Astronomy*. A brief explanation of what the qualities mean is needed here, as Roger has abbreviated this so heavily that some of it becomes meaningless, as we'll see below.

Each sign is broken down as follows, using Aries as an example – the first few relate to planetary dignities, and are described in more detail in Appendix Two of this book.

House: this gives the ruling planet. Aries is the house of Mars.

Exaltation: where this applies this gives not only the planet exalted in this sign, but a specific degree at which the planet is most exalted. The Sun is exalted at 19 degrees of Aries.

Triplicity: signs are grouped into elements, also known as triplicities, and each element has a daytime ruler, a night-time ruler, and a participating, or common, ruler. The Sun is the daytime ruler of fire signs, Jupiter the night-time ruler, and Saturn the participating ruler.

Terms: each sign is divided into five unequal segments called terms or bounds, ruled by a planet. Aries has the first 6 degrees ruled by Jupiter, the next 6 by Venus, the next 8 by Mercury, the next 5 by Mars, and the final 5 by Saturn. There are numerous errors in the various manuscripts that get this part wrong. Sometimes the figures do not even add up to thirty degrees!

Faces: each sign is divided into three 10-degree segments called faces, ruled by a planet. The first 10 degrees of Aries is ruled by Mars, the next 10 by the Sun, and the final 10 by Venus.

Gender of degrees: each sign has degrees that are described as male or female – again, this section has various errors, and some signs do not even add up to thirty degrees. Aries has the first 7 degrees as male, the next 2 female, the next 6 male, the next 7 female, and the final 8 male.

Quality of degrees: each sign is divided into bright, dark, smoky, and empty degrees, which Roger abbreviates to their Latin letters: l for lucidi (bright), t for tenebrosi (dark), f for fumosi (smoky), and v for vacua (empty). For Aries, the values given are t.3, l.6, f.8, t.4, l.5, v.1. This does not add up to 30 degrees, so this is yet another section that has various errors.

Full and empty degrees: Roger has abbreviated this section to the point of making it useless. Each sign contains full and empty degrees, outlined in the Hellenistic text *Mathesis* by Firmicus Maternus. Firmicus describes Aries as having the first 3 degrees empty, the next 5 full, the next 9 empty, the next 4 full, the next 5 full, and the final 4 empty. This description is useful, since it can be seen that a planet at, say, 19° Aries will be full, and Firmicus explains what this means (natives lucky enough to have all seven planets in full degrees will be "elevated like gods").[71] However, Roger simply notes that there are 12 full and 18 empty degrees for Aries – and without knowing which degrees are empty and which are full, this is useless information.

Element of sign: each sign falls into one of four elements: fire, earth, air, and water. Roger's text describes Aries as masculine, fiery, and oriental. In fact, simply the element is enough – all fire and air signs are masculine, while earth and water signs are feminine. Fire signs are eastern (oriental), earth signs are southern, air signs are western (occidental), and water signs are northern.

Table A1.5 summarises all of these.

---

[71] Mathesis IV.22.4, p.147.

Sign	Ruler	Exal + deg	Trip D/N /P	Terms	Faces	Sex	Bright-ness	F/ E	Char Sex/El Dir
♈	♂	Su 19	Su Ju Sa	Ju 6 Ve 6 Me 8 Ma 5 Sa 5	Ma Su Ve	m7 f2 m6 f7 m8	d3 b6 s8 d4 b5 e1	12 18	M F E
♉	♀	Mo 3	Ve Mo Ma	Ve 8 Me 6 Ju 8 Sa 5 Ma 4	Me Mo Sa	m7 f8 m15	d4 b4 e5 b4 e5 b7 d2	20 10	F E S
♊	☿	NN 3	Sa Me Ju	Me 6 Ju 6 Ve 5 Ma 7 Sa 6	Ju Ma Su	f5 m11 f6 m4 f4	b4 d3 b5 e4 b6 d5 e4	21 9	M A W
♋	☽	Ju 15	Ve Ma Mo	Ma 7 Ve 6 Me 6 Ju 7 Sat 4	Ve Me Mo	m2 f6 m2 f2 m11 f4 m3	b12 d2 e4 s2 b8 e2	19 11	F W N
♌	☉	_	Su Ju Sa	Ju 6 Ve 5 Sa 7 Me 6 Ma 6	Sa Ju Ma	m5 f3 m7 f7 m8	d10 s10 b5 e5	21 9	M F E
♍	☿	Me 15	Ve Mo Ma	Me 7 Ve 10 Ju 4 Ma 7 Sa 2	Su Ve Me	f7 m4 f8 m10	d5 b3 e3 b5 s6 e5 d3	14 16	F E S
♎	♀	Sa 21	Sa Me Ju	Sa 7 Me 8 Ju 7 Ve 7 Ma 2	Mo Sa Ju	m5 f10 m5 f7 m3	s5 d5 b8 d3 b7 e3	19 11	M A W
♏	♂	_	Ve Ma Mo	Ma 7 Ve 4 Me 8 Ju 5 Sa 6	Ma Su Ve	m4 f10 m4 f8 m5	d3 b5 e6 b6 s2 e5 d3	16 14	F W N
♐	♃	SN 3	Su Ju Sa	Ju 12 Ve 5 Me 4 Sa 5 Ma 4	Me Mo Sa	m2 f3 m7 f12 m6	b11 d3 b5 s4 e7	_	M F E
♑	♄	Ma 28	Ve Mo Ma	Me 7 Ju 7 Ve 8 Sa 4 Ma 4	Ju Ma Su	m11 f8 m11	d7 b3 s5 b4 d3 e3 d5	_	F E S
♒	♄	_	Sa Me Ju	Me 7 Ve 6 Ju 7 Ma 6 Sa 5	Ve Me Mo	m5 f10 m6 f4 m5	s4 b5 d4 b9 e4 b5	_	M A W
♓	♃	Ve 27	Ve Ma Mo	Ve 12 Ju 4 Me 3 Mar 9 Sa 2	Sa Ju Ma	m10 f10 m3 f5 m2	d7 b6 d6 b4 e3 b2 d3	_	F W N

Key: Sa=Saturn, Ju=Jupiter, Ma=Mars, Su=Sun, Ve=Venus, Me=Mercury, Mo=Moon, NN=North Node, SN=South Node. D/N/P=Day/Night/Participating, F/E=Full/Empty, Brightness: b(right), d(ark), s(moky), e(mpty), Sex/El/Dir=Gender, Element, Direction.

Table A1.5: Virtues of the planets in the signs.

Summary Tables

Roger's reference section ends with a set of lists and tables, as follows:

Joys of the planets in houses and signs

Each planet is said to rejoice in a particular house, as shown in Table A1.6. Guido Bonatti, writing in the thirteenth century, attributed this to Abū Maʿšar and al-Qabisi.[72] However, other than very briefly listing the joys, neither Abū Maʿšar nor al-Qabisi have much to say about them and do not give any reasons for their placement.[73] Bonatti, though, did give reasons for why each planet rejoices in a particular house; for example, he said that the fifth house is the house of pleasure, and Venus signifies this, so she rejoices there, and that Saturn, the great malefic, rejoices in the twelfth house which is the house of grief and sorrow, which Saturn rejoices in. The logic behind both is straightforward, although Roger did not dwell on it. One can consider that the seven planets are three pairs, plus Mercury. The greater light (the Sun) is diurnal, the lesser light (the Moon) is nocturnal. The greater benefic (Jupiter) is diurnal, the lesser benefic (Venus) is nocturnal. The greater malefic (Saturn) is diurnal and the lesser malefic (Mars) is nocturnal. Mercury can be either diurnal or nocturnal, according to whether he appears as a morning star or an evening star. Using this model, Mercury rejoices in the first house, which (if one uses the original whole-sign houses) straddles the Ascendant so can be either above or below the horizon. Each of the remaining pairs rejoice in opposite houses, one diurnal and one nocturnal – so the Sun (a diurnal planet) rejoices in the ninth house, above the horizon, and the Moon (a nocturnal planet) in the opposite third house below the horizon. Diurnal Jupiter rejoices in the eleventh house which is above the horizon, nocturnal Mars in the fifth, below the horizon; and diurnal Saturn rejoices in the twelfth, above the horizon, while nocturnal Mars rejoices in the opposite sixth, below the horizon.

Similarly, each planet rejoices in one of the signs that it rules, with diurnal planets preferring male signs (fire and air), and nocturnal planets preferring

---

[72] Bonatti, *Book of Astronomy*, Chapter 11, pp.140-141.

[73] Al-Qabisi, *Introduction* I.70, p.55; Abū Maʿšar, *Abbreviation*, I.121, p.31.

female signs (earth and water). The Sun and Moon only rule one sign each, so have to rejoice there; Saturn rules both Aquarius and Capricorn, but prefers masculine Aquarius as he is diurnal. Jupiter rules both Pisces and Sagittarius, but prefers masculine Sagittarius. Mars rules both Scorpio and Aries, but prefers feminine Scorpio because although he is male, he is nocturnal. Venus rules both Taurus and Libra, but prefers feminine Taurus because she is nocturnal. Mercury is the odd one out as he can be either diurnal or nocturnal, and al-Kindi said he rejoices in Gemini if he is a morning star and Virgo if an evening star, although Roger only allocated him to Virgo.[74]

Planet	House	Sign
Saturn	12	Aquarius
Jupiter	11	Sagittarius
Mars	6	Scorpio
Sun	9	Leo
Venus	5	Taurus
Mercury	1	Virgo
Moon	3	Cancer

Table A1.6: Planetary joys.

What testament a planet has in its dignities

This is very simply the "scoring system", described in Appendix Two, for calculating how strong a planet is in a particular degree of a sign. A planet scores five points for rulership, four points for exaltation, three points for triplicity rulership, two points for term rulership, and one point for face rulership.

[74] Al-Kindi, *Forty Chapters*, p.85.

Friendship and enmity

Table A1.7 is a list of planets, and which planets they consider friends, and which they consider enemies. The list is not necessarily two-way; for instance, Jupiter hates Mars, but Mars does not hate Jupiter.

Planet	Friendship	Enmity
Saturn	Jupiter, Sun, Moon	Mars, Venus
Jupiter	All but Mars	Mars
Mars	Venus	Everyone except Jupiter and Sun[75]
Sun	Jupiter, Venus	Mercury, Moon
Venus	All but Saturn	Saturn
Mercury	Jupiter, Venus, Saturn	Sun, Moon, Mars
Moon	Jupiter, Venus, Saturn	Mercury, Mars
N. Node	Jupiter, Venus	Saturn, Mars
S. Node	Saturn, Mars	Sun, Moon, Jupiter and Venus[76]

Table A1.7: Friendship and enmity.

Strengths

This is a summary of planetary dignities. Essential dignity relates to the essence of a planet – Mars is always dignified in Aries, as he rules it. Accidental dignity is when a planet, regardless of essential dignity, is fortunate because of something happening at the time – for example, it is making a beneficial aspect to another planet, or is fast-moving, and most of this list is a summary of accidental dignities that a planet can have.

[75] This seems to conflict with the friendship that Mars supposedly has with Venus.
[76] The earliest manuscript also lists Mars, but this must be an error.

- In a good place from the Ascendant (that is, not cadent or non-aspecting)
- In its own dignity
- Direct or tending towards direct
- If it does not have a malefic in its sign, or square or opposite
- Not cadent or in fall or detriment
- It has reception
- Masculine and diurnal and oriental in a compatible sign
- In a fixed sign
- In the heart of the Sun (within 17 minutes of the Sun – this is called being **cazimi**)
- In the eastern half of the chart (from the tenth sign to the third sign)
- Fast moving
- In a good degree, bright or full

This completes the reference section of *Judicial Astrology*, and accounts for more than half the book in those manuscripts that include it. As mentioned earlier, the fact that it isn't present in all manuscripts suggests that it is considered a separate reference guide to be used independently of Roger's main book. It was quite common in medieval texts to provide introductions that explain basic concepts, and it seems that this is what Roger was doing here.

Indeed, I've done so myself in this very book – I'm aware that some readers will be familiar with medieval astrology, and others will not be. For this reason, I, like Roger, have included a separate appendix giving the principles of medieval astrology, which I hope will act as a useful primer for astrologers not familiar with medieval techniques.

APPENDIX TWO: MEDIEVAL ASTROLOGY PRIMER

I'm making the assumption that if you're reading this book, you already know some basics of astrology. However, the astrology that most of us astrologers in the twentieth and twenty-first centuries learned was modern astrology, which differs somewhat from the astrology that Roger was familiar with, and so this section covers some of the basic principles of medieval astrology that are useful to know to understand Roger's discussion. This Appendix does not relate directly to Roger's book, but is simply a primer to give some of the basics of medieval astrology to help you appreciate its outlook and techniques.

Planetary strength

Modern astrology, in its usual presentation within magazine horoscope columns, places a lot of emphasis on the significance of signs of the zodiac. Most people know their "zodiac sign" and a few choice keywords associated with that sign – Virgos are analytical, Capricorns work too hard and so on. In fact, when somebody claims "I'm a Taurus", what they actually mean is that the Sun was in the sign of Taurus on the day they were born. On that same day, all the other planets would also have been in various signs, but the Sun sign has the unique advantage that it is not necessary to know the year of birth to calculate it – if you were born on 15 May, regardless of the year, the Sun was in Taurus on that date, which makes it very easy to memorise your Sun sign, or simply look it up in a short column in a magazine.

Medieval astrology, however, did not place nearly so much emphasis on signs. Planets were seen as the active agents in a chart, and they were stronger in some places in the chart than others, and each planet had its own personality traits – Saturn was sombre and Jupiter generous. Saturn and Mars were considered **malefic** planets with a negative influence, while Jupiter and Venus were **benefic** positive planets. Many of these characteristics have made their way directly into the English language – martial arts and martial law derive from Mars' warlike demeanour, jovial from Jupiter's (or Jove's) generosity and general beneficence, and venereal disease from Venus' lustful traits. Methods were used to identify the strongest planet or planets in a chart, and the characteristics of that planet were used to describe the person or event that the chart represented. Hence in medieval astrology, rather than a person being described by their Sun sign, they might be described as Saturnian, relating to the strongest planet in their chart.

To illustrate some of these examples, I'm going to use the chart of a particular historic event that links the medieval and modern worlds: the reburial of King Richard III of England. Richard III was the last Plantagenet king of England, and was killed at the Battle of Bosworth near Leicester in 1485. Richard's body was brought to Leicester, but the exact location of his body was unknown; some legends claim it had been thrown into the local river. In fact, after much painstaking work in recent decades, his probable burial site was identified, in the city centre of Leicester, in a place that at the time was a car park. It seemed very unlikely that they would be able to find his remains, but an excavation was organised of the car park by archaeologists from the University of Leicester in 2012, and to everyone's astonishment Richard III's body was found – and not only found, but positively identified by DNA evidence. Richard III's body was reburied in Leicester Cathedral on 26 March 2015 at 12:05, in a ceremony watched across the world.

Figure A2.1: Richard III's coffin in Leicester Cathedral prior to his reburial.

Credit: Chris Mitchell, CC BY-SA 4.0.

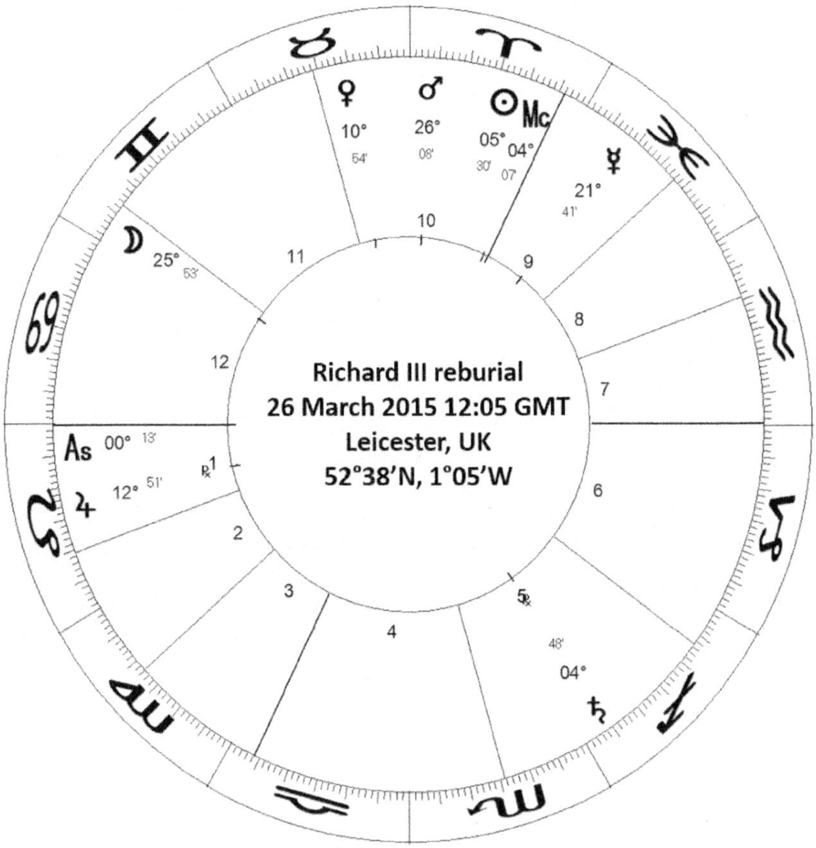

Figure A2.2: The chart of Richard III's reburial at Leicester Cathedral.

There were five techniques for determining planetary strength, called **dignity**, used by medieval astrologers, although their provenance is earlier and are described by Ptolemy: sign rulership, exaltation, triplicity rulership, terms (also called bounds), and faces.

Sign rulership is the strongest of these. There are seven planets and twelve signs (planets beyond Saturn weren't known to medieval astrologers), but two of these planets have special significance as the lights – the Sun and the Moon. The Sun is given rulership of the sign Leo, and the Moon rules the adjacent sign Cancer. This leaves five remaining planets and ten signs, and so each planet is given two signs to rule: Mercury, the fastest moving, is given rulership of Gemini and Virgo, the two signs closest to Leo and Cancer; Venus, the next fastest moving, is given rulership of Taurus and Libra, the next signs out and so on in a symmetric pattern shown in Figure A2.3.

Any planet in a chart that is in the sign that it rules is particularly strong. For example, in the Richard III reburial chart shown in Figure A2.2, Venus is in the sign of Taurus, which it rules, so Venus is particularly strong in this chart. Similarly, Mars is in Aries, which it rules. In addition, every chart has a ruler, which is the planet that rules the sign of the Ascendant, usually known in medieval texts as **the Lord of the Ascendant**. In the Richard III reburial chart, Leo is the Ascendant, and Leo is ruled by the Sun, so the Sun is the Lord of the Ascendant.

If a planet is in the sign opposite to the one it rules – for example, if Mars is in Taurus or Libra – the planet is said to be in **detriment**, and therefore weak. In the Richard III reburial chart, Mercury is in Pisces and so is in detriment as Pisces is opposite Virgo, one of the signs that Mercury rules.

The next strongest dignity is **exaltation**. Unlike the elegant symmetry of sign rulership, there is no obvious logic to exaltation. Saturn is exalted in Libra, Jupiter in Cancer, Mars in Capricorn, the Sun in Aries, Venus in Pisces, Mercury in Virgo (which it also rules), and the Moon in Taurus. Many texts even assign precise degrees to exaltation – the Sun is exalted in all of Aries, but particularly at 19° of Aries. In the Richard III chart, the Sun is in exaltation.

If a planet is in the sign opposite to the one in which it is exalted – for example, if Mars is in Cancer – the planet is said to be in **fall**, and therefore weak.

Figure A2.3: Sign rulership.

By the Middle Ages, all signs were considered as being related to Aristotelian elements, as follows: Aries, Leo, and Sagittarius are fire signs, Taurus, Virgo, and Capricorn are earth signs, Gemini, Libra, and Aquarius are air signs, and Cancer, Scorpio, and Pisces are water signs. Ptolemy did not make the link between signs and elements, although he did group them into the same four sets which he called triplicities or triangles, and so rather cumbersomely referred to the "Aries-Leo-Sagittarius triplicity" instead of the simpler "fire signs". For this reason, the elemental rulerships are called **triplicity rulerships**. Each element (or triplicity) has three planets ruling it. Some schemes made use of all three planets, others had one of the planets as the day ruler, one as the night ruler, and one as the common ruler, as shown in Table A2.1.

Element	Day			Night		
Fire	Sun	Jupiter	Saturn	Jupiter	Sun	Saturn
Earth	Venus	Moon	Mars	Moon	Venus	Mars
Air	Saturn	Mercury	Jupiter	Mercury	Saturn	Jupiter
Water	Venus	Mars	Moon	Mars	Venus	Moon

Table A2.1: Triplicity rulers.

For example, in the Richard III chart, the Sun is above the horizon, so it is a daytime chart. The Sun is in Aries, a fire sign, so has dignity because it is one of the triplicity rulers of fire signs, and it is in a fire sign. Jupiter is also in a fire sign (Leo) and is also one of the rulers of fire signs, but less powerful in a daytime chart than the Sun – but Jupiter still has dignity here. Saturn is also in a fire sign (Sagittarius), and so has some dignity here as it is one of the rulers of fire signs, but not as much dignity as either Jupiter or the Sun.

Terms or **bounds** are unequal segments of a sign. Each sign has five such segments, each one ruled by a particular planet excluding the Sun and the Moon, and there is no obvious logical pattern to them. The origin of these terms was apparently Egyptian, and the lack of logic appears to have frustrated Ptolemy, who developed his own system of terms to replace the illogical Egyptian ones (although as he gave very little in the way of explanation of his method, the logic of his supposedly improved system is still hard to see to a modern eye), which some medieval astrologers used in preference to the Egyptian ones.

The final sort of dignity involves **faces**, or **decanates**, which are ten-degree segments of each sign. The first decanate (that is, the first ten degrees) of Aries is in the face of Mars, the next decanate in the face of the Sun, and the final decanate degrees in the face of Venus. The first decanate of Taurus is in the face of Mercury, the middle decanate in the face of the Moon, and the final decanate in the face of Saturn. The sequence of faces for each ten-degree segment proceeds in the ever-repeating **Chaldean order** of planets: Saturn, Jupiter, Mars, the Sun, Venus, Mercury, and the Moon, so the first decanate of Gemini is in the face of Jupiter, since the previous decanate (the final ten degrees of Taurus) was in the face of Saturn.

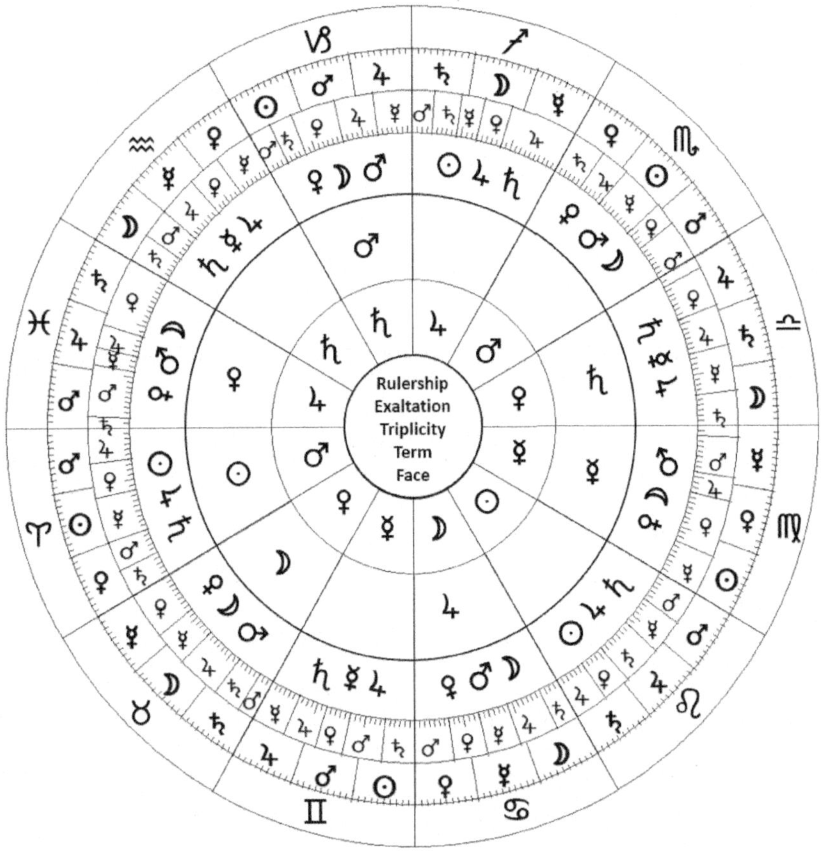

Figure A2.4: Essential dignities.

Figure A2.4 is a visual representation of all the dignities, referred to as **essential dignities**. The outermost ring shows the signs and each degree marked with a tick. The planets in the central ring show the signs ruled by those planets; the next ring out shows the exaltations of each sign; the third ring out shows the three triplicity rulers for each sign, the fourth ring out shows the term rulers; and the outer ring shows the face rulers of each ten-degree segment.

Using the Richard III reburial chart as an example, we can see which planets are particularly dignified, and which have weaknesses (detriment or fall). We can draw up a table for each planet, look at the position of that planet, and then say which planet rules that particular position in all five dignities.

Using Jupiter as an example, we note that Jupiter is at 12°51′ of Leo. Leo is ruled by the Sun. No planet is exalted in Leo. Leo is a fire sign, so the triplicity rulers are the Sun, Jupiter, and Saturn (in that order of priority in a daytime chart). To work out the terms, we can see from Figure A2.4 (or by referring to one of the many tables in medieval manuscripts, or from a Hellenistic source such as Ptolemy) that the first six degrees of Leo are ruled by Jupiter, the next five by Venus, and the following seven by Saturn, so the term ruler for 12 Leo is Saturn. Finally, Jupiter is in the second ten-degree decanate (or face) of Leo, and the face ruler of the second decanate of Leo is Jupiter. Hence we can see that although Jupiter isn't in the sign of its own rulership or exaltation, it is in a sign that it rules by triplicity, and in a part of that sign that it rules by face, so it has dignity. We can draw up a list for all the planets as shown in Table A2.2 (bold and underlined shows where a planet is in its own rulership):

Planet	Position	Ruler	Exalted	Triplicity	Term	Face
Saturn	4 Sag	Jupiter	None	Sun Jupiter **Saturn**	Jupiter	Mercury
Jupiter	12 Leo	Sun	None	Sun **Jupiter** Saturn	Saturn	**Jupiter**
Mars	26 Ari	**Mars**	Sun	Sun Jupiter Saturn	Saturn	Venus
Sun	5 Ari	Mars	**Sun**	**Sun** Jupiter Saturn	Jupiter	Mars
Venus	10 Tau	**Venus**	Moon	**Venus** Moon Mars	Mercury	Moon
Mercury	21 Pis	Jupiter	Venus	Venus Mars Moon	Mars	Mars
Moon	25 Gem	Mercury	None	Saturn Mercury Jupiter	Saturn	Sun

Table A2.2: Essential dignities for the Richard III burial chart.

We can see from this table that Mars and Venus are in the signs of their rulership, and the Sun is in the sign of its exaltation. The Sun is also in a fire sign (Aries), and the Sun is one of the triplicity rulers of fire signs, so the Sun has two types of dignity, as does Venus. Mercury is in Pisces, which is the sign opposite to Virgo, where Mercury is both the sign ruler and the exalted ruler. Mercury is in both detriment and fall, and is the weakest planet. Finding the strongest planet is often a matter of judgement by the astrologer, although a number of points systems were in operation by the twelfth century. The simplest of these scored five for rulership, four for exaltation, three for triplicity rulership, two for term rulership and one for face rulership. Using this formula, Venus would score the highest, with the Sun a close second. The astrologer would also note that the Lord of the Ascendant was the Sun (since Leo is the Ascendant, and its ruler is the Sun) in a daytime chart, which would probably give the Sun the edge despite its lower score.

Houses

Planets were seen, then, as the active agents in a chart, each with their own personality, and whose relative strengths were determined by their placement within signs. In addition to their placement within a sign, their placement with respect to the horizon was also significant. Jupiter may be in Leo in a particular chart, but it will behave differently when it is high up in the sky to when it is setting, or rising, or below the horizon. This distinction is significant, because it is this that makes a chart unique to a location. At the moment that Richard III was reinterred, the Sun was in the sign of Aries all over the world, but its position in the sky differed from place to place. The Sun was high in the sky in Leicester, but below the horizon in Sydney.

An astrological chart represents this location feature by a second division of the ecliptic. The first division is the universal division into equal thirty-degree segments, or signs, from a universal point – the equinox point where the ecliptic and the celestial equator cross. The second division is the division of the ecliptic starting from the Ascendant into twelve segments called **houses**. These houses are not necessarily all thirty degrees in extent. Astrologically, while planets manifest traits, houses represent areas of life in which these traits manifest. For example, the fifth house represents children, the seventh house marriage, the ninth house travel.

Medieval astrology makes use of several methods of dividing the ecliptic into houses, many of which derived from Arabic methods that became known in Europe from the twelfth century. The terminology in Hellenistic astrology was rather confusing, since different English translations use different words for the same thing, and the term "house", "sign", and "place" are often used interchangeably, and most Hellenistic astrologers used something called the whole-sign house system, which meant that houses were in fact thirty degrees. The terminology made a clear distinction by the time of the Arabic translators, who used the terms "house" and "sign" in the sense that we use them today.

In all house systems, the location of the Ascendant is the basis for the division of the ecliptic into houses. In Hellenistic astrology, a whole sign system was used, in which the sign containing the Ascendant was the first house (or "place"), the second house is the whole of the next sign, and so on. For example, Figure A2.5 shows a sample chart where the Ascendant is at 20° Leo. Any planet in Leo is considered to be a first house planet, any planet in Virgo a second house planet, any planet in Libra a third house planet, and so on.

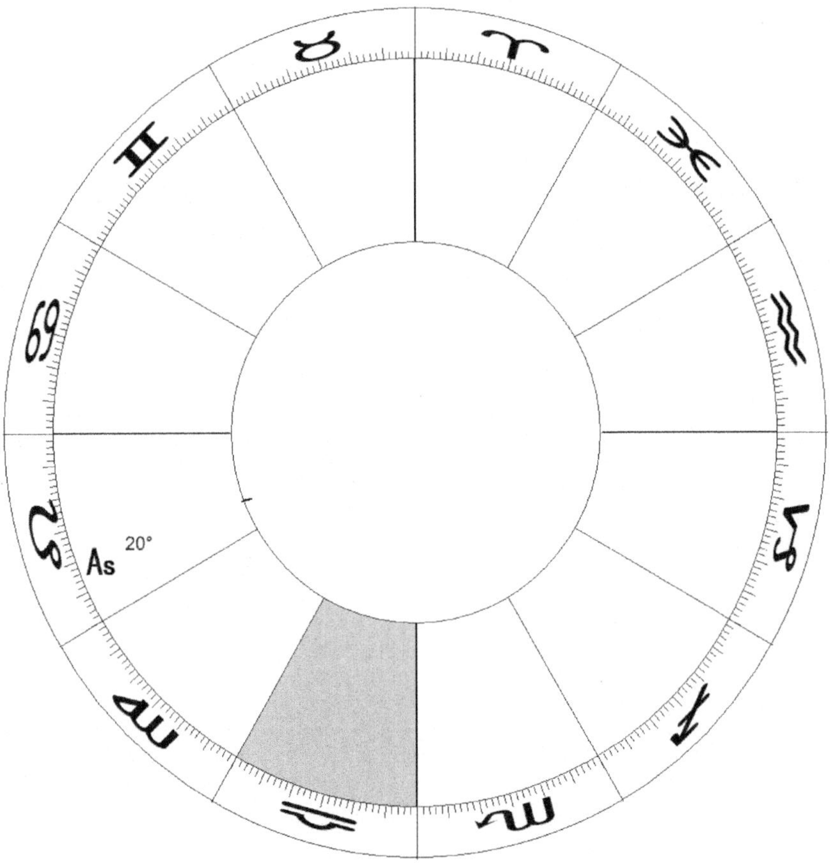

Figure A2.5: Hellenistic whole sign houses, with the third house highlighted.

Later house systems, such as those adopted by the Arabic writers, used a **quadrant house system**. From an observer's visual point of view, there are four key points in space when observing planets in the sky. The first is the **Ascendant**, the point where the ecliptic crosses the observer's eastern horizon. The second is the **Midheaven**, due south in the northern hemisphere, where the ecliptic is at its highest elevation. The third is the

Descendant where the ecliptic crosses the observer's western horizon, and is directly opposite the Ascendant. The fourth is the **Imum Coeli**, or IC, the point where the ecliptic is at its lowest elevation. It is invisible as it is under the horizon, but is directly opposite the Midheaven (the Midheaven is also called the **Medium Coeli**, which is why it is abbreviated to MC). These points are all represented on a chart, but as the IC is always opposite the MC and the Descendant is always opposite the Ascendant, conventionally only the Ascendant and MC are labelled. These four points define the four **quadrants** of the chart, and a quadrant house system will use various techniques to divide these quadrants into three houses each.

Figure A2.6 shows an example of this. In this diagram, the Ascendant (shown as Asc on the diagram) is at 7° Sagittarius, and the Midheaven (shown as MC on the diagram) is at 7° Libra. As can be seen from the diagram, the houses do not correspond directly to signs – the first house begins at the Ascendant, so a planet in the earlier degrees of Sagittarius would not be in the first house (as it would be in the Hellenistic whole sign system), but in the twelfth house. Houses are not all the same size – the third house, highlighted, is clearly much bigger than the fifth house in this example, and is so large that it includes an entire sign (Pisces) plus parts of two other signs (Aquarius and Aries) within it. Note also that there is no link between houses and signs; one could have two planets in Taurus, but with one planet in the fifth house and one in the sixth. Similarly, one could have two planets in the eighth house, but one of them in Cancer, the other in Leo. There are a wide range of quadrant house systems, and all have the feature that opposite houses have the same number of degrees in them. One quadrant house system widely used in medieval Europe was the Alcabitius system, developed by and named after the Arabic astrologer al-Qabisi, known as Alcabitius in Latin-speaking Europe.

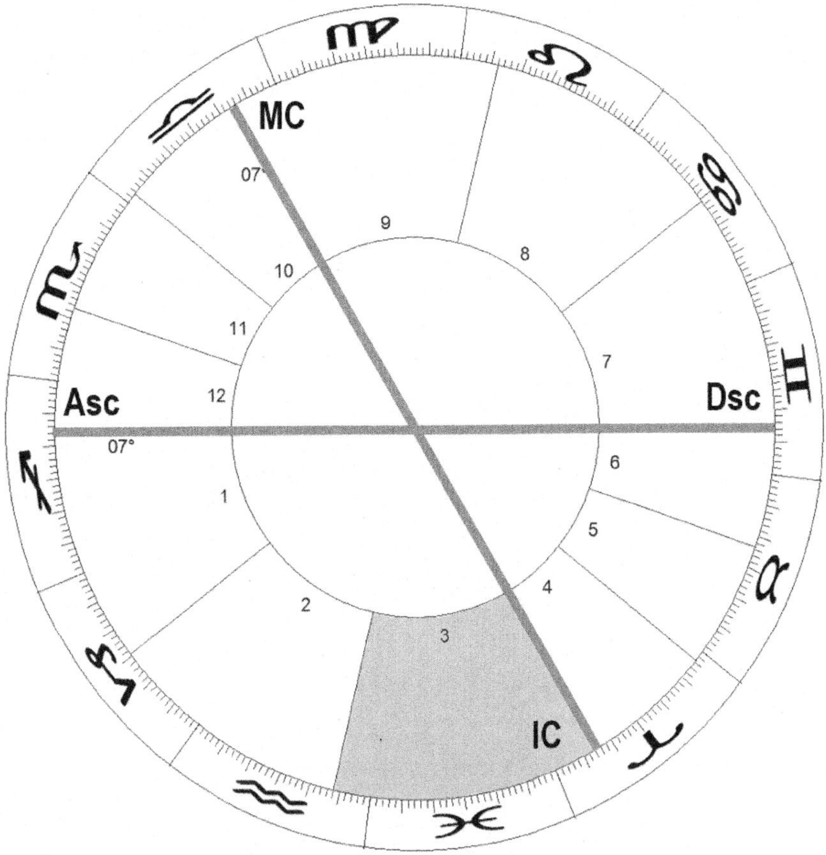

Figure A2.6: Quadrant house system.

Houses in the chart represent areas of life. The ninth house, for example, indicates long journeys. Thus if someone wanted to know whether it was safe to undertake a long journey, the astrologer might draw up a chart for the proposed time of the journey, and look at the position of the start of the ninth house. In the example chart in Figure A2.7, that is the very last degree of Capricorn. Even though most of the ninth house is in Aquarius, Capricorn is the start, or **cusp**, of the ninth house, so the ruler of Capricorn – Saturn – would be the "Lord of the ninth" and the planet that would suggest the outcome of the journey. Without going into too much detail about techniques, as these are covered elsewhere in this book, a brief glance at the sort of analysis that a medieval astrologer might make is in order here. In this case,

Saturn being the ruler of the ninth house is a mixed blessing, since although Saturn itself is in Capricorn and therefore strong (in rulership), it is in the eighth house, and that house represents death. Saturn itself is also associated with death and considered a very negative planet. The Lord of the Ascendant, Mercury, is in Pisces, so is in fall and in detriment. The client may elect to postpone the possibly fated journey to a date and time where the planets are more favourable!

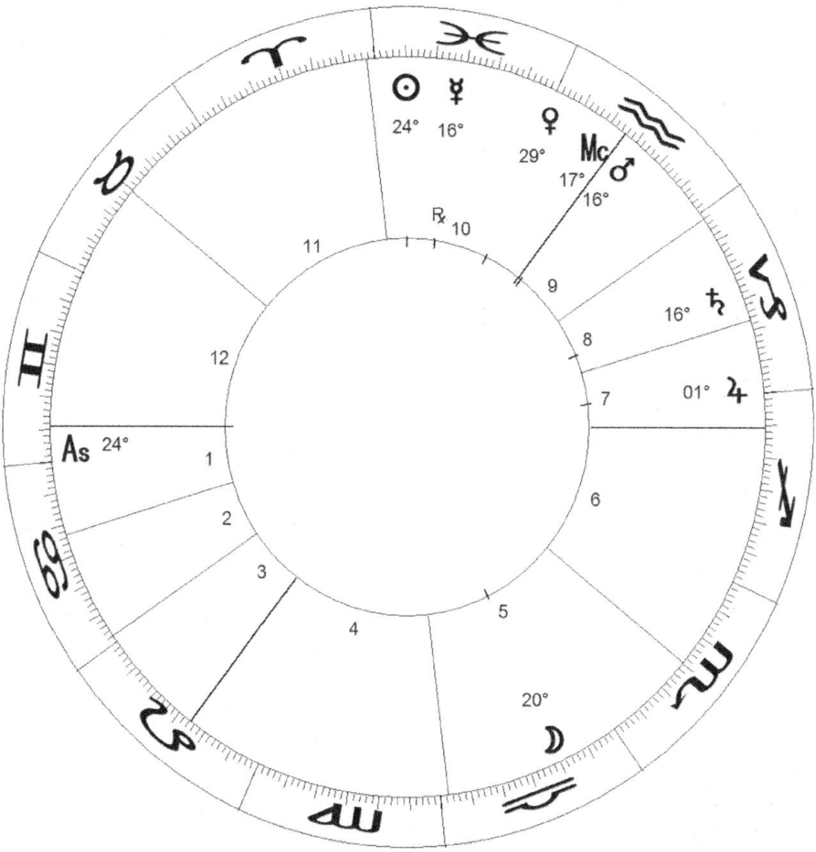

Figure A2.7: A sample chart for a question about travel.

Medieval charts

The charts in this book have been presented as circular, and produced using modern software, which makes it easier and more intuitive to visualise relationships between planets and signs and houses. In medieval texts, however, it was more usual either simply to write out the position of the planets and houses and not have a diagram at all, or to draw a square chart. Square charts are less intuitive than circular ones, but they do emphasise the first, fourth, seventh, and tenth houses, which were considered strong houses, and had the advantage of being much easier to draw than circles. The house layout in a square chart is illustrated in Figure A2.8, and an actual example of one (a horoscope for Henry VI drawn up in 1421) is shown in Figure A2.9.

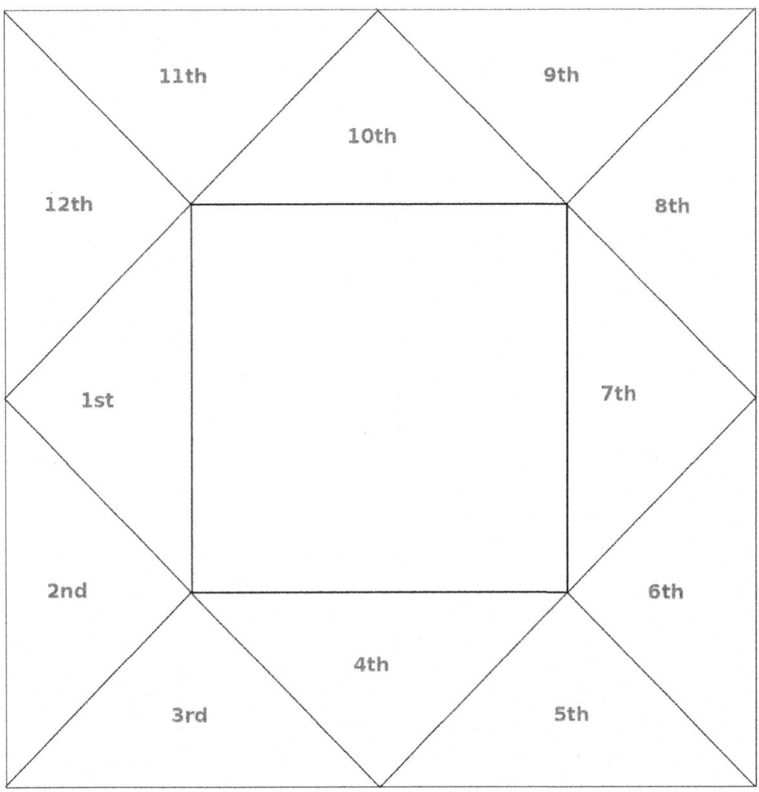

Figure A2.8: Square chart layout.

The chart for Henry VI is shown in Figure A2.9, with a Latin inscription saying that he was born on 5 December 1421 at 3 hours 20 minutes and 56 seconds in the afternoon. Even today, people don't generally know their birth time to the nearest second, and they certainly wouldn't have done in the fifteenth century! This apparently ridiculous level of accuracy was actually because clock times were so uncertain; it was therefore traditional to correct a chart using a technique described by Ptolemy called **rectification**, which supposedly resulted in a more accurate Ascendant (and hence birth time). The degrees and signs of the house cusps are written along the lines, such as "Canc 3 34" along the second house line, while the planets' positions are written in the relevant house, such as "Sol 22 44'" in the seventh house (the Sagittarius is assumed since the signs are written against the house cusps either side).

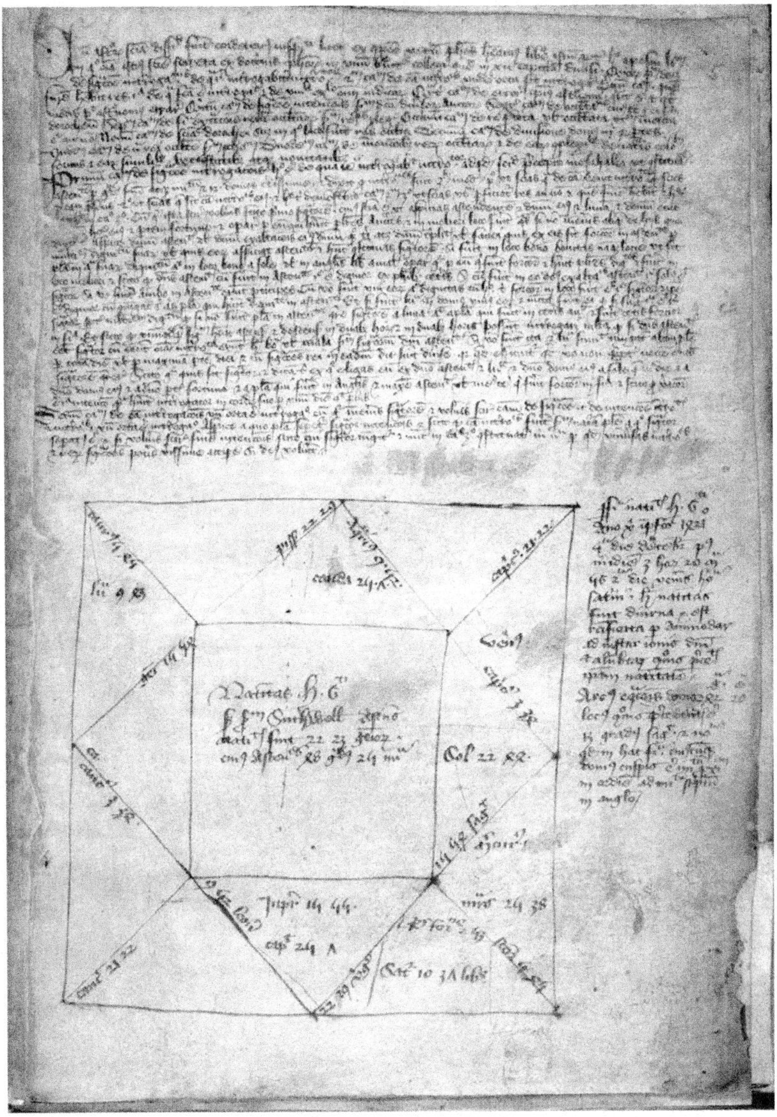

Figure A2.9: Chart for Henry VI, London, British Library MS Egerton 889, f.5.

Aspects

We have now seen how planets act in charts; they have individual characteristics, and have strength by virtue of their placement within signs. For any particular chart, planets will rule certain houses, which represent various areas of life – marriage, death, travel, and so on. Planets may also relate to each other in a particular chart, by virtue of their positions relative to each other. These relationships are called **aspects**.

An aspect is simply a particular angle between two planets, and five aspects are used in medieval astrology, as shown here:

Aspect	Angle
Conjunction	0°
Sextile	60°
Square	90°
Trine	120°
Opposition	180°

Sextiles and trines are considered to be harmonious aspects, while squares and oppositions suggest conflict between the two planets. A conjunction is where two planets occupy the same location, and can either work together or conflict, depending upon the planets. It is very rare for planets to occupy the same degree in a chart, so a certain amount of leeway of a few degrees, called an **orb**, is allowed. In medieval astrology, the orb depended on the planets in question – the Sun and Jupiter had bigger orbs than smaller planets like Mercury or Venus.

Figure A2.10 shows a typical chart, where planets aspect each other. The Moon, in Cancer, is almost 60° from Venus in Virgo (within two degrees) – close enough to be considered a sextile, shown by a dotted line. The Moon is also opposite Saturn, within a degree, shown by a solid line. Venus in Virgo is just over 120° from Saturn in Capricorn, which is a trine, shown by a dotted line. Venus is also just over 90° from Mars, which is a square, shown by a solid line. The Sun is also trine Jupiter, at just under 120°, shown by a dotted line. Mercury is sextile to Mars, also shown by a dotted line. A medieval astrologer would consider that the Moon and Saturn are hostile to each other, as are Mars and Venus, while Mars and Mercury are cooperating, as are the Moon and Venus, Venus and Saturn, and the Sun and Jupiter. This would be used in making a judgement – for example, if this were the chart for a proposed dangerous journey, the astrologer would look at the Lord of the ninth house of journeys, which in this case is the Sun. The Sun is in rulership, and has a harmonious trine aspect to Jupiter, also in rulership, Lord of the Ascendant, and a benevolent planet, so this would bode well.

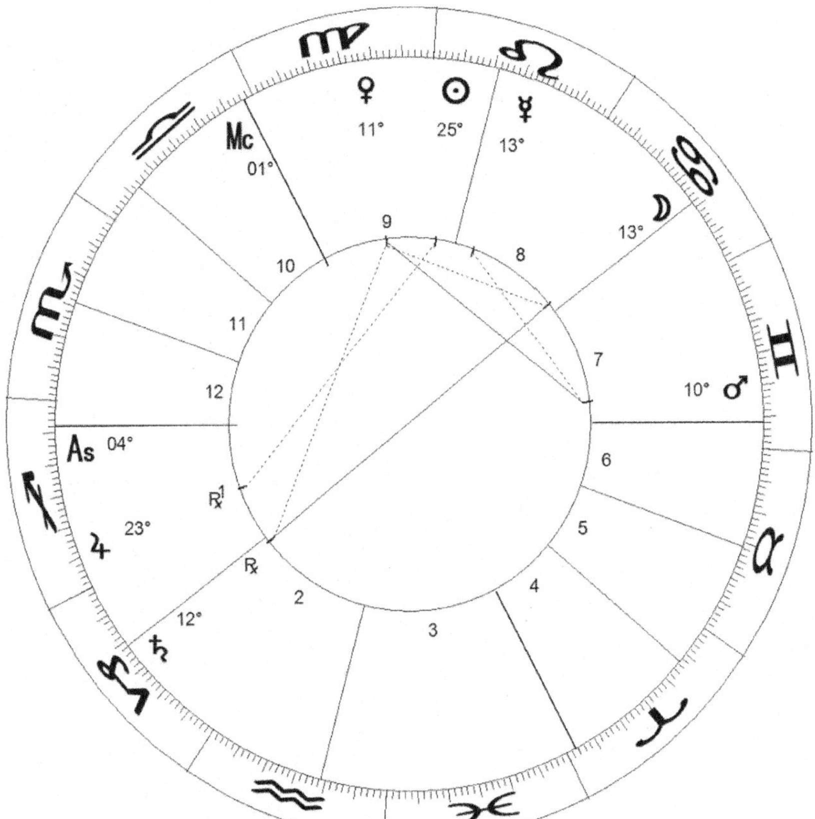

Figure A2.10: Illustration of planets aspecting each other.

Summary

An astrological chart is a representation of planets in the sky, and their relationship to the observer in a given location. In astrological terms, planets act like personalities, some positive and some negative. Planets, whether favourable or unfavourable, are given strength by virtue of the signs they are in. Medieval astrology had a complex system of dignities to evaluate planetary strength based on which part of the zodiac they occupied.

A chart is also divided into houses, from a point defined by the Ascendant rising at the time and place for which the chart was cast. These houses identify areas of life, and are ruled by particular planets dependent upon time and place. Planets also work in relation to each other in medieval astrology. They may cooperate or fight, depending upon the aspects they make to each other, with some aspects harmonious and others conflicting.

A chart, then, is a unique snapshot of a moment in time at a particular location. This snapshot can be for a person's birth, called a **nativity**, such as the chart drawn up for the birth of Henry VI. It can be a chart of a proposed event, called an **election**; a famous example of this was the foundation chart of Baghdad mentioned in Chapter Two. It can also be a chart drawn up when a client visits an astrologer with a question in mind, such as whether a relative will die or whether a shipment of goods will arrive safely, and the chart is then drawn up for the time and place the question is asked. This form of astrology is called **horary** or **interrogational** astrology. Astrology was also used in medicine, when a chart would be cast for the moment a person became too ill to work and took to their bed, known as a **decumbiture chart**.

Medieval astrology therefore had many applications, but they were all based on the concept of drawing up an astrological chart for a specific moment of time at a specific location. The purpose of this Appendix has been to introduce some astrological terminology as a pre-requisite for understanding the concepts behind drawing up a chart and for appreciating the technical chapters of this book, since Roger's *Judicial Astrology* assumes a familiarity with the subject.

BIBLIOGRAPHY

Manuscripts

Unknown author, Sagittarius Calendar, London, British Library, Cotton Tiberius B V/1.

Holbrooke, John, Chart of Henry VI, London, British Library MS Egerton 889.

Pseudo-Ptolemy, *Iudicia*, Paris, Bibliothèque nationale de France, Lat. 16208.

Pseudo-Ptolemy, *Iudicia*, Munich, CLM 848.

Roger of Hereford, *Judicial Astrology*, Oxford, Bodleian Selden Supra 76.

Roger of Hereford, *Judicial Astrology*, Cambridge, University Library Gg VI.3.

Roger of Hereford, Note on ingress dates, London, British Library, Arundel 377.

Books

Abū Maʿšar, *The Abbreviation of the Introduction to Astrology*, Charles Burnett (trans.) (Leiden: Brill, 1994).

Abū Maʿšar, *Liber introductorii maioris ad scientam judiciorum astrorum*, John of Seville (trans.), Richard Lemay (ed.), Volume 5 (Napoli: Istituto Universitario Orientale, 1995).

Abū Maʿšar, *Liber introductorii maioris ad scientam judiciorum astrorum*, Hermann of Carinthia (trans.), Richard Lemay (ed.), Volume 8 (Napoli: Istituto Universitario Orientale, 1995).

Al-Biruni, *The Book of Instruction in the Elements of the Art of Astrology*, R. Ramsay Wright (ed.) (London: Luzac & Co, 1934).

Al-Kindi, *The Forty Chapters of al-Kindi*, Ben Dykes (ed., trans.) (Minneapolis: Cazimi Press, 2011).

Bede, *Bede: The Reckoning of Time*, Faith Wallis (trans.) (Liverpool: Liverpool University Press, 1999).

Bonatti, Guido, *Book of Astronomy*, Ben Dykes (trans.) (Golden Valley, Minnesota, 2007).

Burnett, Charles, *The Introduction of Arabic Learning into England* (London: British Library, 1997).

Cameron, Alan, 'The last days of the Academy at Athens', *Proceedings of the Cambridge Philological Society* 195 (1969), pp. 7-29.

Campion, Nicholas, *A History of Western Astrology Volume II - The Medieval and Modern Worlds* (London: Continuum, 2009).

Dykes, Ben, *Hermann of Carinthia: The Search of the Heart* (Minneapolis: Cazimi Press, 2011).

Dykes, Ben, *Works of Sahl and Māshā'Allāh* (Minneapolis: Cazimi Press, 2008).

Freely, John, *Aladdin's Lamp: How Greek Science Came to Europe Through the Islamic World* (New York: Alfred A. Knopf, 2009).

Firmicus Maternus, *Ancient Astrology Theory and Practice: Matheseos Libri VIII*, J.R. Bram (trans.) (Park Ridge, NJ: Noyes Press, 1975).

Ibn Ezra, Abraham, *Book of Reasons*, Shlomo Sela (ed., trans.) (Leiden: Brill, 2007).

Isidore of Seville, *Etymologies*, S. Barney, W.J. Lewis, J.A. Beach, O. Berghof (eds) (Cambridge: Cambridge University Press, 2006).

Leach, Arthur, *The Schools of Medieval England* (London: Methuen, 1915).

Māshā'Allāh, *On Hidden Things*, in Dykes, *Sahl and Māshā'Allāh*.

Māshā'Allāh, *On Reception* in Dykes, *Sahl and Māshā'Allāh.*

Metlitzki, Dorothee, *The Matter of Araby in Medieval England* (New Haven: Yale University Press, 1977).

Mitchell, Chris, 'Roger of Hereford's Judicial Astrology: England's First Astrology Book?', PhD thesis (2019), https://doi.org/10.25392/leicester.data.11793636.

Moreton, Jennifer, 'Before Grosseteste: Roger of Hereford and Calendar Reform in Eleventh and Twelfth-Century England', *Isis*, 86.4 (1995), pp.562-586.

Pliny, *Natural History*, Volume I: Books 1-2, H. Rackham (trans.), Loeb Classical Library 330 (Cambridge, MA: Harvard University Press, 1938).

Pullin, Chris, 'Cathedrals as Centres of Learning' in A. Johnson and R. Shoesmith (eds), *The Story of Hereford* (Woonton, Herefordshire: Logaston Press, 2016).

Russell, Josiah, 'Hereford and Arabic Science in England about 1175-1200', Isis, 18.1 (1932), pp.14-25.

Sahl ibn Bishr, *Introduction* in Dykes, *Sahl and Māshā'Allāh*.

Tolan, John, *Petrus Alfonsi and his Medieval Readers* (Gainesville: University Press of Florida, 1993).

Valens, Vettius, Anthologies, Book IX Mark Riley (trans.) (2010) online at http://www.csus.edu/indiv/r/rileymt/Vettius%20Valens%20entire.pdf.

Von Stuckrad, Kocku, 'Interreligious Transfers in the Middle Ages: The Case of Astrology', *Journal of Religion in Europe*, 1.1 (2008), pp.34-59.

Yamamoto, Keiji, and Charles Burnett (eds), *The Great Introduction to Astrology by Abū Ma'šar* (Leiden: Brill, 2019).

INDEX

Printed in Great Britain
by Amazon

77543134R10139